101 WONDERS
OF THE WATERWAYS

A Guide to the Sights and Secrets of Britain's Canals and Rivers

STEVE HAYWOOD AND MOIRA HAYNES

ADLARD COLES

LONDON • OXFORD • NEW YORK • NEW DELHI • SYDNEY

ADLARD COLES
Bloomsbury Publishing Plc
50 Bedford Square, London, WC1B 3DP, UK
29 Earlsfort Terrace, Dublin 2, Ireland

BLOOMSBURY, ADLARD COLES and the Adlard Coles logo are trademarks of
Bloomsbury Publishing Plc

First published in Great Britain 2023

A catalogue record for this book is available from the British Library
Library of Congress Cataloguing-in-Publication data has been applied for

ISBN: 978-1-4729-9177-5; ePub: 978-1-4729-9178-2; ePDF: 978-1-4729-9179-9

2 4 6 8 10 9 7 5 3 1

Designed by Austin Taylor
Typeset in Quadraat by Phil Beresford
Printed and bound in India by Replika Press Pvt. Ltd.

To find out more about our authors and books visit www.
bloomsbury.com and sign up for our newsletters

Contents

Introduction 5

Some Basics
1 The Inland Waterways Association 8
2 Locks 10
3 Distance and Mile Posts 12

The Midlands
4 Bancroft Basin, Stratford-upon-Avon 16
5 Barrel-roofed Lock Cottages, South Stratford Canal 18
6 The Birmingham Canal Navigations 20
7 BCN Challenge 22
8 Braunston 24
9 Charity Dock 26
10 The Chesterfield Canal 28
11 Cosgrove to Grafton Regis, Grand Union Canal 30
12 Cromford Mills and the Cromford Canal 32
13 Fotheringhay 34
14 Foxton Locks and Inclined Plane 36
15 The Great Northern Basin 38
16 The Harecastle Tunnels 40
17 Hatton Locks 42
18 Lichfield Canal Aqueduct 44
19 Napton and the Oxford Summit 46
20 Royal Ordnance Depot, Weedon 48
21 Shardlow 50
22 Stoke Bruerne and Blisworth Tunnel 52
23 Stourport-on-Severn 54
24 South Stratford Split Bridges 56
25 Tixall Wide 58
26 Toll Islands, Birmingham 60

Arts and Crafts
27 Roses and Castles 62
28 Towpath Art 64

The North
29 Anderton Boat Lift and The River Weaver 68
30 Barton Swing Aqueduct 70
31 Bingley Five Rise Locks 72
32 Bugsworth Basin 74
33 Burnley Embankment 76
34 Chester 78
35 Ellesmere Port 80
36 Gargrave 82
37 Glasson Dock and Basin 84
38 Hebden Bridge and the Rochdale Summit 86
39 Hest Bank 88
40 The Liverpool Link 90
41 Naburn Lock 92
42 The Ribble Link 94
43 The Rochdale 9 96
44 Saltaire 98
45 The Springs Branch 100
46 Standedge Tunnel 102
47 Wardle Canal 104
48 Wigan Pier 106
49 Worsley Delph 108

Canal Curiosities
50 Roving Bridges 110
51 Tow Rope Grooves 112
52 Hobbit Houses 114

The South
53 Blow-up Bridge (Macclesfield Bridge), Regent's Canal 118

54 Camden Lock 120
55 Little Venice 122
56 The Thames Tunnel 124
57 Maritime Greenwich 126
58 The Thames Barrier 128
59 Three Mills Island 130
60 The Royal Gunpowder Mills 132
61 The River Thames between Goring and Windsor 134
62 Swan-upping 136
63 The Wey Navigation 138
64 Port Meadow and Oxford 140
65 Cropredy Festival 142
66 Southern Oxford and Llangollen Lift Bridges 144
67 Tooley's Boatyard 146

Travelling Players
68 Mikron Theatre 148
69 Tim and Pru 150

The East
70 The Broads 154
71 The Cambridge Backs 156
72 Denver Sluice 158
73 Ely 160
74 The Glory Hole, Lincoln 162
75 Reed Cutters 164
76 Wicken Fen 166
77 Tributaries of the Great Ouse 168
78 The Wash 170

Waterways Wildlife
79 Water Voles 172
80 Water Birds 174

Wales and the West
81 Bridge-keepers' Cottages, Gloucester & Sharpness Canal 178
82 Bristol Floating Harbour 180
83 Caen Hill Lock Flight 182
84 The Ellesmere Lake District 184
85 Gloucester Docks 186
86 Pontcysyllte Aqueduct 188
87 Pulteney Bridge, Bath 190
88 Horseshoe Falls 192
89 Ironbridge 194
90 The Rennie Aqueducts 196
91 Sapperton Tunnel and the Cotswold Canals 198
92 The Severn Bore 200
93 Whixall Moss 202
94 Woodseaves Cutting 204

A Water Way of Life
95 Waterways Pubs 206
96 Traditional Boatman's Back Cabin 208

Scotland
97 Caledonian Canal 212
98 Crinan Canal 214
99 The Falkirk Wheel 216
100 The Kelpies 218
101 Neptune's Staircase 220

Index 222
Acknowledgements 224

Introduction

The idea of 'Wonders' of the waterways was the brainchild of Robert Aickman, the founding chairman of the Inland Waterways Association (IWA), who was an exemplary publicist for the canals and rivers of the UK at a time when their future was uncertain. In the early 1950s, Britain was still recovering from the Second World War. Factories had been devastated; major cities were peppered with bomb sites where once there'd been housing; food was still rationed. The waterways were hardly going to be a priority of post-war reconstruction and the 3,220km (2,000-mile) network, which had had a brief renaissance during hostilities, now lay decaying and becoming more derelict by the year, forgotten except by a handful of enthusiasts. Aickman hit on the idea of publicising the waterways by focusing on some of the remarkable structures that could be found on it. Nowadays, we recognise these as important historical sites, part of our industrial heritage; but at that time, when industrial archaeology was in its infancy, heritage was country houses and grand palaces, and few were interested in the crumbling remnants of an Industrial Revolution that was already so remote it was lost in history.

Aickman's idea was to link his contemporary waterways Wonders to the Seven Wonders of the Ancient World. Today, people would barely know what you were talking about if these came up in conversation, but in those days kids like us were taught them at primary school and we were as familiar with the Colossus of Rhodes and the Hanging Gardens of Babylon as we were with Buckingham Palace and the Houses of Parliament – all of which seemed equally fantastical places to us.

Aickman homed in on the Pontcysyllte Aqueduct, the Standedge Tunnel, the Caen Hill flight of locks, the Barton Swing Aqueduct, the Anderton Boat Lift, the Bingley Five Rise Locks and the Burnley Embankment – all of which feature in this book. His campaign was successful beyond his wildest dreams and his legacy is the thousands who use the canal today and take them for granted as part of the tapestry of their lives. Some may just walk their dogs along the towpath; others may cruise the canals in boats worth as much as a small house. Regardless, both think the canal is theirs; both feel ownership of it.

So why keep banging on about waterway wonders, much less write a book broadening the scope of them? Aren't seven Wonders of the Waterways more than enough, let alone more than a hundred? And what do we mean by 'wonder' anyhow, you may ask. Looking at the Pontcysyllte Aqueduct for the first time, that may seem an absurd question. However many pictures you've seen of it, or videos you've watched, it is nevertheless awe-inspiring when you first lay eyes on it, something that stops you dead in your tracks with pure... wonder. But there's so much else on the waterways that engenders the same feeling, from tunnels to bridges, embankments to cuttings. You wonder that all these things could have been built in an age without machinery when everything had to be done by hand, wonder at the men who did it, and the dangers they faced to achieve what they did. On a more pedestrian level, there's a lot about the canals that you just wonder about with idle curiosity: walls that seem to have no purpose, signs that are meaningless, doors in bridges that are incomprehensible. We hope this book will explain at least a few of these oddities.

It struck us in compiling our inventory that it was unnecessarily restrictive to be bound by the arbitrary number of seven – a number that seems to have been plucked out of the air by various Greek (or was it Byzantine?) scholars sometime around 200 BC. Seven seemed to us a laughably inadequate number to communicate what is so valuable about our waterways, both in their scale and their detail. It wasn't nearly enough to convey any sense of the waterways as a linked network, a system stretching from Bristol to the Lake District, Wales to the flatlands of the east country.

Besides, waterways haven't stood still in the 70 years since Aickman devised his list. New canals have been opened, older ones restored; features exist now that didn't then, and others that were derelict at the time Aickman highlighted them – like the Caen Hill locks, for instance –

have been completely restored so that we can see them now, not as just the ruins of another age but as living and functioning parts of our own.

This miraculous renaissance has come about mainly as a result of the enthusiasm of so many volunteers, some who work behind the scenes planning and fundraising, others who roll up their sleeves on work camps and the like, literally getting their hands dirty grubbing up trees, excavating muddy ditches and rebuilding locks and bridges. They do it because it's something they feel passionate about in an almost spiritual way. But they also do it because – like the woman walking her dog or the man on the tiller of his posh boat – they feel a sense of ownership of the canals. They feel the waterways belong to them and they'll go to any lengths to protect them, especially when it seems over the years that so many official bodies charged with that task have been happy enough to sit back and watch them be destroyed.

It is to these people – to the local Inland Waterways Association (IWA) groups and canal societies around the country whose determination and vision has ensured the survival and growth of Britain's inland waterways, to the

Waterways Recovery Group who for the last 50 years have been involved in every major canal restoration, to those countless other volunteers who over the years have dedicated their time and energy to canal restoration – that we dedicate this book.

Finally, we have to apologise in advance. We are aware that every waterways Wonder we cite has its experts: its engineering specialists, its social historians, its local enthusiasts who have studied it for years. We don't claim to be experts in anything except how to enjoy the canals, and we crave indulgence from those that are. Inevitably, mistakes will have crept in, either from lack of attention on our part or because we've had to truncate our descriptions of some features about which books have been written into a meagre 500 words. But we hope that the odd slip on a detail of construction, or a date, won't impair your enjoyment of the book. The inland waterways of Britain really are full of wonders. They are – quite literally – wonderful. And at least we won't be directing you towards sights that aren't there, as those scholars compiling their Seven Wonders of the World did all those years ago. Those Hanging Gardens of Babylon, for instance. Many contemporary commentators today doubt they ever existed.

Apologies too to those who will be left tearing their hair out at what sometimes must seem totally arbitrary decisions on our part. Why have we included some canals as Wonders in their own right, but not others? Why have we chosen some features over others? Some may think Scotland gets a raw deal here; others will find it hard to believe we've not highlighted places like York or other locations and features they would have included. Our only defence is to say that this list represents our personal choice, and it's inevitable that others would choose differently. To arrive at our selection has been a difficult and sometimes fraught process, with one of us championing one element for inclusion and the other championing another. It has meant that hard choices have had to be made. So you may find mention of some features – like the Crofton Pumping Station on the Kennet & Avon Canal or Galton Bridge in Smethwick, for instance – that could have been Wonders in their own right. Others, like the Monmouthshire & Brecon Canal in Wales, St Katharine Docks in London, the Exeter Canal, the Grantham Canal or the three great aqueducts on the Union Canal in Scotland, don't even get a mention. How could we do that? The 12-arched Avon aqueduct at Linlithgow is extraordinary.

We can only hope the book generates some friendly debate on the topic and reminds us what a rich and varied resource are the waterways of Britain, and how important it is that we should fight to preserve every bit of them against assaults by insensitive politicians and developers who would bulldoze the lot of them to bolster their votes or add another couple of points to their share price.

Ted Ellis, a local East Anglian naturalist, described the Broads as 'the breathing space for the cure of souls'. We think our whole network of waterways could be described in the same way.

Steve Haywood and Moira Haynes

1 The Inland Waterways Association

We baby boomers – 'Children of the Revolution', as T. Rex's Marc Bolan would have it – think we invented political activism. After all, we grew up in the era that spawned the Campaign for Nuclear Disarmament (CND), Greenpeace and Amnesty International. In fact, the claim is typical of our arrogance.

The truth is political activism has been a feature of life in Britain as long as Britain has existed, and the fight to preserve inland waterways has an honourable place in this history. Indeed, judging by how successful it has been in achieving its aims, the Inland Waterways Association (IWA) is arguably one of the most effective – if not the most effective – post-war pressure groups.

Consider this: after the Second World War, which had temporarily revived the canals as an industrial network, they were left with no real function. Carrying declined, along with the infrastructure of the waterways; though what finally did for the canals wasn't the railways of the 19th century, but governments of the 20th that increasingly committed themselves to roads as the primary system of industrial transport. By the time the idealist, polemicist, engineer and author Tom Rolt retreated to a converted narrowboat in 1939 to live with his new wife Angela, the canals network was on its last legs. Not only had it

deteriorated to the stage we found it at 40 years later, but getting on for 20 per cent of it had disappeared, surreptitiously abandoned through disuse.

However, Rolt's account of his honeymoon journey in his book *Narrow Boat*, published in 1944, touched a chord in a country that had been at war for five years and where civilians were as much on the front line as the military. With the arrival of peace, people began searching for what was important in an age where old colonial certainties were breaking down. They wanted to know what they had been fighting for. They wanted to know what the country stood for in this new, post-war world.

As a direct result of the book, the Inland Waterways Association was formed in 1946 on a platform of reviving the canals by stressing, among other things, their heritage and the way they could be developed for pleasure boating. When the campaign began, even the association's founding chairman – Robert Aickman – recognised that most waterways enthusiasts, 'few in number at the best, were as gloomy about the prospects (of success) as any official, and often more so'. One can only wonder with awe what they would feel now, were they able to see the major restorations that have taken place over the years as a result of IWA campaigning, often in ways that involved direct action and confrontation with the authorities: the Kennet & Avon Canal, the Huddersfield Narrow, the Rochdale Canal, the Stratford Canal, the Peak Forest Canal, the River Avon ... the list goes on. Even more impressive are the restorations that are in hand, not all of them directly managed by the IWA, but every one of them inspired and supported by it: the Chesterfield Canal, the Cotswold Canals, the Cromford Canal, the Grantham Canal, the Lichfield and Hatherton canals...

And the IWA's assistance isn't just academic. Its associated organisation, the Waterways Recovery Group

For more info about IWA activities and membership:
| waterways.org.uk

If you fancy getting your hands dirty in the cause of canal restoration, contact the WRG:
| waterways.org.uk/waterways/sites/
| waterway-recovery-group

(WRG), has arranged work camps at virtually every major restoration since the 1960s, providing plant, equipment and phalanxes of volunteer labour, trained in the skills needed to make a derelict ditch navigable and build a lock from scratch.

Seeking pleasure on canals

When Tom Rolt and Robert Aickman worked together they were an unstoppable force. But their relationship soured and Aikman eventually engineered Rolt's expulsion from the organisation they had jointly formed.

Mr. R. F. Aickman (left) and Mr. L. T. C. Rolt, chairman and secretary of the Inland Waterways Association, taking water aboard their boat on the Aire and Calder Canal yesterday. They were leaving to complete a survey which will, it is hoped, lead to the use of canals for pleasure cruising and extended commercial use. A note on the proposal appears in This World of Ours. (A "Yorkshire Post" picture.)

② Locks

Anyone who walks the towpath regularly may think they know all there is to know about locks. However, their style and design differ significantly across the country, and being familiar with your local ones doesn't give you any sense of how different they can be in other places. Locks appear to defy gravity by allowing water to travel uphill – which is an astonishing concept. More astonishing is that without locks, there couldn't be any canal system.

There are 1,569 of them across England and Wales, and another 94 or so in Scotland. Some of them are single locks, built to accommodate just one full-length 22-metre (72ft) narrowboat at a time; some are double locks, which are two single locks, side by side. By comparison, broad locks, as they're called, can take two narrowboats in the same lock at the same time. Some broad locks though, like those on the Leeds & Liverpool, are only 18 metres (60ft) long. Some are huge. Teddington barge lock on the Thames, for instance, is 198 metres (650ft) long by 7.5 metres (25ft) wide. Some, like Tuel Lane Lock in Sowerby Bridge in Yorkshire, the deepest in the country at nearly 6 metres (20ft), are very deep. And to confuse matters further, some are very shallow. They're not even there to raise or lower boats. They are called stop locks and have a fall of only a couple of inches, if that. They were designed so that one canal company couldn't 'steal' water from another.

Locks differ in other ways too. Their long balance beams, for instance – designed to counteract the weight of the lock gates. These can sometimes be made of beautifully tapered hardwoods; sometimes they can be little better than rough-hewn tree trunks; some are just ugly iron girders. Some don't have lock beams at all because they're mechanised. And what is true of lock beams is especially true of paddle gear, the apparatus that opens and closes the sluices of a lock by means of a windlass or 'lock key' – or sometimes a wheel – allowing water to flow in and out of the lock chamber. The most familiar of these is probably the spindle-and-ratchet mechanism that you see all over the place, though these vary widely in design and age, some of them such old and beautiful pieces of machinery you wonder why they're not in a museum rather than abused on a day-to-day basis by boaters. Sometimes – in odd places on the Leeds & Liverpool Canal – you raise them by inserting a windlass not at the side but at the top. Some work by lifting wooden handles. Others – like a few on the Calder & Hebble Navigation – don't operate by lock keys at all but by 'spikes', 1.2-metre (4ft) wedges of wood with tapered handles, fashioned to fit into crude ground cogs. They look like offensive weapons. Steve was once questioned by an officious police officer in Brighouse who saw ours on the top of the boat and was concerned he was going to use it for nefarious purposes.

If this isn't enough variation, some locks are built so that paddles draw water through culverts under the ground, others open paddles set directly into lock gates, which if you open them at the wrong time can swamp a boat with a wall of water. Some paddles operate hydraulically, like those on the Hatton flight (see Wonder 17) and along the Grand Union; some operate by lifting gates upwards in the manner of a guillotine blade, like those in the east country.

And that's not all. A standard lock consists of two sets of gates. You enter by one set, going either up or down, and – after you've adjusted the water levels – leave by the other. However, there are other locks called staircase locks, in which the upper gates of one chamber also act as the lower gates of the next, effectively creating a set of steps where

the usual pounds of water between locks are missing. Some staircase locks – like the famous ones at Foxton (see Wonder 14) or the Five Rise at Bingley (see Wonder 31) – were built to tackle steep gradients in short distances that made conventional lock flights impractical. Some, you suspect, were just built to save money. How else can you explain the odd configuration of double and triple staircase locks towards the summit of the Chesterfield Canal (see Wonder 10)?

Navigating staircase locks requires care and they can confuse even the most experienced boater. Failure to open and close the right paddles in the right order can lead to locks flooding and deluging the towpath, as Steve was allowed to demonstrate spectacularly once while he was making a film at the three-lock Grindley Brook staircase on the Llangollen Canal.

Listing all these different lock variations has made us feel more like anoraks than anything else we've written in this book. But we'd argue that these differences between what is, after all, THE key component of the canal environment add to the richness of the system; and standardisation would make it poorer.

3 Distance and Mile Posts

You'd wonder, wouldn't you, with all the research into industrial archaeology over recent years, how it could be possible that there are still aspects of canals that aren't fully understood? Take these 'DIS' markers you find on the southern Oxford Canal, for instance. They're low cast-iron posts, bevelled at the top so that the letter 'D' points in one direction, the letter 'S' in the other and the 'I' at the apex. Presumably it's because of this they're generally known as distance posts, though no one seems to know for sure.

Because they're always positioned on the approach to locks, the accepted story is that they were put there to prevent disputes between boatmen travelling in different directions as to which had right of way. It's said the first boat to reach a DIS post took priority, cracking a horsewhip or sounding a klaxon to establish their precedence.

We've never bought into this nonsense. Rather than resolve disputes between boatmen, a system like this seems better designed to generate them. After all, the posts are 55–65 metres (60–70 yards) from locks – that means boats approaching from different directions would be a long way from each other. Without a referee, who could determine with any precision who'd got to the posts first? And all this horsewhip rubbish. What was to stop anyone just cracking a whip before they got to the posts?

Our friend Phil has a much more rational explanation. He thinks that in the days when boats travelled in pairs – the motorised or horse-drawn boat hauling a 'butty' – the posts were there to alert skippers that they were getting close to locks and it was time to ease off pulling. Remember, boats don't have brakes. A boat being towed had to be brought to a gentle stop to avoid a collision.

Distance posts remind anyone walking or cruising a canal that

there's a lot to watch out for on the towpath. Mileposts, for instance. These were important in the days when canal haulage was charged by the mile and there are hundreds of them across the country, all very different. Some are metal, some stone, some a mixture of both. Most are fairly obvious. For example, posts on the old Grand Junction Canal, part of today's Grand Union, measure from London to the once important canal village at Braunston (Wonder 8). Some had two measurements, to either end of the canal. Mileposts along the Gloucester & Sharpness Canal, for instance, are marked with the letters 'G' and 'S', indicating distances between these two places. However, some are bewildering if you're not up on your canal history. On the Caldon Canal in Staffordshire, the posts display the distance to the terminus of the old Uttoxeter Canal, which was

Keep your eyes peeled when you're walking and cruising canals: there's a lot of this stuff around. Weirs, for instance, built to keep the canal at a consistent level. The bollards for securing boats in locks, which vary a lot. Embankments, which you may not even notice under tree cover. Our top tip is when you see a wall at the side of the cut, be nosy and look over it. Most likely you'll see a culvert with a small stream or sometimes a sizeable river passing under the canal: part of its construction you'd never think of.

an extension of the Caldon … and abandoned more than 170 years ago.

Time has taken its toll on these old relics of the past but in recent years canal societies have taken to restoring and replacing missing ones, preserving another small but charming feature of our waterways' heritage for future generations to enjoy.

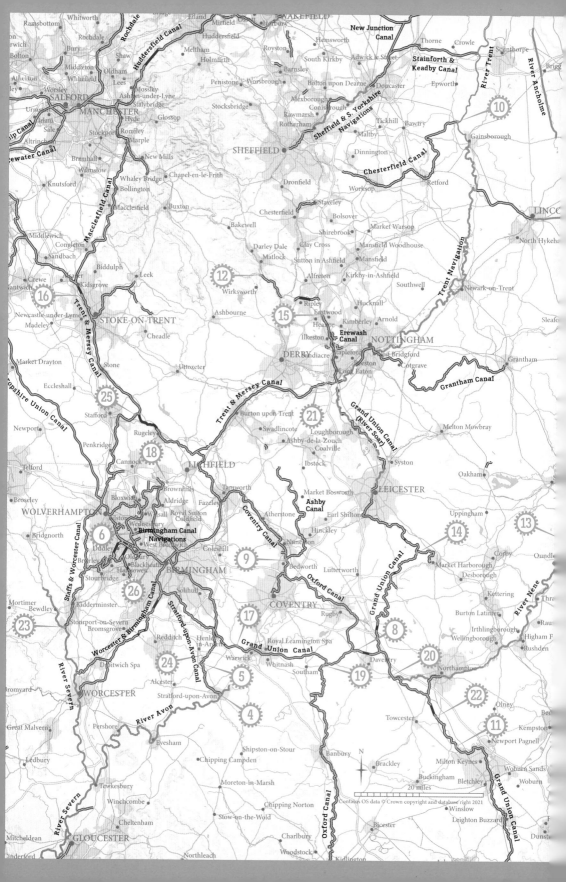

The Midlands

Cromford Canal

Bancroft Basin, Stratford-Upon-Avon

Lying between the Royal Shakespeare Theatre – Stratford-upon-Avon's most iconic building – and a giant Ferris wheel – its most recent tourist attraction – Bancroft Basin provides a gentle transition from the Stratford Canal to the River Avon. The basin itself is surprisingly large for somewhere in the town, and since the installation of 'finger' moorings a few years back, there's a generous number of places to tie up alongside pretty and well-tended flower gardens.

You make a dramatic entrance from the canal, emerging from the darkness and muffled silence of a low bridge into a spacious auditorium with crowds milling around the waterside. As Shakespeare himself famously said, all the world's a stage – but this is a custom-built theatre-in-the-round, boaters the performers, the crowds the audience.

Leaving the basin for the river requires careful rehearsal if you're not to end up with scathing reviews. You pass through a picturesque lock where you are certain

The iconic Royal Shakespeare Theatre in Stratford-upon-Avon overlooks the river, after which the town is named.

to have critical onlookers watching your every move. We canal folk call them gongoozlers, and with so many eyes on you, you're practically guaranteed to make an embarrassing mistake. This is the moment you'll drop the windlass in the water or ram the lock gate as you try to make a graceful exit.

When we first ventured here, we were on a 9-metre (30ft) boat that was easy to tuck into awkward gaps parallel to the bank – the only way you could moor here in those days. It was like being in a goldfish bowl: day trippers who wouldn't be so rude as to stare through the windows of your house had no such compunction when it came to peering through portholes into your boat. All you could do was smile through gritted teeth.

Of course, we couldn't be in Stratford without seeing a play. The Royal Shakespeare Company was putting on *The Winter's Tale* – the one with perhaps the most famous stage direction of all time: 'Exit, pursued by a bear.' That year it was Jeremy Irons being chased; but for us it was equally thrilling to be able to step on to the terrace with our interval drinks and see our boat just a stone's throw away. The following night we sat on deck watching actors in full costume get some fresh air outside their dressing rooms before curtain-up. We were so close we felt we'd practically joined the company ourselves.

We had an enormous tabby cat with cerebral palsy at the time and he wanted to get in on the act too. He spent the night communing with the statue of Hamlet we were moored next to. Who knows what he got up to? After all, to quote the tormented prince himself, 'There are more things in heaven and earth, Horatio, than are dreamt of in your philosophy...'

Finger moorings in Bancroft Basin from the lock which takes boats from the canal to the River Avon.

Visit

In the area

The RSC has not one, but three theatres in Stratford. For details of productions and ticket information:
| rsc.org.uk

For Shakespeare's birthplace and details of his wife Anne Hathaway's cottage, a pleasant half-hour walk up the canal from the town centre:
| shakespeare.org.uk

You can take your pick when it comes to boat trip options.

Canal and river trips:
| canalandrivertours.com

River trips:
| bancroftcruisers.co.uk

Rowing boats and punt hire:
| avon-boating.co.uk

Restaurant cruise:
| countessofevesham.co.uk

Barrel-roofed Lock Cottages, South Stratford Canal

Lock cottages with curiously barrel-shaped roofs are a distinctive feature of the South Stratford, unusual and strikingly picturesque. They were built in the early 19th century to house the lock-keepers and 'lengthsmen' who looked after the canal. These days, one of them belongs to the Landmark Trust and is available as a holiday let, but if you want one yourself these modest erstwhile homes for workmen occasionally come up for sale. One was on the market a year or two back for not much short of £¾ million.

We were smitten with them the first time we found ourselves cruising this gorgeous canal. It was love at first sight. We spent hours imagining what it must be like to live under those rounded eaves, which were the shape of Nissen huts, though infinitely more attractive – especially when adorned as many were with brightly coloured window boxes and hanging baskets.

Actually, it was the window boxes that got us into trouble. Or, to be precise, got Moira into trouble. One lock cottage was selling them, and she couldn't resist buying one to show off on our boat. She positioned it and stepped back in admiration. The shocking-pink petunias were dazzling, the geraniums like exploding fireworks. She adjusted the display slightly and stepped back to admire it again ... this time stepping straight into the lock. Luckily, the water was level with the towpath and so although her dignity

In the past, lock cottages like this used to sell flowers to passing boats, their merchandise enhancing the simplicity of their structure.

was shattered, she was unhurt. This was probably just as well, since Steve would have been incapable of rushing to her assistance. He'd found the whole incident so hilarious – like something out of a cartoon – that he'd literally collapsed to his knees in hysterics. Even after he'd pulled himself together, it was the camera he reached for rather than Moira's hand. She was left to drag herself out of the water while he played David Bailey, framing his close-up shots to make the most of her bedraggled state. She was not amused.

Construction of the Stratford Canal started in 1793, not long after the French Revolution. The political turmoil had economic consequences and the project soon ran out of money and ground to a halt. Eventually, a canny local land agent called William James stepped into the breach to complete the connection with Stratford and the River Avon, which was completed in 1816. Money problems continued to dog the project though. There was constant pressure to cut costs, and it's said that James's engineer William Whitmore – who was more accustomed to building bridges than houses – simply adapted materials he had available. These included recycling the wooden frames used for building traditional humpback bridges as rafters for the cottages, giving them their characteristic shape.

Visit

In the area

Among the many delights of the Stratford Canal is Mary Arden's farm at Wilmcote. Mary was Shakespeare's mother. To find out more, see:

shakespeare.org.uk/explore-shakespeare/shakespedia/mary-ardens-farm/about-mary-ardens-farm/

A couple of miles north is Edstone Aqueduct, the longest cast-iron trough aqueduct in England, one of three on this canal built to the same design and unusual in that the towpath runs at the same level as the bottom of the trough so that on foot you have a duck's-eye view of boats crossing.

To rent

The Lowsonford Lengthsman's Cottage:

landmarktrust.org.uk/search-and-book/properties/lengthsmans-cottage-8857/#Overview

Today, many of the 'cottages' have been extended and modernised to become much larger (and more expensive) homes. Only the surviving barrel roof facing the canal is a reminder of the original function of the house.

The Birmingham Canal Navigations

6

OK, let's settle this once and for all. Or at least let's try to. Does Birmingham *really* have more canals than Venice or is this just an urban myth, the creation of some frustrated PR exec charged with raising the city's international profile?

Well, it certainly has more MILES of canal than Venice – about 56km (35 miles) to Venice's 42km (26 miles). But even bending over backwards to be fair to Birmingham, none of its canals are exactly on a par with Venice's Grand Canal. The Italian canal is only 3.8km (2.4 miles) long, but in places it's nearly 90 metres (300ft) wide, which is roughly twice as wide as the shortest British canal is long (see Wonder 47). Besides, the Grand Canal in Venice is lined with sumptuous palaces and ancient churches. Birmingham's got its new library and the BT Tower, which, with

Built by the great engineer Thomas Telford in 1829, the Grade I listed Galton Bridge crosses the canal in a single 150ft (46m) span.

the best will in the world, just doesn't hack it.

However, Brum does have a trick or two up its sleeve, which evens up the score somewhat. For the canals within the boundaries of Birmingham itself are only a part of a system known in its entirety as the Birmingham Canal Navigations, or the BCN. Despite its name, this incorporates canals in Wolverhampton, parts of the Black Country and Walsall. Originally 257km (160 miles) of waterway, 160km (100 miles) is still navigable, and this is not just more than Venice, but more than Venice and Amsterdam combined, which sort of settles the matter, no?

The BCN is built on a hill – which is not exactly the cleverest of things for a place that's indisputably the centre of Britain's waterways' system; but once you've climbed the long flights of locks necessary to get up there, it's relatively flat, built on three levels. So it's easy to move around and there's a lot to discover once you do, whether you're walking, biking or boating. There are reservoirs and grandiose pumping stations like the one at Smethwick, and fine bridges like the Grade I listed Galton Bridge. There are curiosities like the Birchills

Canal Museum at Walsall, the site of the former Boatman's Rest, commissioned as a chapel and coffee room in an attempt to keep boatmen out of pubs. There are other museums, too, like Cadbury World at Bournville and the Black Country Living Museum in Dudley – one of the best of its sort in the country – where there's a reconstruction of a 1930s' street, a mine, a canal dock and much, much more. And of course there's Brindley Place, one of Birmingham's more recently built attractions with its bustling abundance of restaurants, clubs and bars.

Sadly, the BCN puts off a lot of boaters who, to their great loss, never visit it. This is because much of the former industrial system is still waiting to be developed, which is happening year by year, sometimes with breathtaking speed. It was to get people to explore the network that the BCN Challenge was devised, a sort of peculiar waterways endurance marathon (see Wonder 7).

Visit

Cadbury World is located in Bournville (satnav postcode B30 1JR. Tel: 0121 3936004), a model village built by the Quaker Cadbury family around their 'factory in a garden':
| cadburyworld.co.uk

Black Country Living Museum (Tipton Road, Dudley, DY1 4SQ. Tel: 0121 5576943):
| bclm.com

Galton Bridge is reached easily: a station is named after it with regular services from Birmingham New Street.

Despite the canal cutting through one of Britain's biggest cities there's a wealth of safe and attractive moorings in central Birmingham. Cambrian Wharf lies in the shadow of the city's impressive new library.

BCN Challenge

The BCN Challenge is one of those loopy ideas that could only have been dreamed up by someone with a peculiarly British sense of humour. Is it a race, an endurance test, a competition – or a combination of all three?

Put simply, it's an annual 24-hour boat marathon around some of the lesser-used backwaters of Birmingham's Byzantine canal system, otherwise known as the Birmingham Canal Navigations – or the BCN, as it's usually called by boaters (see Wonder 6). These are what give Brum it's much vaunted reputation for having more canals than Venice.

Birmingham is a very different city from the towpath. The motor car might never have been invented for all that it

intrudes into this water-world. For every Brindley Place and Gas Street Basin, where the busy bars and restaurants stretch down to the water's edge, there are obscure parts known only to the true canalaholic: the Curly Wyrley, Titford Pools, the Soho Loop...

It all harks back to the time when Birmingham was the workshop of the world. Then, the branches, arms and basins of the BCN extended an incredible 257km (160 miles), 160km (100 miles)

Birmingham is awash with extraordinary urban vistas. Here, contemporary motorways, rail bridges and earlier road bridges dwarf the canal, creating a striking image as sunset falls. The BCN Challenge encourages boaters to explore underused parts of the network.

of which are still navigable today. The BCN Challenge aims to encourage more boaters on to these rarely used parts of the network – a case of 'use it or lose it'. The rules are arcane. There's a common finishing point, where everyone celebrates completing the challenge with a bit of a beano, but you can start where you like. You plot your own route and you're honour bound not to cheat. Your score depends partly on the number of miles and locks you do, but you get bonus points for tackling out-of-the-way sections – a bucketful for legging your way through Dudley Tunnel, for example.

The winner is presented with a shield, and everyone taking part gets a commemorative plaque. To suggest the winner is occasionally a foregone conclusion would be to impugn the integrity of the BCN Society, who organise the event. However, the year we took part it was won by a short, flat-bottomed boat owned by ... the BCN Society. Not that it mattered. As the society says, 'It's not about winning, it's about exploring and getting deeply involved with the Birmingham canals.'

When we did the challenge with friends Bob and Rosemary some years ago, we left the route planning to them and merely supplied the necessary boat, with ourselves as crew. Just as well, since we didn't have the first idea what we were supposed to be doing. But then it became clear that they didn't either. Firing the starting gun all on our own in Walsall Basin seemed bonkers, but the challenge was the most fun we've ever had in Birmingham.

Locking up Farmer's Bridge flight in the early hours was magical. Bemused party animals spilling out of adjacent bars and clubs wanted to know what on earth we were doing. If it sparked their interest in exploring the hidden waterways of their home city – well, it was job done.

Visit

To find out more about the BCN Society, or taking part in the challenge:
| bcnsociety.com

8 Braunston

It was clever of the 18th-century engineers digging their way across Northamptonshire to construct their canal close to the M1. Except, of course, they didn't – the canal pre-dated the motorway by some 180-odd years. Even so, the serendipity of the motorway's location hasn't been unhelpful to the small village of Braunston, near Daventry, built on the low escarpment overlooking the junction of the Grand Union and Oxford canals.

It ensured that long after canals ceased to have any commercial importance, the village continued to thrive. Today, it is the capital of canal leisure boating, attracting hirers and owners from all parts of the country who find it a handy base for their boating, partly because of its convenient motorway links. Braunston itself only has about 800 or so houses. We'd guess that there are easily as many boats moored in marinas in or around the village, not to mention the regular streams of other craft stopping for a night or two as they're passing through.

Braunston is a living canal village that has always owed its prosperity to the cut. And that continues today, for unlike other comparably sized communities, which can barely boast a functioning pub, Braunston has four of them. It also has a wealth of other facilities, ranging from a well-stocked supermarket to a highly recommended butcher. It's a popular tourist spot, too, a fascinating place for a day out; and despite the odd curmudgeonly period when we've dissed it for being too busy, and too filled with brass-polishing obsessives who never actually move their boats, the fact is you can't help but like the place.

Approaching from the west, you pass a unique triangular junction spanned by a couple of distinctive black-and-white-painted Horseley Ironworks bridges, with their decorative lozenge-shaped railings. There's another of these elegant Horseley bridges a little further on, carrying the towpath over what is now an arm to a busy marina. At one time, boats travelling the newer Grand Junction Canal, as it was then, were forced to pay punitive tolls to the older Oxford Canal. This was the sort of commercial extortion that wouldn't shame some of our contemporary software companies. But the two were in bitter competition for London trade and the gloves were off. All's fair in love, war and making money, then as now.

Today in Braunston it doesn't take a lot to imagine yourself back in a different age. This is particularly the case in summer, when it holds its annual historic narrowboat rally and canal festival, where the industrial past comes to life with the inspiring sight of fleets of

Braunston's celebrated Admiral Nelson pub: a close up view of the lock or what?

the enormous working boats that once serviced British industry.

There's an imposing toll house along the canal, which is worth a look. Further along, on the opposite bank, is an interesting but relatively industrial part of the village, where boats are still built and repaired. Beyond, at a dry dock adjacent to a small shop – one of the best places on the canal to buy canal books – is the beginning of a pretty flight of six locks, which take you to the start of the 1,867-metre Braunston Tunnel. That's 2,042 yards in old money, more than a mile. It's a lovely walk, but if you want something longer you can continue across the top, along the track where towing horses were led to the other side to rejoin their boats, which were being 'legged' through by labourers stretched across the width of the tunnel on precarious planks.

But where is the village, we hear you ask – the actual village, the one with houses and all the facilities? For that, you have to make your way up the escarpment, either by a lovely public footpath across the fields from the bottom lock or by the road, from the other end of the towpath, where you'll pass the fine church of All Saints, known as the Cathedral of the Canals, where in the past boat people were christened and married and where many of them lie in the surrounding churchyard.

Visit

Access
On a boat, all routes seem to lead to Braunston; sadly, no railways do. The nearest stations are Long Buckby or Rugby, both of them a half hour's taxi ride away. By car, from the south, leave the M1 at Junction 16. From the north come off at Junction 18 and follow the A5. But be warned: though there is limited parking at the Canal & River Trust's Braunston office (charges may apply), the rest of the village can be difficult.

For details of the historic narrowboat festival and canal rally:
| braunstonmarina.co.uk

9 Charity Dock

More than anything, it's the beauty of the canals that attracts people to them today, something that can strike you as forcibly in the middle of a city as in the deepest countryside. It wasn't always like this though.

In the 1970s, the system was collapsing. Towpaths were crumbling, and canals themselves – even those that today are some of the most popular cruising routes – were so shallow they were almost unnavigable. The cut in those days resembled a once-loved garden that, through neglect, has been allowed to go to seed. In towns, it was the same picture. People turned their back on the water as if it represented a threat. They segregated themselves behind high fences, which soon got covered in graffiti. Or worse, corrugated iron stockades, mile upon mile of them sometimes. It was not pretty.

Charity Dock is not pretty either. Perhaps that's why we love it. Perhaps it's a reminder of what the canals were like at a key turning point in their history. It lies on a bend on the Coventry Canal at Bedworth (pronounced Bed'uth), just a little up from Hawkesbury Junction, where it meets the northern Oxford Canal; and coming across it, unprepared, is startling to say the least. It's a study in canal-side kitsch, which, depending on your perspective, is either a messy, rat-infested scrapyard or an installation you'd find at Tate Modern. Wrecked cars, the skeletons of motorbikes, and rusted engines sit alongside the sort of junk you'd find at a council recycling centre.

There are mannequins salvaged from department stores. Some are dressed as clowns, others as circus performers or pirates. One female figure, sheltering in a camouflaged bivouac, wears khaki hotpants; another sits on a model horse posing provocatively in stockings and suspenders, a parody of the local icon, Lady Godiva. Scattered around at random are flags, old street signs and Polynesian fertility masks. There are garden gnomes, huge ice-cream cones, old advertising hoardings, an enormous hare's head ... You get the picture. Unfortunately, a lot of people don't. They think it's a ramshackle eyesore that doesn't fit the sanitised image of modern canals. We think it's wonderful.

Charity Dock has become an unlikely, but much photographed, feature of the waterways.

We stumbled across the place in 1981 when our engine broke down, and we ended up staying for years. It was no tidier then, worse even, managed by a cantankerous old rogue called Joe Gilbert, who at that stage was still repairing wooden narrowboats. The place was a complete mess, but it was a mess with an impeccable historical lineage that stretched back to the 1830s, when it was the wharf for the nearby and long since abandoned Charity Colliery. Today, it sits in the middle of an unprepossessing council estate where, in 1963, when the Great Freeze effectively signalled the end of commercial canal carrying in the UK, families from the boats were rehoused after they'd been heartlessly turfed out of their homes by the British Waterways Board.

The old boatmen were stocky, taciturn folk who used to wander down to Charity Dock as if drawn there by some inexplicable bond to the water. You'd catch them looking wistfully up the cut as if waiting for boats they knew would never arrive. When we pass the dock today, they still seem to be standing there like ghosts from a lost past.

Visit

In the area

Charity Dock lies close to the fascinating Hawkesbury Junction – known to boaters as Sutton Stop after a family of lock-keepers who once lived there. There – at the site of one of the waterway's more famous pubs, The Greyhound (Sutton Stop, Longford, Coventry, CV6 6DF. Tel: 02476 363046) – the Coventry Canal meets the northern Oxford Canal, another spur veering off to Coventry itself:
| thegreyhoundlongford.co.uk

Around the corner from Charity Dock is the entrance to the 35km (22-mile) Ashby Canal, a delightful virtually lock-free waterway that winds its way into the heart of Leicestershire through the site of the Battle of Bosworth, where there's a visitor centre:
| bosworthbattlefield.org.uk

10 The Chesterfield Canal

The Chesterfield Canal owes a large part of its charm to its seclusion. The only way to get there by boat is via the tidal Trent, which is no river for cissies. And the canal is a dead end – a delightful dead end, but a dead end nonetheless. Most people on the river pass it without a second glance on their way to destinations less off the beaten track. We did the same ourselves more than once. When curiosity finally got the better of us, what we found was a revelation.

As soon as you leave the hazards of the river behind and pass through the lock at West Stockwith, you find yourself in a tranquil basin where, with a couple of pubs – one serving mean fish and chips – it's tempting to linger.

Once on the move, though, it doesn't take long to realise that this is a traditional Brindley canal (see Wonder 23), following the contours of the land as it winds through remote countryside, with views across flat, open farmland, broken by occasional low hills. There are vast fields of loamy soil turned over by the plough. Sheep, cattle and horses graze in green pastures, which are sometimes shared with chickens. The derelict remains of old brickworks give way to wooded stretches strewn with wildflowers, and there are so few boats passing that even the ducks seem alarmed by their presence.

Woods bordering the top end of the canal are carpeted with bluebells in the spring.

The Midlands

The Chesterfield is like canals used to be: shallow, narrow, weedy and reedy, its ragged banks fringed with high bulrushes and splashes of yellow flag. Water lilies like lotus blossoms float undisturbed on the water, the deep silence of the surroundings broken only by the sound of songbirds and the shrill call of an occasional coot.

At the top end of the canal is one of the most attractive lock flights in the country – a flurry of narrow, slow-filling double and treble staircase locks set beside woods carpeted with bluebells and scented with wild garlic. It's hard to believe this was once an important coal mining centre and the canal a hive of activity, with nearby Anston Quarries the source of the stone used to rebuild the Houses of Parliament after they burned down in 1834.

The canal comes to an abrupt end just before the entrance to the derelict Norwood Tunnel. At more than 2.5km (1.5 miles) long, it's the biggest obstacle to the ambitious restoration that has seen the Chesterfield Canal Trust reinstate 19km (12 miles) of canal, 37 locks and 11 bridges since 1989. Its bold aim is to open the tunnel and the remaining unnavigable 14km (9 miles) of the canal by 2027, the 250th anniversary

of its original opening, making it possible to cruise its entire length for the first time since 1907. From the tunnel, you can cycle, as we did, the 24km (15 miles) or so into Chesterfield itself on the Trans Pennine Trail. This follows the route of the original canal, parts of which have already been restored in anticipation of the tunnel reopening.

Visit

In the area

You can walk or cycle all 74km (46 miles) of the canal towpath – through Derbyshire, Nottinghamshire and South Yorkshire – along the Cuckoo Way, named after the so-called cuckoo boats unique to this canal: essentially narrowboats with mast, sail and oars, enabling them to navigate the Trent as well as the canal.

For those who want to get on the water, Chesterfield Canal Trust runs trip boats from various locations:
| chesterfield-canal-trust.org.uk

The canal passes through two sizeable towns, Retford and Worksop; and at Bassetlaw Museum (Amcott House, 40 Grove Street, Retford, DN22 6LD. Tel: 01777 713749), a five-minute walk from the canal, is a gallery dedicated to the Pilgrim Fathers who all came from this area:
| bassetlawmuseum.org.uk

Others celebrated locally are the Straws, local grocers whose house (5–7 Blyth Grove, Worksop, S81 0JG), frozen in time and packed with Edwardian artefacts, is now owned by the National Trust (NT). Pre-booking is essential (Tel: 0344 2491895, or online), though you can sometimes be lucky as we were and squeeze in on a cancellation:
| nationaltrust.org.uk/mr-straws-house

Calm waters wind through a peaceful landscape of rolling farmland.

Cosgrove to Grafton Regis, Grand Union Canal

To be honest, you could blink and miss the small Northamptonshire village of Cosgrove, 9.7km (6 miles) north of Milton Keynes on the Grand Union Canal. And as for Grafton Regis a few miles away, you wouldn't need to blink because even if your eyes were propped open with matchsticks you wouldn't be able to see it from the canal. So why do these two apparently undistinguished villages get a mention in a book featuring 'wonders' of the waterways? What is so wonderful about them?

To understand the answer to this question, you need to realise the canals aren't just a procession of flashy artefacts you can tick off one by one. Often, what makes the waterways remarkable is the accretion of different elements along them, one feature layered upon another in such a way that together they create a vivid narrative of Britain. It is as if a still picture becomes a movie, as if something flat and two-dimensional suddenly attains a depth and perspective that makes you see it in an entirely different way.

So it is with these two places. You

Fancy bridges are rare on the cut and no one seems sure why this one was built, a confusion mirrored in the differing names by which it is known.

approach Cosgrove over a trough aqueduct supported by a single brick pier made of cast iron; it's known as the Iron Trunk, and it crosses the River Great Ouse, the border of Buckinghamshire and Northamptonshire. At a fraction of its size, this is no Pontcysyllte (see Wonder 86). Even so, it's an impressive structure and at 4.57 metres (15ft) broad, it's wider than its Welsh counterpart, allowing bigger boats to cross. The Great Ouse was always a major obstacle on the canal, and originally boats traversed it by a couple of flights of locks on either side of the river valley, remnants of which can still be seen. Eventually, they got around to building a traditional brick and stone aqueduct to the design of the famous civil engineer William Jessop, but this collapsed in 1808 after less than three years in use. After that, in the wake of the success of Pontcysyllte, the existing trough aqueduct was built.

A little further up the canal is the now disused arm of the Buckingham Canal, which was prone to freezing, so much so that the owner of nearby Cosgrove Hall used to harvest the ice, which he stored in a still surviving ice house and sold in the summer. Further along, under the canal, is the unusual horseshoe-shaped Cosgrove foot tunnel, so designed to accommodate the broad shoulders of horses passing underneath – though it's used more nowadays to access the Barley Mow pub from the towpath. Leaving the village, you pass under the surprisingly decorative Bridge 65, known as the Ornamental Bridge, Solman's Bridge or sometimes Samson's Bridge. These fancy bridges are rare on the cut and they're usually associated with local landowners who wouldn't allow the canal on to their property without it being tarted up (see Wonder 24). But there's controversy about this one, reflected in its many names, and no one seems to know for sure why it was built.

However, if it's controversy you want, there's enough of this to be had a pleasant hour's walk up the canal at Grafton Regis – a place, as its name suggests, that has royal connections. Barely a hundred people live there today, but in the 1500s it was an important manor, owned at one stage by Henry VIII, who'd inherited it through his grandmother Elizabeth Woodville, King Edward IV's wife, who was born there. So imbued with Tudor history is the place that it seems unsurprising that some 400 years later a painting on an oak panel acquired by a family called the Smiths should still be hanging on the wall of their unassuming cottage. It was dated 1588 and depicted a young, delicately featured man who'd probably been presented with it as a birthday gift, since his age, 24, is emblazoned in the top-left corner. The painting found its way to County Durham, where for many years it hung in a pub and where the belief grew that it was a portrait of the young William Shakespeare. The main reason for this being that, well … it looks like Shakespeare, who in 1588 was indeed 24 years old. The fact is that if the painting's not him, he's an exact contemporary of the real subject.

Experts have been arguing about the authenticity of this Grafton Portrait, as it's known, for years. They still are.

An unusual aqueduct, a canal junction, a horse tunnel and some lovely canalside cottages: unremarkable it all may be, but the combination of its features makes Cosgrove a fascinating village to explore.

Cromford Mills and the Cromford Canal

It's impossible not to link these two extraordinary features of the waterways. The Grade I listed mill – the world's first cotton-spinning mill, built in 1771, and progenitor of factory production the world over – is a few minutes' walk from the Cromford Canal. Today, the waterway is largely unnavigable, but for its entire 8km (5-mile) length to Ambergate it's a Site of Special Scientific Interest, home to rare damselflies, grass snakes and the increasingly threatened water vole (see Wonder 79). It's also a delightful and undemanding stroll, suitable for both wheelchairs and buggies.

However, mill and canal are not quite as closely connected as you'd think. Originally, when a waterway was first mooted to link Cromford to the River Trent by way of the Erewash Canal,

it needed support to get it built from powerful local dignitaries – men like Sir Richard Arkwright, whose mechanised mill at Cromford was powered by water brought into the mill by an

Leawood Pumphouse, one of the features of the Cromford Canal: kept in pristine working condition thanks to the dedication of the Middleton Top and the Leawood Pump Volunteer Group.

aqueduct and an intricate complex of subterranean culverts. It was this question of water supply that created division between Arkwright and the canal sponsors.

At the eleventh hour, before a bill giving the canal the go-ahead was presented to Parliament, Arkwright saw a way of turning things to his advantage by demanding that water to feed the canal should come not from sources previously agreed but from the River Derwent by way of a raised weir. This was a solution that would have benefited his own mill more than the canal; and though a compromise between the two was eventually cobbled together, there was no love lost between them afterwards.

Arkwright's mill was what we'd now call a sweatshop, with workers – many of them children as young as six – earning a pittance for shifts 13 hours a day, six days a week. Today, it's part of a UNESCO World Heritage Site, and an ideal day out for a family jaunt. There are cafes, independent shops and – paradoxically – a lot of fun kids' activities on offer, along with regular theatre and music events. Lectures, exhibitions and guided tours around the site are available too – a site that made Arkwright so rich it's said that at one time he could have personally paid off the National Debt.

Those of a hardier disposition, looking for a more demanding challenge, can branch off the canal at what's now called High Peak Junction, where at one time the Cromford and High Peak Railway linked with the Peak Forest Canal over the other, western side of the Pennines, at Whaley Bridge (see Wonder 32). Here, the old bed of the railway rises up a vertiginous incline to a 27km (17-mile) trail for

(see Wonder 32)

Visit

In the area
Cromford Mills is in the Derbyshire Dales, close to the inland holiday resort of Matlock, a great centre for hillwalking.

For details on visiting the former factory (entry is free):
| cromfordmills.org.uk

For more on the canal, including details of boat trips from Cromford Wharf on the historic narrowboat *Birdswood*, contact Friends of the Cromford Canal:
| cromfordcanal.org

For Leawood Pumphouse:
| middleton-leawood.org.uk/

Facilities
There are cafes at both the mill and the wharf.

walkers and cyclists. At the top, the going gets a lot easier, and from a virtually level course you can enjoy dramatic views over this splendid part of the country.

A former warehouse at the end of the canal, a short walk from the mill, is now a popular stop for tea.

13 Fotheringhay

Nowhere is the word 'magical' better fitted to a waterways' location than the castle at Fotheringhay on the banks of the River Nene in Northamptonshire. It's just a mound – the old castle 'motte'. Few remnants of the castle itself survive. Even so, the place is magical in all the ways a dictionary defines: it's bewitching, beguiling, entrancing.

But it's magical in a more literal, other-worldly sense, too. The castle was where Mary, Queen of Scots, was tried and brutally executed, beheaded by an inept axeman who missed her neck and hit her head with his first blow. Fotheringhay is where her entrails – her guts – are buried. In the mornings and early evenings, moored underneath it, the place can sometimes be wreathed in thick mists, its chilling history all too present.

The tiny hamlet of Fotheringhay, adjacent to the castle, has a population of little more than a hundred living in a scattering of honey-stone houses grouped close to the church of St Mary and All Saints, the distinctive tower of which dominates the surrounding flatlands. You'd be inclined to call the architectural style of the place Tudor – except that would be a gaffe on a par with asking for a Turkish coffee in a Greek restaurant. For Fotheringhay Castle was a fortress of the Yorkists, a branch of the House of Plantagenet from which three English kings sprang. The last of these was the ill-fated Richard III, who was born in the castle and died fighting the upstart pretender Henry Tudor at the Battle of Bosworth in 1485.

From the top of the mound as the evening shadows fall across the fields. But melancholic clouds of history always hover above Fotheringhay.

Fotheringhay, though, is most associated with the story of Mary. As a former queen of Catholic France, she was embroiled in religious politics almost from the moment of her birth, a vulnerable patsy to those who would use her to replace the Protestant Elizabeth I – granddaughter of that self-same Henry Tudor who had founded a new dynasty on the back of his victory on the battlefield. Mary had already been incarcerated for 18 years when she allowed herself to be drawn into an assassination plot that galvanised Elizabeth into action, first putting Mary on trial and then, after months wrestling with her conscience on the matter of killing queens, finally signing her death warrant.

There's an awful melancholy that even now still hangs over Fotheringhay as a result of these events all those years ago. We walked to the top of the mound one evening on our first visit and had to tread carefully to avoid the thick clumps of thistle that had grown – or been planted – on the slopes. We were alone, and at the summit we looked across the river in silence as a dramatic sunset fell over the featureless fields, staining the countryside a blood red. Until then, it had been a warm evening, but now it suddenly seemed cold. We left immediately. We wouldn't have wanted to be stranded there after dark.

Visit

Access

Fotheringhay is out in the sticks. From Peterborough, which is the nearest station, it's about 8km (5 miles); buses are few and far between. Parking in the village is easy because there's nothing there apart from a lovely pub. There are extensive moorings for boats, but they are on private land where charges will apply.

Facilities

The Falcon Inn (Fotheringhay, PE8 5HZ. Tel: 01832 226254):
| thefalcon-inn.co.uk

The church of St Mary and All Saints with its distinctive tower. Inside is a mausoleum to prominent Yorkists killed in the Wars of the Roses.

Foxton Locks And Inclined Plane

There's an old black-and-white photograph of Foxton Locks, probably one of the earliest ever taken there, thought to date from around 1899. It shows a boat in one of the locks, a woman standing next to it holding a rope and a man opposite with a horse. In the foreground is a girl, hand on hip, sitting on a lockbeam.

All of them are looking directly at the camera, unsmiling. It's a winter's day, there is a light dusting of snow on the ground, and it is wet and slippery underfoot. The family are bundled up against the cold but their clothes are dirty and ragged, and they look as if the icy conditions have penetrated to their very core. Their faces are pinched, their expressions not just weary, but wary too, as if they are suspicious not only of the photographer who is taking their picture,

A haunting image of the past: a copy of this picture has hung in different boats of ours for decades.

but of the successive generations of people like us who will look at it, staring at them like exhibits in a museum. The girl in particular looks wretched, as if she'd rather be anywhere but where she is.

The photograph was hanging in a pub at the bottom of the flight the first time we went through on a cold and very wet March day in the mid-1970s, and as soon as Moira saw the girl she instantly felt an affinity. It was as if she'd found a boating sister-in-arms, a ghost from another age speaking to her directly about the hardship of being one of a working boatman's family. Moira was drenched herself from our trip down the locks, and she knew immediately how the girl must have felt, soaked to the skin, shivering, exhausted and probably famished, too. The image haunted her, and when we got home she made it her mission to find a copy of the photograph. It's hung in the cabin of our boats ever since.

Set on an escarpment with extensive views over the undulating Leicestershire countryside, Foxton Locks have long been a favourite day out for local families. Steve, who grew up not far away, went there himself many times as a kid. The two staircases of five locks each,

The locks clamber up the hill carrying the canal out of the valley of the River Soar on its route to London. Today the flight is a popular tourist destination.

with a passing pound in the middle, is remarkably unchanged since its opening in 1814, a key link between London and the East Midlands coalfields. But the flight was always a bottleneck and boat progress was invariably delayed.

In 1900, an ingenious alternative opened: a boat lift on an inclined plane. This worked on the basis of two counterbalanced caissons filled with water and connected by a steel cable. As one ascended the 1 in 4 gradient, the other descended the 23-metre (75ft) slope at the same rate, carrying up to four loaded boats at a time. A 25hp steam winch controlled the operation. Nothing like it had ever been seen on British waterways, but revolutionary as it was in engineering terms, it kept breaking down and the canal company could never make it pay. It closed after only ten years in operation.

Visit

Access
There is parking at both the top and bottom of the flights; charges may apply. Boat crews need to check in with the duty lock-keeper before proceeding.

Facilities
There is a cafe at the top lock and two pubs at the bottom of the flights, the Foxton Locks Inn (Tel: 0116 2791515, restaurantfoxtonlocks.co.uk), and the highly recommended and more traditional Bridge 61 (Tel: 0116 2792285).

In the area
There's a small museum and visitor centre on the site, run by the Foxton Inclined Plane Trust, where the workings of the lift are explained. Surrounding it, you can explore the remaining traces of the lift, and wander around the locks and the delightful side ponds adjoining them, built as a water-saving device:
| foxtoncanalmuseum.org

Passenger boat trips run most weekends in the summer:
| foxtonboats.co.uk

The Great Northern Basin

15

You may wonder what on earth the people who named the Great Northern Basin were thinking. You'd probably have a case against them under the Trade Descriptions Act because the place is neither Great, nor Northern, nor much of a Basin either when all's said and done.

In fact, this junction on the border of Nottinghamshire and Derbyshire where the Erewash Canal meets two unnavigable canals – the Cromford and Nottingham canals – is more accurately described by its workaday alternative title: Langley Mill. The miracle is that it exists at all. It was restored, along with Langley Lock, by the Erewash Canal Preservation and Development Association (ECP&DA), a determined group of local people hastily convened to save the canal when it was under threat of closure in 1968, after being silted up for years by coal waste. Now it's a delightful green oasis – beautifully maintained by volunteer working parties – with good moorings, an interesting collection of boats and a welcome pub.

The towpath is in excellent condition for walking or cycling and the canal is regularly restocked with fish for anglers. Despite this, it's still something of an achievement for boats to get here. It's less than 16km (10 miles) and only 15 locks from the River Trent at Trent Junction, with some surprisingly attractive rural sections for an area so scarred by heavy industry; but it's not on many holiday routes, since the Erewash has a reputation as a no-nonsense, rufty-tufty kind of canal that makes you earn your passage: lock gates are heavy and the paddle gear sometimes feels like it needs a hefty clout to get it working.

The rewards for persistence are worth it, though, because a short walk from the top is Eastwood, one of Britain's best-known mining towns thanks to local lad DH Lawrence, the novelist famous for *Sons and Lovers*, *Women in Love* and the notorious *Lady Chatterley's Lover*, which overturned outdated obscenity laws in a landmark 1960 trial at which jurors were famously asked by the prosecution: 'Is it a book that you would even wish your wife or your servants to read?'

For such an industrialised canal passing through built-up areas it's surprising to still find rural sections harking back to a different age.

Trade from local collieries, brickworks and ironworks made the Erewash Canal one of the most profitable in the country, with shares quickly rising in value from £100 to a whopping £1,300. But the canal was also important to one of Nottingham's defining industries: lacemaking. Raw materials and the finished lace articles were both transported by water.

The whole area in these parts is threaded through with the rich seams that once formed the Notts/Derby coalfield, and mining subsidence has played havoc with local canals. There's good news to celebrate, though: the Friends of the Cromford Canal (FCC) finally have the green light to begin work on restoring a short section beyond Langley Mill at the Great Northern Basin, marking a start on realising a dream of someday perhaps reconnecting to the top of the canal, which is unnavigable but still in water (see Wonder 12).

(see Wonder 12).

Visit

In the area

Sandiacre Lock Cottages (1779) comprise the only surviving lock cottage and toll house on the Erewash Canal. Restored, managed by volunteers from the ECP&DA, and open to the public as a museum, opening hours are limited to the third Sunday of each month plus bank holiday Mondays. Entry is free and freshly made cakes, hot drinks and an open fire add to the attraction:
| ecpda.org.uk/sandiacre

For details of the Friends of Cromford Canal:
| cromfordcanal.org

David Herbert Lawrence was born and brought up in Eastwood and his childhood home is open to the public; you can take a guided tour and have tea there afterwards. The local library houses a collection of his letters and books, including first editions:
| lleisure.co.uk/d-h-lawrence-birthplace-
| museum

16 The Harecastle Tunnels

Tunnels can be an adventure when you're cruising canals. They can also be a pain. Even on the sunniest of summer days they're cold, dark and more often than not wet as well. For most boaters, they're an obstacle to be negotiated as quickly as possible, something to be endured rather than enjoyed. This is particularly the case with the Harecastle Tunnel between Kidsgrove and Tunstall north of Stoke-on-Trent in Staffordshire, which, at 2.6km (1.6 miles), is not only very long but very narrow, too, and so low that travelling through it, you can touch the roof with your hands. Claustrophobia doesn't begin to describe it.

Although only one is still functional now, there used to be two canal tunnels under Harecastle Hill and the entrance to the old one is still visible by the side of the newer one, blocked and inaccessible. It was completed by James Brindley in 1777 after 11 years of hard labour by a huge workforce using picks and shovels. In those early days, when tunnelling was in its infancy, the process was all a bit hit-and-miss. The course of the tunnel was marked out on the hill above and shafts were dug at various points along its length. Miners were then lowered in baskets to dig outwards, joining them up. When construction of the tunnel began, nothing on this scale had ever been attempted before and it was seen as the 'eighth wonder of the world'. It was hazardous work, fraught with danger. Many lives were lost.

Unfortunately, as with so much of the British canal system, cost-cutting decisions were made that quickly proved a false economy. The tunnel had no towpath, so boats had to be 'legged' –

The imposing southern portal to the tunnel. Note the hanging gauges indicating how low parts of the tunnel are.

literally inched along by men lying on the roofs 'walking' them through, an arduous process that took about three and a half hours. It was too narrow for boats to pass too, which meant one-way traffic and inevitable delays. Eventually, a new tunnel – with a towpath, since removed – was built under the direction of star engineer Thomas Telford. This was opened in 1827 and though it was still too narrow for boats to pass, having two tunnels in operation allowed traffic in both directions, cutting journey times significantly. That stopped when the original Brindley tunnel collapsed in 1914. Today, the surviving Telford tunnel has to carry all modern leisure traffic. Tunnel keepers oversee a one-way system that allows boats to travel northbound for parts of the day, and southbound the rest of the time.

Inside, it can be hard keeping a steady hand on the tiller. Under your headlight, the dank, dripping walls of 200-year-old brick take on an eerie dimension and your senses play tricks with you, so that you see odd shapes in the shadows. There's a point when you can't see even a pinprick of daylight at either end, but then you pass under an air shaft and see a circle of sky at the summit of what seems an impossibly tall brick cylinder like a chimney. It's easy to get

Visit

Access

Passage through Harecastle can be booked online:

canalrivertrust.org.uk/ notices/21498-harecastle-tunnel

spooked, especially when you discover that the tunnel is said to be haunted by a headless ghost. You can end up losing concentration and accidentally scraping the tunnel wall, as we once did years ago. Our steering has improved since, but we still have a half brick, dislodged at the time, that we keep as a souvenir.

The northern entrance to the tunnel with the mouth of the original, now disused, tunnel visible to its right. The distinctive colour of the water is caused by iron oxides leaching from rock formations.

17 Hatton Locks

Long before Led Zeppelin penned their most famous song, working boatmen had christened the Hatton flight of 21 locks on the Grand Union Canal the 'stairway to heaven'.

Perhaps it was because looking downward from halfway up, there's a fine view of the tower of the Collegiate Church of St Mary, Warwick, perfectly framed by trees and the balance beams of the locks. A more likely explanation, it's generally agreed, is that after the hard work involved in getting through the locks, boatmen could count on a much easier run into Birmingham, where they'd get paid.

The Hatton flight is unusual in that the original narrow locks dating from 1799 were widened in the 1930s to make them more commercially viable. This was a high-stakes gamble by the newly formed Grand Union Canal Company, which in 1929 took over the eight canals connecting London and the Midlands, of which the Warwick & Birmingham Canal – home to the Hatton flight – was one. It was a brave plan, the last throw of the dice; canal transport was in decline, already superseded by rail freight and road haulage.

The new company was banking on the corporate restructure and modernisation making the canal profitable. With the

country in the grip of the Great Depression, the project was bankrolled by the government, a job creation scheme of its day. Another risky innovation was using concrete – untested in canal building at the time – to line lock chambers and cap banking. Remains of the long-disused original brick-built narrow locks still survive alongside the newer and wider locks; and the old wharf and maintenance yard now houses a heritage skills training centre. Historic boats *Malus* and *Scorpio*, which used to work this route, can sometimes be seen tied up alongside the wharf.

There's no getting round the fact that ascending the flight by boat is a slog. The striking white hydraulic paddle gear seems to need winding forever, and the gates are heavy. If that wasn't enough, the locks are spaced out over more than 3km (2 miles) and it's a trudge between them, though at the top there are rewards with the popular Hatton Locks Cafe in converted canal stables and the Hatton Arms gastropub a short walk away.

Once when we tackled Hatton, we'd agreed to pair up with friends on another boat – which seemed a good idea at the time. Unrelenting torrential rain should have made us reconsider, but for some reason we soldiered on grimly as the towpath turned to mud and we all got soaked, literally, to the skin. Things got so bad we had to stop halfway to change clothes and have a hot drink. As we reached the top, the sky brightened. It was at that moment, bringing tea to the tillerman, that Moira slid gracefully into the water from the gunnels. She emerged dripping like some strange mermaid, still clutching two mugs tightly in her hand.

Sunset with both the modern and the disused original flights clearly visible.

18 Lichfield Canal Aqueduct

If anything encapsulates the indomitable optimism of canal enthusiasts nowadays, and the strategies they have to adopt to restore waterways, it's the aqueduct over the M6 toll motorway a little north of Birmingham.

This is no ordinary aqueduct. For a start it's relatively modern, built in 2003. At 46.8m (154ft) long, it's something of a landmark to motorists speeding underneath, though few probably know what it is, and of those that do, hardly any would know its secret. The fact is, it's never had a boat go over in its history and it'll be a few years yet before it does. Until then, it's empty of water, connected to nothing but thin air on either side, waiting for the canal to reach it.

The background to this strange structural *Marie Celeste* floating above a modern motorway says a lot about the demands of contemporary canal restoration. Eventually, it will connect

Borrowcop Locks on the Lichfield Canal awaiting only gates and water to be operative after fifty years of dereliction.

to the Lichfield Canal, part of a major restoration incorporating the Hatherton Canal – the long-term aim of which is to link the Staffordshire & Worcestershire Canal in the west to the Coventry Canal in the east. To this end, the Lichfield & Hatherton Canals Restoration Trust was founded in 1988, though from the outset it had to surmount what you'd think were insuperable obstacles. The section from Brownhills to Lichfield is only about 11km (7 miles) long, for instance, but to restore it meant crossing a railway line and several major roads. Additionally, the canal had been built over in various places and a number of diversions would be required to complete it, meaning that substantial lengths of new canal would have to be dug from scratch. And then there was the small matter of some 30 locks that would need reinstating as the canal dropped 75 metres (247ft) to the valley of the River Trent...

If all this wasn't enough, the trust's problems were compounded by plans to build the M6 toll road, which would cut across the proposed restoration further. After what were at times difficult discussions, a compromise agreement was eventually brokered whereby the road company had to pay for the foundations of the aqueduct but left the

A vaguely forlorn bridge to nowhere that passes over it the M6 Relief Road. It awaits connection to the Lichfield and Hatherton canals.

trust to pay for the structure itself. Given that any delayed attempt at erecting it would be disruptive and even more expensive than it was going to be anyway, the trust had no alternative but to have it built during motorway construction.

It was a tough ask, financially challenging and in many ways irrational. But the trust had already taken to working like this: not attempting to restore the canal in a linear fashion from one end to the other, but restoring it in bits, as and when it was feasible. Spearheaded by the renowned actor Sir David Suchet CBE – the trust's vice chair, patron and a long-time waterway enthusiast – an appeal was launched, one that eventually raised enough from private donations and grants and European Union funding to erect the aqueduct.

The appeal attracted much publicity and, incongruously perhaps, the most enduring result of it may be not the aqueduct itself – which is still some years off ever being connected to any canal – but revised government guidance it gave rise to, stating that new road building should make provision for any abandoned waterways along its route that might be restored in the future. Or putting it another way: where there is

a possibility of restoration, aqueducts, bridges and culverts associated with it should be integral to the road scheme, not something canal societies have to fund themselves.

Visit

For the latest on the restoration and for donations and offers of help, contact:
| lhcrt.org.uk.

In the area

You may not be able to visit Lichfield by water yet, but it's a remarkably attractive city, its cathedral the only medieval one with three spires and its close one of the most complete in the country.

Lichfield's most famous son is the polemicist and poet Samuel Johnson, best known for his acerbic dictionary, who was born in the town. His birthplace in the centre (Breadmarket Street, Lichfield, WS13 6LG. Tel: 01543 264972) is now a museum:
| samueljohnsonbirthplace.org.uk

Nearby is the Grade I listed house of Erasmus Darwin (Beacon Street, Lichfield, WS13 7AD. Tel: 01543 306260), grandfather of Charles Darwin and a renowned scientist in his own right:
| visitlichfield.co.uk/attractions/
| erasmus-darwin-house

19 Napton and the Oxford Summit

Remember those geography lessons at school that had you poring over Ordnance Survey maps studying the contour lines – those subtly shaded, fingerprint-like whorls indicating heights of hills above sea level and precise gradients of valleys? Well, the 18km (11-mile) summit of the Oxford Canal is the most perfect example of why they're useful, because in the early days of canal building, in order to avoid the expense of building locks, engineers would religiously follow the lie of the land.

These 'contour canals', as they're called, wind around the countryside in a hypnotic, hallucinatory way that is guaranteed to disorientate you and have you wondering if you can trust your senses, especially in the early morning mists or on a late summer's evening when the world hangs precariously between day and night and the slightest rustle in a hedgerow can set the imagination racing. On the Oxford summit you pass a radio mast that seems positioned to confound you. It appears on one side of the canal, and then seems to switch to the other. Even when you think you've left it behind it reappears in front of you, jumping about like a grasshopper. The canal corkscrews so much that at one point you could get off the boat and, in ten minutes, walk between two bridges that – with the canal being as shallow as it is – can take you getting on for an hour to cruise by water.

Best to just relax and enjoy the unspoiled scenery: classic English countryside with the outline of lost villages and strip farming still embossed

The Oxford Canal winds around Napton-on-the Hill before starting its long ascent to the summit.

on undulating fields, punctuated by occasional copses, and views that open spectacularly across the rich Warwickshire Plain. You get a sense of an England marooned in a rural past here, but don't go fretting about it being too old-fashioned for the modern world; it won't be around for much longer. They're routing HS2 through the middle of it. They call it 'progress', though 'vandalism' is a better word in our lexicon.

The focal point of the summit is Napton-on-the-Hill, where a flight of delightful narrow locks cascade into a shallow valley, which rises on the other side to a windmill, its classic domed brick tower and huge white sails dominating the lush landscape. Napton village itself is just a step or two away, easily accessible on foot from the canal. More demanding is a climb up to the windmill, where one summer's evening at dusk we once happened on a family of badgers out taking the air and as surprised to see us as we were to see them.

Sheep graze freely around the precincts of Wormleighton village, a bucolic scene that barely seems part of the modern age.

Visit

Facilities

There's a freehouse at Napton called The Folly (Folly Lane, Napton, CV47 8NZ. Tel: 01926 815185), conveniently positioned in an old farmhouse near the bottom lock and perennially popular, serving Oxfordshire ales and homemade food in an unspoilt rustic setting:
| follyatnapton.co.uk

If you're up to it, it's a 14km (9-mile) walk across the summit to The Wharf Inn at Fenny Compton (Wharf Road, Fenny Compton, CV47 2FE. Tel: 01295 770332), where you'll find a welcome in a more contemporary gastropub that has a large garden bordering the canal, and where you can order a taxi back to your starting point.

In the area

A shorter walk from Fenny is to head to Wormleighton, once the ancestral home of the Spencer family (as in Diana, Princess of Wales). Beyond the lovely church you'll find a farm track to the canal, where you can cross a bridge to the towpath and back to your starting point. Wormleighton is unmissable, a tiny hamlet preserved in aspic without shop or pub, where sheep graze the verges and churchyard undisturbed by the 21st century.

Royal Ordnance Depot, Weedon

Imagine for one moment a Georgian house grand enough to be a royal palace. Imagine it surrounded by barracks capacious enough to house 500 men, as well as warehouses and magazines to store enough gunpowder, cannons and small arms to resist a siege. Imagine the scene back in the day bustling with red-coated soldiers and officers with their brass buttons and epaulettes gleaming in the sunshine, their ladies in empire-line muslin dresses like characters from a Jane Austen novel. Imagine it today. It would be a tourist hotspot, wouldn't it? A National Trust honeypot where you'd have to pay 20 quid before you could get a glimpse inside.

Actually, it wouldn't be like that at all. Today, you'd find the place intact, but a bit run down – messy almost – an industrial estate filled with a mix of small businesses, everything from furniture makers to motor repair shops. The place is the Royal Ordnance Depot in the small Northamptonshire village of Weedon.

It's said that Italy has too much history to be able to preserve it properly, and Weedon proves that we might have the same problem in the UK. Positioned strategically to be as far away from the coast as possible, the Weedon complex was built during the Napoleonic wars. Its most fascinating feature is a set of

This once strategic complex now lies neglected, peopled only by the ghosts of the soldiers that once thronged the garrison.

buildings collectively known as The Pavilion. These were used as quarters for the garrison's top brass, but plausible arguments have been advanced that it was earmarked as accommodation for George III in the event of a French invasion.

The place was once connected to the Grand Union Canal by a short arm, which entered the complex by way of a portcullis. It's easy to trace the old connection to the main canal, though part of it has been infilled to build houses. Travelling along the canal it's a different matter and you could easily miss it, hidden as it is behind a small marina. We missed it for years until we moored in the village on an embankment above the church and stumbled across it on an afternoon walk. Part of the canal still exists within the depot, though it's silted up and in disrepair, home only to a patch of bulrushes and a couple of disreputable-looking mallards. The clock tower above the portcullis is in perfect repair, the clock accurate to the minute. We got talking to one of the tenants in the place who we thought at first was going to kick us out, but who finished up taking us inside and showing

Visit

Access
You can't help but wonder when the complex is going to be restored in the way it deserves. There is a once-a-year opportunity to visit the site as part of the national Heritage Open Days:
| heritageopendays.org.uk.

The village website talks of plans for a more permanent visitor centre. For updates, see:
| weedonbec-village.co.uk

us the clock's internal workings, beautifully maintained and meticulously greased. Underneath it was a sickening, foot-high pile of dead flies. It seemed that in order to discourage spiders and their webs from the mechanism, the flies had to be regularly exterminated.

The portcullis leading to an arm, now built over, which once linked to the Grand Union canal. It defended the entrance to the barracks.

(21) Shardlow

The small village of Shardlow, 9.6km (6 miles) from Derby, is today considered Britain's best surviving example of an inland port, though Stourport-on-Severn (see Wonder 23) may have something to say about that. It consists of more than 50 listed buildings ranging from former wharves to warehouses, from artisans' cottages to stylish town houses built for the rich, as well as all the other trappings you'd expect from what was once a busy transport hub.

Positioned on the important Manchester–London turnpike, Shardlow had always been an important interchange, where river barges transferred their cargoes from the nearby Trent to packhorses; but after the construction of the Trent & Mersey Canal in the late 18th century, it became more important yet as the ceramics industry

developed around Stoke-on-Trent, spearheaded by Josiah Wedgwood, one of the canal's most important investors.

The village is home to what is arguably the most iconic single building on the canals, the Clock Warehouse. Elegantly proportioned and commanding a dominant position adjacent to the lock, there's no mistaking its distinctive,

The famous Clock Warehouse in the 1970s before it became a pub. Despite various incarnations it is still instantly recognisable, as much of a waterways icon as ever.

instantly recognisable facade. Or its proud declaration, in letters several feet high, capitals and all, that this is the NAVIGATION FROM the TRENT to the MERSEY.

Shardlow holds a special place in our hearts. It's where we took possession of *Pelikas*, our first narrowboat, though it barely warranted the name 'boat' at all. It was a homemade affair built by a welder who was, unfortunately, no boatbuilder. It was twisted and bent. Even so, we loved that boat and for more than a decade we cruised large parts of the canal system on it.

In those days, Shardlow was badly neglected, some of its historic warehouses not far off becoming derelict. The place seemed to be going to rack and ruin. The state of the brickwork on some of the original canal buildings was atrocious, stained with damp and badly in need of repointing. Some barely had roofs and even those that did were scarred with gaping holes, tiles broken and displaced. One or two had been

cheaply weatherproofed after a fashion, but some important ones had already been demolished, among them a stable block capable of accommodating a hundred horses used for towing boats. It's a great shame it was lost, but we should be grateful that for the most part, thanks to the efforts of local volunteers, the village has survived and much has been renovated, a shrine to the glory of canals in their heyday. Recently, it's received Heritage Inland Port status from the Maritime Heritage Trust, which should help ensure its future.

Visit

- -

Shardlow Heritage Centre, located in an original salt warehouse (Canalside, London Road, Shardlow, DE72 2GA. Tel: 01332 792489), is run by volunteers to research and preserve the history of the village. Guided walks can be arranged: | shardlowheritage.eclipse.co.uk

Once badly neglected, today Shardlow's warehouses have been restored and adapted to new uses.

Stoke Bruerne and Blisworth Tunnel

Stoke Bruerne, a tiny, picturesque Northamptonshire village straddling a flight of seven locks on the Grand Union Canal, is part of canal folklore. It's where one of the country's first waterways museums was established, in an old corn mill in 1963.

It's also where thousands of working boats would pause in their journeys between London and Birmingham for the rare opportunity to get health advice from one of the few outsiders they trusted, a woman who became a waterways legend.

Anyone familiar with TV's *Call the Midwife* would recognise the figure of Sister Mary Ward – midwife, district

Waterways legend, Sister Mary Ward was born in and worked in Stoke Bruene.

nurse, heath visitor, confidante – who ministered to the working boat families in her care with an intimate understanding and respect for their lives and culture. Her vocation was the welfare of this proud, self-reliant and close-knit travelling community, who were more often than not illiterate because as children they were never in one place long enough to go to school, and whose health was barely attended to for similar reasons. Mutual mistrust meant boat people were largely misunderstood and treated with disdain and suspicion by folk living settled lives on dry land. By the same token, working boat people had little reason to put much faith in authority. Sister Mary Ward was the exception. Universally loved by the community she chose to serve, those surviving boat people who came under her care remember her with awe, affection and gratitude.

Born in Stoke Bruerne in 1885, she grew up on familiar terms with the many boat people who regularly passed through her home village. As she said of the families she knew: 'People think my boat people are dirty and crude and want to get rid of them, but they are wonderful, proud, wise people.' After ten years spent in convents in Europe and the United States as a nursing sister, she came home to Stoke Bruerne and set up an ad hoc surgery next to Lock 15, in what's now the local Indian restaurant. There, she ministered to the working boat community until her retirement in 1962, having been awarded the British Empire Medal in 1951, and appearing on TV's *This is Your Life* in 1959. As she told the *Nursing Mirror*: 'You can't take me away from boat people. There isn't one of them wouldn't die for me, or one I wouldn't die for.' She died in 1972.

Half a mile up the towpath, Blisworth Tunnel, at 2,812 metres (3,075 yards), is one of the longest and oldest in Britain. It was not easy to build. Navvies armed only with picks, shovels and wheelbarrows started digging it out in 1793 but work came to an abrupt halt three years later when the tunnel collapsed due to quicksand, killing 14 men. Work resumed in 1802 and it finally opened to boat traffic in 1805. It was wide enough for two narrowboats to pass travelling in opposite directions but there was no towpath, so crews had to 'leg' their boats through, taking about three hours, while their horses were led across the top. From 1871, steam tugs pulled boats through, and later on, motor boats got through under their own steam. But by 1980 it had become dangerous and was closed for an astonishing four years, dividing the entire northern canal system from London and the south and setting back the development of the pleasure boat industry. It reopened following major rebuilding work involving lining the middle section with precast concrete rings. If you've ever travelled on a Eurostar train then you have Blisworth Tunnel to thank for making it possible: the project was used to test new materials and techniques later used in the Channel Tunnel.

With its museum, pub, café and boat trips, the village is a popular destination for a day out.

Visit

In the area

The canal museum (Bridge Road, Stoke Bruerne, NN12 7SE. Tel: 01604 862229) is a highlight of any visit to Stoke Bruene: | canalrivertrust.org.uk/stokebruerne

Boat trips are available. Stoke Bruerne Boat Company runs a skippered trip boat, *Charlie* departing from outside the canal museum, also available to charter: | stokebruerneboats.co.uk

Alternatively, the historic Boat Inn (Bridge Road, Stoke Bruerne, NN12 7SB. Tel: 01604 862428), situated across the locks from the museum, runs trips along the canal and through the tunnel in its trip boat, *Indian Chief*. | boatinn.co.uk/boat_trips.html

Stourport-on-Severn

The coming of canals shaped the Britain we know, and the attractive riverside town of Stourport is about as good an example as you'll find of how this happened.

In the 1760s, when the pioneer canal engineer James Brindley was planning the Staffordshire & Worcestershire Canal, he had a choice to make about where it joined the River Severn. His first preference was the town of Bewdley, at that time a thriving river port. But nimbyism prevailed even then and they didn't want it, so he decided to bring it out ... at a small hamlet a few miles downstream where there were only a dozen people living who might object. Fast-forward 30 years and a prosperous town of 1,300 inhabitants had developed there around a state-of-the-art inland

It still retains the name of the hotel it once was but this fine riverside building has now been converted to up-market apartments.

port. Modern Stourport has seen its ups and downs but today it boasts a population of over 20,000. Bewdley, on the other hand, is about half the size, the river there unnavigable because of silting.

The remarkably intact docks complex at Stourport is still the heart and soul of the place, its focal point the charming warehouse, on which was later built a distinctive Georgian clock tower. Around it is a handsome complex of warehouses, workshops, former canal offices and a dry dock. A map of the site in the early 19th century shows seven basins. Not all of them survive today, though there is an ongoing strategy of repair and restoration, in the vanguard of which was the opening of Lichfield Basin Dock in 2007. Stourport is packed with moored boats (leisure craft, of course; commercial trade ended long ago). Even so, wandering around the dock, it's not hard to imagine what it might have been like in its heyday.

With its fine Georgian architecture and riverside setting, Stourport became a fashionable resort town for a while in the late-18th century, with people flocking there in carriages to enjoy the 'regattas' or water parties that were common at the time. You can still sense something of this about it now. Perhaps it's the permanent funfair by the river that gives it a holiday feel. Or maybe it's just that anywhere with boats and water lifts people's spirits, which explains why Stourport is still a popular day-trip destination.

Sadly, the once magnificent Grade II listed Tontine Hotel, wonderfully positioned on the banks of the river, closed in 2001. Purpose-built by the canal company around 1772, it had 100 beds, stables, and a ballroom that doubled as a boardroom for canal company directors and shareholders, a template for the great railway terminus hotels that followed. Over the years, it had shrunk to a rather shabby pub in the centre of the building. Now it's been turned into smart, privately owned apartments.

The Staffs & 'Wusts' Canal, as it's generally known by boaters, was a key arm of James Brindley's ambitious 'Grand Cross' scheme – his plan for an inland waterways system that would link England's major navigable rivers: the Severn, Mersey, Trent and Thames. The idea was to create a comprehensive network of inland trade routes spanning the whole country and extending overseas from the ports it connected – Bristol, Liverpool, Hull and London.

Visit

In the area

For information on guided tours and boat trips through the canal basins, plus guided walks and 'Heritage Room' tours of the Old Ticket Office and the Tontine Stable:
| stourporttown.co.uk/visit/attractions/

Also available are group trips on heritage working boat *Bramble*, built in 1934 for canal carrying company Fellows, Morton & Clayton, restored by local volunteers and back in use since 2016:
| stourporttown.co.uk/attraction/
  bramble/

The *River King* trip boat based in Stourport offers turn-up-and-go day trips as well as private hire, and is even available for ash-scattering ceremonies:
| riverboathire.co.uk

Joining his Trent & Mersey Canal (then known as the Grand Trunk Canal) to his new Staffordshire & Worcestershire Canal at Great Haywood (see Wonder 25) recharged the Industrial Revolution.

South Stratford Split Bridges

What marks out the South Stratford Canal as special is not just the glorious countryside through which it threads, but its defining features: its utterly original style of lock cottages (see Wonder 5) and its pretty yet functional split bridges.

These are cantilevered on either side with a gap in the centre to accommodate tow ropes. This allowed horse-drawn craft to pass under a bridge effortlessly, without the palaver of unhitching the horse from the boat – crucial here because, unlike most canals, the bridges weren't built wide enough for a towpath to pass underneath. It was a money-saving measure. Much

canal building was defined by the need to save money on construction. Civil engineering today is the same.

The South Stratford transports you 22km (13.5 miles) from Kingswood Junction near Solihull to join the River Avon. It's what's called 'a narrow canal', meaning its locks and bridges are built to a width of just 2.13m (7ft). The bridges

A money saving solution it may have been, but the legacy of the Stratford Canal lies in its defining features, the most distinctive of which are its 'split bridges'.

A public footpath crosses one of the canal's unique bridges: Bridge 49, south of Preston Bagot.

are of a largely consistent build, too, with guard rails of black-and-white-painted ironwork in a lattice pattern completing what is a harmonious and pleasing design. They add to the beauty of one of the prettiest canals in the country, which reaches its destination in the attractive Bancroft Basin in Stratford-upon-Avon (see Wonder 4), overshadowed by the Royal Shakespeare Theatre. The basin is such a well-proportioned complement to the theatre that it's hard to believe the whole canal was almost lost in 1958 after Stratford Council set in train legal moves to abandon it completely as 'disused'. If it hadn't been for a couple of canoeists who'd fortuitously saved their toll tickets from a recent trip they'd made, there wouldn't be any Stratford Canal today. The tickets were dated, proving that the canal wasn't disused at all. Subsequently it was handed to the National Trust and restored by a workforce of volunteers, armed services personnel and prisoners from HMP Winson Green. It was

reopened by the Queen Mother in 1964, marking a turning point for the waterways restoration movement.

When we encountered it in the 1970s it was still in the care of the NT, if you can call it care, since an organisation whose main expertise was in preserving country houses didn't know much in those days about waterway maintenance. Plus there was a charge to use it – something of a deterrent for impecunious boaters like us. We went down it a few years later though, after responsibility for it had been transferred to the British Waterways Board. It was a slog, so shallow we were dragging along the bottom all the way, but the trip's etched on our memory. It was a perfect English summer and we moored in the basin along the bank next to the statue of Hamlet, enjoying a location money couldn't buy. Memories to last a lifetime. That's what we call the magic of the waterways.

Visit

Access
If you're intending to travel the idyllic River Avon by boat, which is highly recommended, you will need a separate licence, available from the Avon Navigation Trust:
| avonnavigationtrust.org/licence

If you're doing that, further mooring opportunities become available, at a charge, on the river directly opposite the Royal Shakespeare Theatre:
| avonnavigationtrust.org/overnight-
| moorings/overnight-moorings-
| stratford-upon-avon-recreation-ground

In the area
For details of river trips, see Wonder 4, Bancroft Basin.

25 Tixall Wide

Tixall Wide is one place on the canal system that is so broad you can do a U-turn in a boat 21.3 metres (70ft) long. And you have to believe that after travelling along waterways so narrow that sometimes boats moving in opposite directions can barely pass, the temptation to do a pirouette or two is hard to resist.

It's on the Staffordshire & Worcestershire Canal, close to the junction with the Trent & Mersey, where it widens out to form what looks like an ornamental lake. This is no coincidence. In fact, it was built to look like an ornamental lake. This was the trade-off for the Hon Thomas Clifford allowing navvies to cut a swathe through his meticulously laid-out gardens and grounds when the canal was dug in 1772. Fringed by reeds and bulrushes and populated by bevies of swans, it's a popular overnight stop for boaters seeking serenity. Sheep graze peacefully in water meadows. Mayflies hover uncertainly in the sunshine.

Visible from the water stands the magnificent Grade I listed Elizabethan gatehouse, which is all that remains of the grand mansion of Tixall Hall, where Mary, Queen of Scots was briefly imprisoned. To call it a gatehouse is an understatement though. It's more of an exquisitely grand Tudor folly, a turreted, three-storey flight of fancy, built to be a display of ostentatious wealth.

If you're not on a boat you can stay in the Tixall Gatehouse and play lord of the manor yourself, courtesy of its current owners, the Landmark Trust. Friends of ours did this and invited us to share the experience while we were moored

Above: No trace remains of the former grand mansion which was Tixall Hall, but the surviving magnificence of the gatehouse provides an imposing backdrop to a canal built to look like an ornamental lake. Above right: Shugborough Hall from the rear.

at Tixall Wide. The views from the roof were spectacular.

Not far from here is Great Haywood, Steve's natural habitat, where *Lord of the Rings*, author JRR Tolkien lived for a time while recovering from trench fever after the Battle of the Somme. Neighbouring Little Haywood – which is what Steve calls his younger brother – is also on the canal, but less attention-seeking. You can moor canal-side at Great Haywood across the meadows from the neoclassical stately home of Shugborough Hall, seat of the earls of Lichfield, the last noble occupant being the Queen's cousin, society photographer Patrick Lichfield. Now a National Trust property and open to the public, you can walk to it from the canal across an ancient packhorse bridge. From here, you can explore the estate, fashioned to resemble an imaginary Arcadian landscape with the historic hunting grounds of Cannock Chase as a backdrop. On afternoons in high summer, you may even see a hot air balloon drifting soundlessly in a clear blue sky above you.

Visit

To book a stay at the Tixall Gatehouse, contact the Landmark Trust:
| landmarktrust.org.uk

For details of visiting the Shugborough Estate:
| nationaltrust.org.uk/shugborough

If you fancy an aerial view, there are hot air balloon trips flying from Shugborough Hall:
| wickersworld.co.uk

Skippered weekend dining and fish and chip cruises for up to 12 people are available on the traditional narrowboat *Lurcher* (willowcruises.co.uk), moored outside the Canalside Farm Shop and Cafe at Mill Lane, Great Haywood ST1 0RQ:
| canalsidefarm.co.uk

Staffordshire Tolkien Trail:
| staffordshire.gov.uk/environment/ RightsofWay/distancewalks/ Staffordshire-Tolkien-Trail.aspx

26 Toll Islands, Birmingham

Cambrian Wharf in the heart of Birmingham was still shrouded in darkness as we silently slipped our moorings one chilly autumn morning, bound for rural Shropshire. Soon, we were on the long, wide and straight Birmingham main line – heading for the flight of 21 locks at Wolverhampton, beyond which was our route to Wales.

Signs of urban decay and dereliction lay all around us. Empty factories and old pumphouses conjured up images of a time when the canals in the city would have been teeming with industry, boats jostling one another for space, darting in and out of countless low arches leading to private wharves, and loops giving access to innumerable factories.

The air here would once have rung with the shouts of boatmen, the din of a thousand workshops and cargoes being loaded and unloaded. That day, we were the only boat for miles, enveloped by an eerie quietness broken only by the barely audible throb of our engine as we glided through the water on tickover.

Along the way, occasional curious concrete islands blocked the canal, restricting passage to a boat's width on either side. Deserted, overgrown and abandoned, they loomed ghostly in the half-light of dawn, few clues remaining as to their original purpose, which was to collect fees from passing boats. Most of the attractive octagonal brick-built toll

A toll island today. Sadly the toll booth which sat on it has not survived.

booths have sadly been demolished or destroyed by vandals over the years.

Toll houses are a common feature of Britain's canal system, but toll islands are only to be found on those waterways that were wide, deep and busy enough to allow tolls to be collected at the same time from boats travelling in opposite directions. The Birmingham Canal Navigations main line is a prime example. The pinch points created by the island meant no boat could escape payment.

The companies that financed the building of canals were permitted by Act of Parliament to charge and collect tolls from boats using their waterways: it was how they made their money and recouped their investment. Toll rates were also set by Parliament and charged per mile, fees dependent on the type and weight of shipments. Coal and limestone were generally the cheapest, followed by iron ore and finished goods. Perishables and packets (fast passenger boats that occasionally operated along some canals) paid premium prices.

Toll collectors had records of the unladen weight of every boat that passed their way so they could use gauging sticks to work out the fee to be charged, according to how deeply the boat sat in the water – the lower it was, the heavier the load. Fraud, of course, was rife. Ruses included wrongly declaring the cargo, or hiding more valuable consignments under cheaper freight. Plain bribery wasn't unknown either. Tolls were gradually reduced as canals came under competition from railways, and in 1948 they were discontinued entirely. Boaters today pay an annual licence fee to the Canal & River Trust (C&RT).

Visit

A short introductory walk around the city, highlighting the canals as part of its industrial past, can be downloaded from the Royal Geographical Society:
| discoveringbritain.org/activities/west-midlands/walks/birmingham-walk.html

In the area
Toll houses are just one of the many features you can discover walking or cycling the Birmingham Canals. The BCN Society website is a pool of information about others:
| bcnsociety.com

A narrowboat stopped near a bankside toll house at Cambrian Wharf.

27 Roses and Castles

A fairy-tale castle set in a strange, surreal landscape, decidedly NOT the British Isles. Snowy mountains with peaks as sharp as needles, green forests, a river; a blue sky dotted with improbable cotton-wool clouds, the whole thing wreathed in gaudy garlands of bizarrely unnatural flowers.

The imagery of canal folk art known as 'roses and castles' is dreamlike. It depicts an unreal world of magical make-believe far removed from the long hours and back-breaking work of manual labour, which, at the time these images were first painted, was the lot of working people on Britain's canals. This style of painting is the country's only indigenous art, and it's conspicuous as

The livery of the historic boat Gifford, once towed by horses, brings a welcome splash of colour to the National Waterways Museum at Ellesmere Port. She was built in 1926 in Braunston by Nurser Brothers and was used to carry liquids such as crude oil, tar and creosote.

much on the external livery of boats as inside, in traditional narrowboat back cabins (see Wonder 96), where it can cover almost every surface from cabin doors to table cupboards, from buckets to stools.

Though the same themes were – and still are – repeated time after time on boats all over the country, each version is nevertheless unique, different boatyards and painters developing distinctive styles, all of them characterised by bright colours and swift, confident brushstrokes. Some of the earliest practitioners of the craft who painted at the beginning of the 20th century – men like Frank Nurser, who worked in Braunston in Northamptonshire (see Wonder 8), or Jess Owen at Charity Dock near Coventry (see Wonder 9) – had particular aptitude and nowadays, if you want to buy an example of their work, it won't come cheap. Their artistry is apparent, their intention clear: it was unashamedly escapist, the expression of a desire for beauty, a counter to the grim industrial ugliness that characterised boaters' lives then.

These days, colourful 'painted boats' are one of the attractions of the waterways, brightening up even the most forlorn stretch of canal. But the origins of the style are shrouded in mystery and the subject of much speculation. What we know for certain is that by the middle of the 19th century, roses and castles had appeared on the vast majority of narrowboats working the English canal system. There's possibly a link to other strands of folk-art tradition developed in Asia, and perhaps imported through Romany connections. The truth is, no one really knows, though in

You'll see new boats all over the system embellished with traditional decoration, but for the finest original examples you'll need to visit any of the main waterways museums:

Ellesmere Port (see Wonder 35):
| canalrivertrust.org.uk/places-to-visit/
| national-waterways-museum

Stoke Bruerne (see Wonder 22):
| canalrivertrust.org.uk/places-to-visit/
| stoke-bruerne/visit-the-canal-museum

Gloucester (see Wonder 85):
| canalrivertrust.org.uk/places-to-
| visit/national-waterways-museum-
| gloucester

There's no doubt that a portable item decorated with roses and castles makes a perfect souvenir of a canal holiday. You can even learn the skill yourself at one of the many workshops and short courses available, such as the one run at Audlem in Cheshire or the Narrowboat Skills Centre:
| day-star-theatre.co.uk
| nsbc.org.uk/roses-and-castles

the 1980s we saw something strikingly similar decorating horse-drawn carts in Eastern Turkey. The tradition is certainly persistent: we decorated our own back cabin with roses and castles, and we proudly own a traditional water-can – Buckby cans as they're known – painted in similar style.

(28) Towpath Art

With so much of Britain's beautiful countryside visible from the towpath, you'd think it arrogant to try and compete with nature by displaying art along the cut.

Well, this is how we felt when sculptures, paintings and murals first started appearing on the canals a few years back. We thought it was over-indulgent, an imposition on the natural order of things. Now, don't get us wrong. We're not anti-art. Exactly the opposite, in fact. We love searching out art galleries in places we pass through on the cut. No, it wasn't art, as such, that offended us. It was just that we felt towpath art was unnecessary, over the top. We came to the canals to see canals. Why burden us with stuff we could see elsewhere?

But we've changed our minds. Perhaps it's because so much of what we disliked has mellowed and become part of the natural environment. Perhaps

Imagination and recycled materials have transformed this unprepossessing brick wall into a work of art.

it's because art along the towpath has become part of what contemporary canals are. We like to think it's because Britain has taken art to its heart. Sculptures like the Kelpies in Scotland (see Wonder 100) and Angel of the North in Gateshead are important symbols of local pride. But they're national symbols, too, expressing what we feel about ourselves as a country.

And as with these major installations, so with smaller works in towns and small villages across the country. Now every town and village worth its salt has a sculpture or mural representing itself. The Oxford Canal is almost an art trail itself with 'poem sculptures' – at Cropredy, Banbury and Somerton. At Hillmorton near Rugby, poems are actually carved into lock beams. In the same vein, in the small market town of Atherstone in Warwickshire, they have planted a tree protected by a steel frame decorated with exquisite medallions the size of your hand representing the town's history. The walls of the docks of Goole in east Yorkshire are peppered with reproductions of paintings by its favourite son, Reuben Chappell, one of the so-called portside painters who in the 19th century used to paint boats to sell as souvenirs for crews.

In both Wales and Scotland they have a canal artist-in-residence; in England there is a Poet Laureate. Towns have picked up the vibe: in Falkirk there is an art trail along the Forth & Clyde, and in east London a free public art walk – The Line – runs between the Olympic Park and the O2 Arena, following the Lea Navigation and the line of the Greenwich meridian. Even Antony Gormley put a lock-side sculpture on the Stratford Canal. Art is all over the place on the waterways – and not all of it professionally produced. You'll pass many bridges where local schools or community groups have painted murals or created mosaics. Art made from recycled rubbish adorns a wall in London's East End, and further up the Grand Union in west London is an extraordinary installation of 200 strange concrete figures studded with sparkling glass and broken tiling created by pensioner Gerard Dalton, around his modest Westbourne Grove housing association flat, before his death in 2019. The installation incorporates a 15-metre (50ft) mural, an idea that the

The extent of art on the waterways means you're probably not far from some, especially since half of us live within 8km (5 miles) of a canal. The Canal & River Trust (canalrivertrust.org. uk) and Scottish Canals (scottishcanals. co.uk) both run impressive websites packed with information about this and other things. Best, though, is just to keep your eyes open while you're walking or cruising. You'll be surprised what you see, as we were once when – without any grand announcement of their presence – we spotted a series of geometric mobiles hanging discreetly in the trees like an exhibition of Picasso's work during his cubist period.

Canal & River Trust, in conjunction with local councils and artists, have espoused to brighten up graffiti-covered walls and bridges in cities across the country. Today, you'll find them all over the place, from Leeds to Leicester, Glasgow to Gloucester … and everywhere else in between.

The wall of a waterside pub makes a perfect canvas for a mural that brightens up a stretch of urban canal.

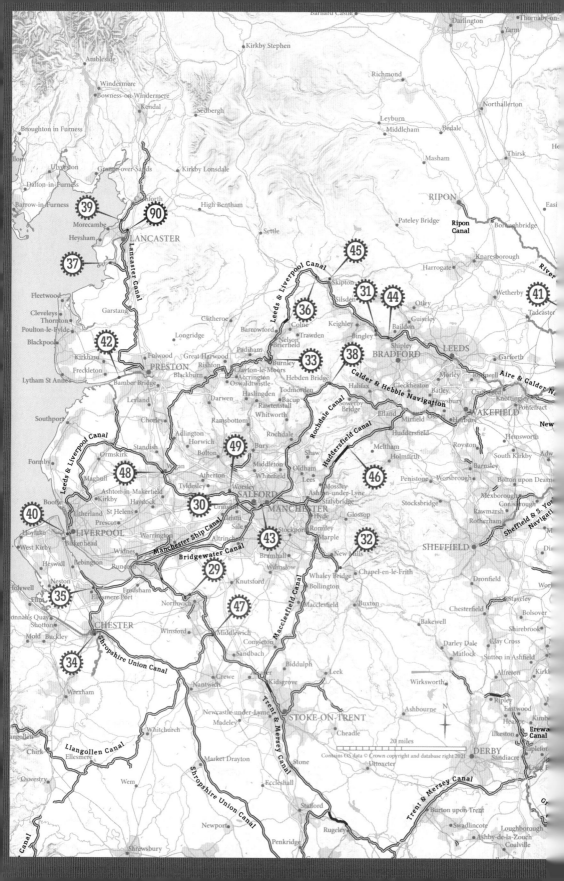

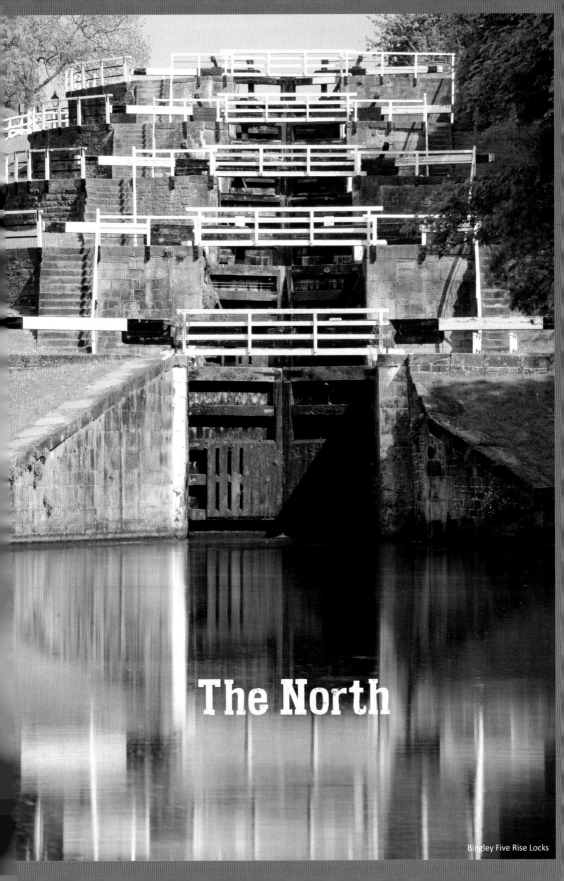

The North

Bingley Five Rise Locks

Anderton Boat Lift and the River Weaver

It looks like a cross between the classic pithead winding gear you used to see in mining areas and one of those towering, terrifying creatures that laid waste the country in *The War of the Worlds*.

However you view it, though, the Anderton Boat Lift near Northwich is wonderfully eye-catching. It's an elevator in which you ascend or descend vertically the 15.2 metres (50ft) between the Trent & Mersey Canal and the River Weaver. But afloat. In a boat.

Built in 1875, Anderton was the world's first commercially successful boat lift. It worked by counterbalancing two iron caissons filled with water,

The lift seen from the level of the River Weaver, a once heavily industrialised waterway which today is mostly pastoral.

contained side by side within an iron framework, each capable of accommodating barges of up to 100 tons. Steer a boat into one and it displaced its own weight in water, leaving the caissons weighing the same. All you then needed was a small engine to control them as they went up and down. Dreamed up by cutting-edge Victorian engineers, it was a groundbreaking project designed to open new trade routes, as important to the Cheshire salt industry as the Staffordshire Potteries.

When we first encountered it, this scheduled historic monument was in an advanced state of disrepair but just about operational. The catch was there was a charge to use it. Being young and broke, we couldn't run to it, so we duly admired it from the top then reluctantly continued on our way northwards without taking advantage of the tempting detour it offered.

The second time we passed, it was no longer working. It had been closed since 1983 because it had become too dangerous to use and too expensive to restore. We went on our way, regretting our earlier missed opportunity, sad that there was unlikely to be another. The Anderton Boat Lift was obsolete. It had come to the end of its useful life. It was a dead parrot and that was that.

But against all the odds, the lift was reopened in 2002 after a £7 million restoration project brought it back to magnificent life. It's now enjoying a renaissance as a breathtaking vertical boat ride for cruising boats and day trippers alike. For us it was third time lucky and there was no way we were going to miss it again.

The contrast between the narrow confines of the canal and the deep, wide water, sweeping bends and densely wooded banks of the glorious Weaver couldn't be greater. The river, which once thundered to the sound of heavy industry, now echoes with birdsong. In one direction it passes through the delightful Vale Royal Cut, where the steep wooded hillsides stretch to the water's edge. In the other it carries you into the heart of Northwich and beyond, to the darker reaches of Runcorn, where the Weaver meets the Mersey and industry still survives in the shape of a huge chemical plant.

Visit

You don't need your own boat to experience the thrill of the boat lift and the pleasures of a cruise on the River Weaver. These days, a trip boat will take you safely up and down so you can see the workings at close quarters for yourself. Cruises can be booked at the top level, where a visitor centre houses an imaginative permanent exhibition explaining the history, importance and mechanics of the boat lift (Lift Lane, Anderton, Northwich, CW9 6FW. Tel: 01606 786777).

Facilities
A light and airy cafe overlooking the river caters to all appetites.

In the area
There are walks and cycle paths around the site as well as picnic spots and even a maze. Adjacent to it – connected by a path alongside the River Weaver – is a nature park, where you can see water birds (see Wonder 80) and rare orchids. Spotters' guides are available from the visitor centre.

Web
canalrivertrust.org.uk/places-to-visit/anderton-boat-lift-visitor-centre

It's an elevator you ascend or descend vertically the fifty feet between the Trent & Mersey Canal and the River Weaver. But afloat. In a boat.

30 Barton Swing Aqueduct

The Barton Swing Aqueduct was built in 1893 to carry the Bridgewater Canal over the much bigger and once busier Manchester Ship Canal. Aqueducts are not an uncommon feature of Britain's waterways but this extraordinary example of Victorian engineering is unique in that it's the only one anywhere in the world that moves.

The structure is ingeniously designed to pivot on a central island. When closed, it allows traffic on the Bridgewater to pass at the higher level; swing it 90 degrees and the shipping lanes below are clear for larger seagoing vessels heading into or out of Manchester on the ship canal. When we first crossed back in 1984, not having done much research on what lay ahead, we were taken aback to find that the canal suddenly stopped dead without warning. Help arrived in the shape of the bridge-keeper, who had logged our arrival from his control cabin and proceeded to set in motion the graceful arabesque that was the aqueduct swinging round slowly to reconnect the canal. Along with the passage, we were fortunate that day to get a guided tour of the bridge from the man who was probably the last surviving full-timer paid to operate it.

So how does it work? Imagine an old-fashioned zinc bathtub, the sort your great-grandfather used before modern plumbing. The swing aqueduct is like that, only much deeper and, at 71.6 metres (235ft), much longer, too. It holds about 800 tonnes of water, which is held back in the caisson by huge

watertight iron gates that close when the aqueduct is favouring traffic on the ship canal and open when it swings back to link the two separated parts of the Bridgewater once more. The docking is done with the accuracy of a space capsule, and with barely any spillage. Think of that and wonder.

Traffic on the Manchester Ship Canal has declined steeply, while leisure boating on the Bridgewater Canal has increased enormously, so the aqueduct is generally to be found fixed to favour narrowboats and small cruisers. Nowadays, it opens once or twice a day,

1984. The Manchester Ship Canal glimpsed through the girders of the swing aqueduct.

The North

more for maintenance than to allow ship canal traffic to pass, but you can be lucky; late afternoons are a good time to catch it moving. A shadow of its former self, the old central island now stands derelict with the bridge-keeper's cabin enveloped in graffiti. These days, most of those crossing the aqueduct by boat will barely notice it, but to those who have seen it swing, it can still conjure up images of the days when Britain was an industrial powerhouse and when ships and narrowboats were part of the same great trading enterprise, transporting coal and cotton across the globe.

The swing aqueduct in its heyday, open to favour traffic along the Manchester Ship Canal. Note the watertight iron gate sealing the canal, and the bridge-keeper's cabin, perched at high level to control operations.

Visit

Access

There are parking spaces both sides of Redclyffe Road, the B5211, which crosses the ship canal a short walk from the aqueduct. More parking is available on Barton Road. Good views are available from the rear of Chapel Place, where there is a viewing platform. However, be cautious, there are warnings that Barton Road can be busy and the platform in poor condition:
| visitmanchester.com

In the area

The architect EW Pugin's 'masterpiece', the church of All Saints, is visible from Redclyffe Road. Currently in the care of the Greyfriars, it's in a bad way, though it's gradually being restored. At the time of writing, it's closed to visitors.

(31) Bingley Five Rise Locks

The five locks at Bingley on the Leeds & Liverpool Canal in West Yorkshire are a staircase flight (see Wonder 2), a spectacular feature in the chain of locks that connect the summit, in the Pennines, to Leeds, some 65km (40 miles) away and almost 91 metres (300ft) below.

From the top, looking towards Leeds above the treeline, you can see the tall, tapered chimney of the Damart mill standing sentinel over the less famous Bingley Three Rise staircase. It's unmistakable – black, with white lettering picking out the name of the factory, which was famous as a purveyor of sensible winter undergarments to all, long before thermals became fashionable. Their hallmark was the sort of no-nonsense white vests and long johns that took proper account of the British climate and could be worn without embarrassment underneath good Yorkshire woollens and Lancashire cottons by labourers and landed gentry alike. In that sense, the factory is emblematic of the importance of those two industries to this canal.

Approaching from the Leeds side, the locks are at their most impressive, rising 18 metres (60ft) from the canal like a cliff face. They seem like a declaration of intent, a daunting obstacle rising above you, clinging to the hillside and announcing to boaters in no uncertain terms that they are about to cross a seriously challenging range of hills, and that they had better get used to locks because there are going to be a lot of them.

The Bingley flight opened with great fanfare in 1774, at the time the locks wider, deeper and steeper than any other British flight of staircase locks. A crowd of 30,000 turned out for the opening and the flight, which is Grade I listed, still attracts lots of visitors today, especially on sunny summer afternoons when crowds picnic on the steep grass banks and peer over the edges of the vertiginous locks.

Measuring 19 metres (62ft) long and 4.2 metres (14ft) wide, they were built to accommodate the distinctive traditional Leeds & Liverpool 'short boats' that used to work this canal, though these days you're more likely to see a couple of narrowboats going up or down them as a pair. But it's the sheer scale of the flight that is its most impressive feature. On rare occasions, when all the locks are drained for maintenance, there are open days when you can walk into the empty staircase. It's the only way to appreciate first-hand just how high the locks rise, and how deep the chambers are, and how massively tall and heavy the gates are within them.

Navigating staircase locks requires care and they can confuse even the most experienced boater. At Bingley – mercifully – a full-time lock-keeper is employed to supervise, thus avoiding this all-too-real risk. For nearly 40 years, Barry Whitelock, the country's longest-serving lock-keeper, did the job, making himself so much of an icon, locally and nationally, that in 2007 he was awarded an MBE for services to inland waterways. He subsequently had a block of flats named after him. We knew him in his early days when, as a youngster, he used to run up and down the locks all day long like a man possessed. We spoke to him last just before he retired, when Steve, in his best grumpy old man mode, was bemoaning some aspect of the contemporary canal world. 'Aye, things have changed,' Barry agreed, 'and not always for the best.'

Visit

Access

There are regular trains to Bingley from Leeds, Bradford and Skipton. The Five Rise Locks are about ten minutes' walk from the station. Closer are the Three Rise Locks, which are less busy; from there, you can amble along the well-maintained towpath to the Five Rise.

Charging up the hill as the canal begins it climb to the summit of the Pennines, the five locks at Bingley are wider, deeper and steeper than any other staircase flight in Britain.

32 Bugsworth Basin

We need to talk about lime. That's limestone, not the fruit. This commonplace British rock may seem a long way removed from the subject of canals, but the two were once intimately connected. For limestone has been intrinsic to human development for millennia. The Egyptians discovered 6,000 years ago that if it was burned and combined with water, it produced a material that hardened over time. They used it to plaster the pyramids. Today, it's a key component in all manner of industries, from steel manufacturing to paper fabrication, water purification to glass-making. And, of course, it's still used in cement production. You get the picture. Limestone is big business.

During the Industrial Revolution the demand for it was insatiable, and since the canals allowed coal to be mined and marketed more cheaply than ever before, and limestone requires a lot of coal to make it into anything useful, the canals became vital in bringing the two minerals together. The White Peak area of the Peak District, named after the limestone plateau landscape of the 'Derbyshire Dome', was a rich source of limestone and a string of quarries sprang up around

The Navigation Inn provides a respite for feet weary after visiting this extensive site.

Buxton to provide it. Key to transporting the material was the 53km (33-mile) Cromford and High Peak Railway, completed in 1831, when carriages were pulled by horses. It wasn't called 'High Peak' for nothing. At one point it was 386 metres (1,266ft) above sea level, the line connected to quarries by a profusion of sidings along its length.

At its south-eastern end it linked with the Cromford Canal at High Peak Junction (see Wonder 12); in the north-west it dropped down to the Peak Forest Canal and the extraordinary basin at Bugsworth. Today, this is recognised as an important industrial archaeological site, but years back, when we first went nosing around it, the place was a complete mystery to us. We had no idea what this bizarre network of ruins and half derelict watercourses could possibly have been. It was an enormous site, mud-filled basins, dilapidated arms and the crumbling remains of docks stretching into the distance.

Since then, the Bugsworth Basin Heritage Trust has done considerable restoration, working out what most of it was used for and erecting a series of interpretation boards to explain it. Today it doesn't take much imagination to picture Bugsworth as it once was – essentially a huge factory for processing limestone: a place where generations of men and women laboured in hardship and dangerous conditions to eke out a rudimentary living.

It's a great place to visit and fascinating to explore. It makes you realise that militarism and imperialism weren't everything that put the Great in Britain. Along the way, ordinary working people had a hand in building the country.

Once a busy 'factory' processing limestone, today Bugsworth Basin provides quiet and pleasant moorings for those wanting to explore the site.

Visit

Access

Bugsworth is a pleasant 20-minute walk from Whaley Bridge, which is on the Manchester to Buxton railway line with a regular service to and from Piccadilly.

Facilities

Bugsworth Basin Heritage Trust runs a small exhibition room and visitor centre on the site (Brookside, Buxworth, SK23 7NE):

| bugsworthbasin.org

A pub, the Navigation Inn (Brookside, Buxworth, SK23 7NE. Tel: 01663 732072), once owned by *Coronation Street* actress Pat Phoenix aka Elsie Tanner, serves food:

| navigationinn.co.uk

In the area

For more ambitious walkers, there's a link to the bed of the old Cromford and High Peak Railway.

Bugsworth is on the Pennine Cycleway, part of the National Cycle Network, Route 68:

| sustrans.org.uk/find-a-route-on-the-national-cycle-network/route-68

⚙(33) Burnley Embankment

So come on, what's all the fuss about? True, Burnley Embankment gives you an impressive bird's-eye view of the town, its streets laid out in neat grey terraces 18 metres (60ft) below, traces of its industrial legacy still visible in the chimneys of disused textile mills dotting the landscape. But otherwise it seems an unremarkable stretch of canal and struggling through wet Pennine weather to prettier locations, you could easily miss it.

Known as 'The Straight Mile' (even though it's actually only three-quarters of a mile long), the embankment carries the Leeds & Liverpool Canal across two river valleys – the Calder and the Brun. This avoided the need for either expensive and time-consuming locks and aqueducts or a detour following the contours of the landscape, which is what the earliest canal engineers would have done. But, increasingly, time was money to commercial freight carriers. They wanted something more direct. The result was this astonishing piece of waterways engineering masterminded by Robert Whitworth and opened in 1801. It's the biggest canal embankment in Britain and the scale and effort needed to build it is mind-boggling. Some half a million tons of earth from a nearby canal cutting and tunnel had to be shifted by shovel to be reused in its construction. And all done by navvies; not a JCB in sight.

There's no doubt Burnley owes much of its former prosperity to the coming of the canal. At first the town was able to take advantage of the rich coal reserve that lay beneath it, and later it created the conditions for it to become what is reckoned to have been the most important cotton weaving centre in the world. Some of the history of textile production in the town is preserved in the attractive warehouses and mills of the Weavers' Triangle alongside the canal, part of which is now an industrial museum.

We first cruised the Straight Mile one wet, misty day in the 1980s and the scene

The wharves and warehouses of the Weavers' Triangle; a reminder of when Burnley was the most important cotton-weaving town in the world.

we looked down on to brought to mind the mournful music and opening titles of *Coronation Street*. The slate roofs of the two-up, two-down terraces shone black with rain, their coal-shed yards and back alleys deserted. The only colour in the monochrome vista came from the front doors opening straight on to the street, and wildflowers clinging gamely to the windy embankment top. We didn't see another soul by the canal, let alone another boat on it. Returning 30 years later, a transformation had taken place. Burnley Embankment was bathed in bright sunshine and the towpath was busy with dog walkers, anglers and families out for a Sunday stroll. The Straight Mile had been reclaimed by local people as a linear park from which to enjoy the waterside panorama of their town.

The mid-1980s when the embankment was wet and deserted. Today, it's a popular and much-loved local amenity giving a wonderful perspective on the town.

Visit

In the area

The Weavers' Triangle visitor centre (85 Manchester Road, Burnley, BB11 1JZ. Tel: 01282 452403), from where you can easily walk to the embankment, is in the former Wharfmaster's House and Toll Office a short walk from the town centre, adjacent to the canal. Admission is free. Manchester Road railway station is five minutes away on foot, with services to Manchester, Wigan, Rochdale and York. For more information:

| visitlancashire.com/things-to-do/free-days-out
| weaverstriangle.co.uk

Situated 5km (3 miles) outside the town centre on the No 5 bus from the bus station, and 5km (3 miles) from Junction 12 on the M65, is the Queen Street Mill Textile Museum (Queen Street, Harle Syke, Burnley, BB10 2HX. Tel: 01282 459996), the last surviving 19th-century steam-powered weaving mill in the world, which still contains more than 300 looms:

| lancashire.gov.uk/leisure-and-culture/museums/queen-street-mill-textile-museum/

 Chester

Chester is a must-visit location on the waterways. Even disregarding its city walls – some of the best preserved in the country – it has its Roman amphitheatre, an impressive cathedral and its unique Rows – half-timbered shopping galleries on different levels dating from medieval times.

It's all so wonderful that it's easy to overlook its waterside attractions, the most remarkable element of which is the way the canal snakes around the city walls along the old moat where the high fortifications of the 13th-century King Charles' Tower rise 21.3 metres (70ft) from the towpath like a cliff wall towering above you.

But there's more yet, for tucked away beyond that are Northgate Locks, a flight of three staircase locks hewn out of sandstone, which drop the canal a precipitous 10 metres (33ft), their height accentuated by a railway and a road bridge that skim along the top of them. From the pinnacle, you can see the Welsh hills in the far distance; underneath, the drop induces vertigo. In our opinion, the Northgate Locks are the most fearsome staircase flight in the country. Beyond them, bordering a substantial

Chester Basin. The fearsome staircase locks are to the right; the canal ahead leads to Ellesmere Port.

Pleasant moorings beneath the city walls. The cathedral and city centre are just a step away.

basin where a short arm connects to the tidal River Dee, is Taylor's Boatyard, a Grade II listed complex incorporating a forge, a blacksmith's shop and a sawmill that was once steam operated. Opposite is an elegant listed warehouse built by Thomas Telford, its design incorporating three graceful arches built over the water to allow boats to unload directly underneath. It's a remarkable example of Georgian industrial building, which has been sensitively adapted by contemporary local architects into a popular pub-restaurant and music venue. Its facade remains unspoiled though, an enduring reminder that Chester was once a major port.

Indeed, long before Liverpool attained its primacy, Chester was the most important seaport in the north-west, and had been since Roman times. But it was constantly silting up, until it eventually became unusable and was turned into a racecourse. For a time, the canal took over its important industrial transportation role, until that trade began to dry up, too. Today, it takes a leap of the imagination to picture how busy the old canal basin must have been, let alone the old port. There are still traces of its Roman past, however. We've never found them ourselves, but we've read that there are overgrown parts of the racecourse where you can still see the stones of the old Roman harbour wall.

Visit

Chester needs more than a brief visit to see even a part of what it has to offer. For boats, there are attractive and free moorings. For more information:
| chestertourist.com
| visitcheshire.com

(35) Ellesmere Port

Not as many boaters as you'd expect get as far as Ellesmere Port at the end of the Shropshire Union Canal. Chester is the problem. Boaters travelling north arrive there and become so enamoured by what the city offers (see Wonder 34) that although Ellesmere Port is only 10 or 11km (6 or 7 miles) away, they turn tail and retrace their steps, deterred from going further by the industrial scenery they'll encounter.

And, of course, they're not wrong. Ellesmere Port IS industrial. The canal joins the River Mersey and flanks the Manchester Ship Canal, how could it be otherwise? It's an unremarkable town – except for its docks, one of the most fascinating canal locations on the whole system.

The name Ellesmere Port, current population around 60,000, derives from what is today the somnolent town of Ellesmere in deepest Shropshire, nearly 40 miles away, current population about 4,000 (see Wonder 84). In the late 18th century, Ellesmere in Shropshire was an important place and ... er, Ellesmere Port on Merseyside wasn't. In fact, Ellesmere Port didn't even exist. Where the canal

The National Waterways Museum at night.

joined the river was the small settlement of Netherpool, which, after the canal had been cut, changed its name to the Port of Ellesmere. But by then the canal had changed its name too. It was originally called the Ellesmere Canal and was scheduled to link the Mersey to the River Severn. But then the money ran out and the link never happened. The section of canal that had already been built – the bit between Chester and the Mersey – would eventually be incorporated into the Shropshire Union. Oh, 'the best laid schemes o' Mice an' Men', as the poet Rabbie Burns says.

Today, there's no Netherpool, no Ellesmere Canal and, with the greatest respect to the good burghers of Ellesmere, Shropshire – not much of importance there compared to how prestigious it used to be. However, the Port of Ellesmere, subsequently renamed Ellesmere Port, continued to prosper, particularly after the opening of the Manchester Ship Canal in 1894, which propelled the city into the major industrial centre it still is today. It was, of course, particularly important for the docks, which had a new lease of life after a period when canal haulage had been contracting in the face of increased competition from railways.

The 2.8ha (7-acre) dock complex fell into disrepair during the 1960s but its handsome Victorian buildings have now been restored to become the National Waterways Museum, an eloquent testament to the importance of water transport in British history. Among other attractions, it houses a fascinating collection of historic craft. There's also an annual Easter Boat Gathering incorporating a beer and sea shanty festival that drew us there one year. Ellesmere Port is a glorious place for a family day out at any time but especially then. We lay in the sunshine on the grass looking over one of the dock basins, where a couple of tugs slowly manoeuvred a huge vessel down the ship canal towards Manchester, the wide Mersey Estuary in the distance a backdrop to their work.

Visit

Access

Mooring is available for visiting boats, included in the price of entrance to the museum:

| canalrivertrust.org.uk/places-to-visit/ national-waterways-museum/boating-at-ellesmere-port

Car parking is available and Ellesmere Port railway station, part of the Merseyrail network, is a ten-minute walk away with regular services into Liverpool and Port Sunlight, below.

In the area

The National Waterways Museum (South Pier Rd, Ellesmere Port, CH65 4FW. Tel: 0151 3555017). For opening times, prices etc:

| nwm.org.uk/Planningyourvisit.html

Port Sunlight, a model village founded by 'Soap King' William Hesketh Lever in 1888 to house his 'Sunlight Soap' factory workers, is now home to a museum and world-class art gallery set in stunning parkland with a backdrop of Arts and Crafts architecture (23 King George's Drive, Bebington, Wirral, CH62 5DX. Tel: 0151 6446466).

| portsunlightvillage.com

36 Gargrave

The village of Gargrave is where the Leeds & Liverpool Canal meets the Pennine Way, the canal towpath converging with one of England's finest ancient footpaths and becoming for a time one and the same.

It's a special sort of place, perched on the edge of the magnificent Yorkshire Dales, sitting between the canal and the infant River Aire, which one of the village roads crosses on an attractive triple-arched bridge. This can sometimes seem a bit of over-engineering, since for most of the year if you're on foot you can as easily cross by a set of pretty stepping stones barely any distance away. However, like all rivers, the Aire is Janus-faced, and what in summer is a babbling brook can in winter, after heavy rainfall, become a forceful river surging towards Leeds and finally into the River Ouse (see Wonder 77).

You can't get away from rain in this part of the world at any time of the year, and neither would you want to, since rain is what makes the Dales what they are. Even in wet weather, the 8km (5 miles) into Skipton along the towpath is a rewarding ramble (see Wonder 45). But if you're looking for a sterner test, you can steel yourself and head out towards Malham Cove along the Pennine Way or another of the comprehensive networks of public footpaths that thread the countryside in these parts.

Gargrave is an ideal place to tie up in a narrowboat for a short stay, and one

glorious summer when we were cruising Yorkshire we kept coming back to it. We often walked to Malham, where we clambered up rocky paths to the top of its 70-metre (230ft) white cliff face, picking our way across the limestone pavement at the top, balancing on what seemed giant cobblestones separated by deep crevices. Longer walks took us to Malham Tarn, where the alkaline waters were sometimes Mediterranean blue. Once, we saw a pair of nesting peregrine falcons and their three chicks, high on the cliff face of the cove, courtesy of a fixed telescope provided by the Royal Society for the Protection of Birds (RSPB). At that distance,

they were invisible to the naked eye, but magnified in perfect focus through the telescope we could see chicks almost as big as their parents, gingerly trying out their wing feathers but reluctant to risk them to a first flight.

Gargrave is a friendly place from which to explore the Dales. One night, we went to see a film in the community hall, which had been transformed for the evening into a cinema. It was already jam-packed when we arrived, but we were ushered to the front row, where everyone shuffled up to make room for us. Bringing your own food and drink to the performance was not only permitted, but almost compulsory, and so we had come armed with a bottle of cheap fizz

Visit

- -

Facilities

There are pubs in Gargrave as well as a fish and chip shop, The Frying Yorkshireman (26 High Street, BD23 3RB. Tel: 01756 748345), an Indian restaurant, Bollywood Cottage (60 High Street, BD23 3LX. Tel: 01756 749252, bollywoodcottage.co.uk), and the famous Dalesman Cafe and Sweet Emporium (54 High Street, BD23 3LX. Tel: 01756 749250).

and a bumper packet of crisps. Everyone else was doing the same, and soon we were chatting to the people sitting next to us as if we'd known them all our lives.

Nestling in the Pennines close to Skipton, Gargrave is an ideal base to explore the Yorkshire Dales. There are good moorings above the lock.

⚙ (37) Glasson Dock and Basin

There's something about coastal junctions that gives you a different perspective on canals. From cruising along the comfortable confines of artificial linear channels, you suddenly arrive at wide estuaries or the sea itself, intimidating in their vastness.

Glasson Dock and Basin, 8km (5 miles) from Lancaster, is one such place. It was opened by the Lancaster Port Commission in 1787 so ships could offload their cargoes of cotton, sugar, spices and – shamefully – slaves, thus avoiding the tides and shifting sandbanks of the River Lune. Slaving was important in this part of the world. At one time, merchants with Lancaster connections were involved in the capture and sale of around 30,000 people, making it the fourth most important slave trading centre in the country.

Glasson Dock was so big it's said it could accommodate 25 ships. Not long after its opening, work began on the Lancaster Canal, and by 1799 the northern part of that was completed from Preston to Tewitfield. Meanwhile, renowned engineer John Rennie was drawing up plans to link the canal to the basin and dock through a branch dropping down to the sea through six wide locks, thus allowing smaller seagoing vessels to use the canal without the need to trans-ship cargoes. This arm was completed in 1826.

The basin is as huge today as it ever was and can accommodate everything from around-the-world yachts to

A solitary narrowboat tucks into the enormous basin at Glasson amidst seagoing sailboats of every sort.

industrial coasters with salt-caked smokestacks. We moored there for a few days once in our narrowboat and got caught in a storm, which so unnerved us we feared we might sink. The wind blew ripples from one side of the basin, which grew visibly until by the time they reached us they were choppy waves topped by white horses, crashing across our deck and smashing us into the wall against which we were moored. However, in more clement weather, it's an attractive place to visit. There's a boatyard, a characterful pub and a smokehouse where you can buy kippers and local potted shrimps. There are some lovely and undemanding waterside walks as well, one of which takes you along the Lancashire Coastal Way footpath, and past the Plover Scar lighthouse and the ancient Cockersand Abbey.

Surprisingly, there are many boaters on the lock-free Lancaster Canal who never venture to Glasson because locks are so unfamiliar to them and ... well, we don't suppose they think it's worth the effort. It is. They're missing a lot.

Visit

In the area

There are also a number of short circular walks from Glasson, such as:

> greatbritishlife.co.uk/things-to-do/walks/lancashire-walk-glasson-dock-circular-7027146

Lancaster Maritime Museum (Custom House, St George's Quay, Lancaster, LA1 1RB. Tel: 01524 382264) explores the legacy of Lancaster and Glasson's involvement in the slave trade:

> visitlancaster.org.uk/museums/maritime-museum/

Glasson is linked the 9km (5.5 miles) to Lancaster by the Lune Estuary cycleway.

It's also on the long-distance Lancashire Coastal Way footpath:

> visitlancashire.com/dbimgs/Lancashire%20coastal%20Way%20leaflet.pdf

38 Hebden Bridge and the Rochdale Summit

It was probably the complete unexpectedness of it that impressed itself on us – and impress it certainly did. We've done a lot of walks around the waterways, but none was quite as startling as this.

We were moored on the Rochdale Canal at Hebden Bridge, and we'd set out that spring morning over the old packhorse bridge to the precipitous path that climbs almost vertically up the valley to Heptonstall. Part way up, we branched off into a wood thickly carpeted with bluebells as far as the eye could see. That would have been an indelible memory on its own, but as we walked on we came across the desolate ruins of a building, heavy with ivy, and lit by beams of sunlight shafting through the trees, highlighting its strangely compelling beauty. A little further on was another, and after that another ruin, and another yet: a string of them following the course of a twisting stream that tumbled through the woodland over mossy rocks. Some were surprisingly intact, others just ruins. All were surrounded by ponds of one sort or another; some were obviously millponds, others more like lakes or lagoons. There were culverts linking them, networks of channels splaying out in all directions, some in water, some just troughs of mud. It was like those romantic Victorian etchings of melancholy ruins, still splendid even in their decay.

The Rochdale Canal follows the course of the Calder Valley, which was for centuries a wool-producing area; and without knowing it we'd stumbled across Hardcastle Crags where, during the Industrial Revolution, mills began to replace the traditional home weaving that families had done to supplement their meagre incomes from hill farming. You can still see – and indeed, stay in – some of these old weavers' cottages in Heptonstall and other places locally. They are frequently three-storey buildings, the top floor, where the looms were sited, invariably built with outsize windows to maximise the light. We found Heptonstall fascinating, but my! it's grim, dominated by its ruined church and burdened – almost stigmatised – as the burial place of the fragile American poet Sylvia Plath, whose husband, fellow poet Ted Hughes, was born and brought up further down the canal at Mytholmroyd.

By comparison, Hebden Bridge is a more joyous community altogether, a place filled with funky shops and organic grocers and newsagents where they sell more of the *Guardian* than all other newspapers put together. It prides itself as being in the forefront of the green movement and for less comprehensible reasons – for who would want to be

The Rochdale Canal cuts through Hebden Bridge in the Calder Valley before reaching its wild moorland summit.

compared with a run-down North London borough? – it's also described as 'the Islington of the north'. Still, whatever turns you on, we guess; all we know is that we love the place.

From Hebden Bridge, the canal climbs through a heavily locked section towards its extraordinary summit, where the surrounding tors and rugged moorlands drop right down to the water's edge. It's an awe-inspiring landscape, at one and the same time forbidding but enticing, too. In bad weather, it can feel physically threatening; in the sunshine, it has such intense beauty it can seem almost unreal, like a Romantic canvas painted by Poussin. Sadly, it's not a long summit and the canal soon begins its descent towards Manchester.

Visit

Access
Hebden Bridge's pretty Victorian railway station isn't just a means of transport, but a tourist attraction in its own right. Recently featured as one of Britain's 100 best railway stations, there are frequent direct services to Leeds, Manchester Victoria and York. More information from:
| northernrailway.co.uk

In the area
For details of other local attractions:
| visitcalderdale.com

Details of Hardcastle Crags, including Gibson Mill, a restored mill:
| nationaltrust.org.uk/hardcastle-crags

Hebden Bridge has a thriving arts scene. The Trades Club (Holme Street, Hebden Bridge, HX7 8EE. Tel: 01422 845265) is worth checking out for its eclectic programme of music:
| thetradesclub.com

39 Hest Bank

Hest Bank on the Lancaster Canal is unique: the only place in England where a canal runs so close to the shoreline you can smell the sea from your canal boat deck. Venture on foot the couple of hundred metres to the foreshore and you'll find not just a stunning view, but traces of the wharf where ships from Liverpool and further afield once unloaded cargoes for transfer to the canal.

Hest Bank gives on to the seemingly endless expanse of Morecambe Bay, the ill-defined hills of the Lake District visible in the far distance. The shifting sands of the bay are notoriously treacherous to cross without detailed local knowledge of the unpredictable changing tides and the rivers draining into the sea, and today at Hest Bank you can't miss the signs warning of the dangers of deep channels, fast-moving tides and quicksands. Pay attention and heed these.

Against the receding tide of Morcambe Bay the shadowy outline of the Lake District hills are prominent.

We did the 11km (7-mile) crossing one year with a group led by the legendary Cedric Robinson, a local celebrity who has since died after a lifetime of safely leading parties of walkers across the shifting sands for charity. For more than 50 years, he was the official Queen's Guide, a position dating back to 1548. His method was to walk the sands alone first, plotting a safe route, which he

marked with laurel twigs. Our crossing took place on a filthy summer's day in torrential rain, the much vaunted seascape obscured by low cloud. But our high spirits were undimmed. Along with a sodden bunch of adults, kids and dogs, we trudged barefoot, paddling through shallow water across the sands, wading at several points through thigh-high, fast-flowing rivers, with Cedric our standard-bearer, a Moses parting the Red Sea. We arrived exhilarated and triumphant at the other end.

For those of a more sedate bent, an hour's walk along the coast road from Hest Bank will take you to Morecambe, where you can drink in the art deco splendour of the recently restored Midland Hotel on the seafront. There are few better places to watch the sun set than its glamorous cocktail bar, where – away from the canal – you can kid yourself you're on the deck of an ocean liner.

Visit

Access

On 5 February 2004, 23 cockle pickers in Morecambe Bay were drowned when they were overcome by fast incoming tides. These sands are dangerous and should NEVER be attempted without a qualified local guide:
| guideoversands.co.uk

Facilities

For details of the Midland Hotel (Marine Road West, Morecambe, LA4 4BU. Tel: 01524 424000):
| midlandhotelmorecambe.co.uk

⚙(40) The Liverpool Link

The Leeds & Liverpool is the longest, oldest – and arguably the most beautiful – of the three canals that cross the Pennines. But for many years its name was a misnomer.

It started in the heart of Leeds, true enough; but at the Liverpool end you could only get to the outskirts, a few miles beyond the famous Grand National racetrack at Aintree. To get into the heart of the city by boat, you had to risk yourself to the potentially treacherous River Mersey, where you weren't welcome anyhow.

All that changed with the construction of the Liverpool Link in 2009, connecting the canal to the city centre. It cost £22 million and is only 2.25km (1.4 miles) long. But what an astonishing 2.25km (1.4 miles) it is – a remarkable route taking you through the old docks. These have been linked together by new locks, connecting culverts and short tunnels,

In the shadow of Liverpool's traditional skyline, startling contemporary buildings line the city's docks.

one of which emerges in startling fashion on the Pier Head below the city's most internationally revered buildings, collectively called the Three Graces. Taken together, the Royal Liver Building, the Cunard Building and the offices of the former Mersey Docks and Harbour Board compose what must be among the most elegant harbour frontages in the world; and seeing it from a narrowboat travelling along the Link is a stunning experience, with views redolent of those that greeted passengers on the great liners in the past arriving from New York after transatlantic crossings. The area is known collectively as Liverpool Maritime Mercantile City, and it claims to have the greatest concentration of Grade I and II listed buildings anywhere in the UK outside London.

When we first travelled the length of the Leeds & Liverpool in the east–west direction nearly 40 years ago, we were disappointed to find the navigable canal fizzled out as it did, and so at Wigan we turned off towards Manchester. Pressing on towards Liverpool seemed a waste of time when we knew we couldn't actually get into the city itself. After the Link opened and we could finally cruise there by boat, it wasn't just the journey that was a delight. We were allotted moorings in Salthouse Dock adjacent to Albert Dock, one of the city's most renowned tourist spots, where attractions such as Tate Liverpool are sited. Nearby is the extraordinarily designed Museum of Liverpool and the International Slavery Museum, where you'll be left in little doubt as to the foundations of the wealth of the city. Frankly, you'd have to pay a fortune in hotel bills to find anywhere half as convenient. We stayed for a couple of weeks during a summer so warm that in the saline waters, jellyfish massed around our hull at night like shadowy ghosts. We could have stayed longer and we'd still have seen only a fraction of what Liverpool has to offer. Yes, we know how associated the city is with The Beatles, but they're only a small part of the story.

The new link to Liverpool gives boaters unrivalled views of the city's iconic Pier Head, lined by the Royal Liver Building, the Cunard Building and the Port of Liverpool Building, collectively known as the Three Graces.

Visit

In the area

For general details of Albert Dock:
| albertdock.com

For Tate Liverpool:
| tate.org.uk/visit/tate-liverpool

For all Liverpool's art galleries and museums, including the International Slavery Museum and Maritime Museum:
| liverpoolmuseums.org.uk

You can't get away from The Beatles in Liverpool: The Beatles Story exhibition is at Albert Dock (booking advised):
| beatlesstory.com

And try the restyled Cavern Club:
| cavernclub.com

However, for our money, nothing beats seeing the inside of John and Paul's childhood homes courtesy of the National Trust, booking essential (online or Tel: 0344 2491895):
| nationaltrust.org.uk/beatles-childhood-
| homes

For boat trips, what else but take a ferry across the Mersey:
| merseytravel.gov.uk/ferry

(41) Naburn Lock

Naburn Lock has been described as the most impressive piece of early canal engineering on any English navigation. It's situated roughly 10km (6 miles) downstream of York – a city that is a wonder in its own right, but one that hardly needs more publicity from us.

By way of comparison, Naburn is virtually unknown, even though it's the gateway to the tidal River Ouse. Above it is the relatively gentle water of an inland river; below is where it rises and falls twice a day as it flows downstream some 110km (68 miles) to join the Humber Estuary and the North Sea.

To say we know Naburn Lock well is an understatement. Let's just say there's probably no one except the resident lock-keeper who knows it better. In fact, we probably hold the record for the longest time a narrowboat's ever spent on a one-hour mooring. Does five months sound like we overstayed our welcome a bit? The rising pontoon designated for boats waiting to use the lock was not just our home for most of one winter: it was our safe haven, our refuge, our sanctuary, our port in a storm.

At only 2.5 metres (8ft) above sea level, the River Ouse is badly prone to flooding. And the winter we were there brought a particularly severe example of it, with the river up and down like a yo-yo. So bad was it that the lock itself disappeared underwater, as the force of exceptionally high tides met a deluge of excessive rain draining into the Ouse from the Yorkshire Dales, bearing

fearsome turbo-charged logs and debris in its white-water wake.

There is no safe place for small boats to moor in York when the river is in flood. Several times – with the river level visibly rising by the minute – we had to make a mad dash out of the city to seek safety at Naburn Lock. Several times, we were not just stranded but marooned for weeks on end. The rising pontoon became an island in a sea of water, and dry land seemed as unreachable as another continent. We were grateful for the watchful, experienced eye of the lockie, Ken, who fixed us up with a supply of fresh drinking water. We were also glad of a plentiful supply of tins and

Overwhelmed by rising floods, the area around the submerged lock becomes a vast and spectacular inland lake.

The North

dried goods on board, as well as coal and booze. Once reconciled to being trapped there, we were able to appreciate the extraordinary beauty and peace of the location, especially the startling flame-red sunsets we experienced.

Dating from 1757, the original design of the lock and weir at Naburn formed an island on which a water mill once stood next to the lock. In Victorian times, a second larger lock was built, along with lock-keepers' cottages, workshops and a blacksmith's forge. The handsome locks are adorned with shrouded paddle gear and cast-iron swing bridges embellished with the York coat of arms. However, the most extraordinary structure on site is a huge hall, like a Greek temple, built by the trustees of the Ouse Navigation simply so that they could celebrate an occasional banquet.

These days, the constant risk of flooding is damaging the historic buildings on the site. Our advice? Go and see them while you can, preferably on a still summer's day when it's hard to believe any of what we experienced could ever have happened.

Visit

In the area

There's an easy but rewarding cycle and walking route between York and Naburn, starting from the riverside path along the Ouse, passing the former Terry's chocolate factory and the racecourse to the old railway line, which was once the route between Kings Cross and Edinburgh. It's Sustrans Route 65 and is perfect for families and novice cyclists. There's a cafe along the way, and an intriguing art installation representing a scale model of the solar system:
| sustrans.org.uk/fi nda-route-on-the-
| national-cycle-network/york-to-naburn/

On the way, don't miss the Brunswick Organic Nursery in Bishopthorpe (YO23 2RF. Tel: 01904 701869), which grows and sells produce as part of its work with those with learning disabilities. Coffee is available, too:
| brunswickyork.org.uk

On a summer's day the approach to Naburn Lock provides a pretty and safe mooring off the River Ouse.

42 The Ribble Link

The Millennium Ribble Link – opened in 2002 at a cost of £5.4 million – is one of the great success stories of the new Canal Age, the first new inland waterway to be built in England for 100 years and the first ever to be built exclusively for leisure rather than commercial purposes.

For 200 years, the Lancaster Canal languished in splendid isolation, cut off from the rest of Britain's navigable inland waterways. The Ribble Link finally connected the Rufford Branch of the Leeds & Liverpool Canal at Tarleton to the 'Owd Lanky' – as it's known to locals – just outside Preston. This brought a fresh lease of life to England's most north-westerly canal, depositing audacious boaters on the doorstep of the Lake District.

However experienced a canal boater you are, crossing the Ribble Link is an adventure. It's like one of those computer games in which you are challenged to overcome ever more difficult obstacles. The crossing takes the best part of a day – an undeniably adrenaline-fuelled day – starting with a hair-raising departure from the tidal lock at Tarleton. Waiting there for the off is like being a rider under starter's orders at the Grand National. As soon as the gates open, you have to punch the incoming tide in the River Douglas using all the engine power you can muster; but even then, the breathtaking force of the

Savick Brook. This barely navigable canalised ditch links the once isolated Lancaster Canal to the rest of the English canal network.

water can bring your boat to a standstill or – worse – begin to push it backwards. This is what happened to us. Cue total panic. To get anywhere, Steve had to go down to the engine room to manually tease more power from it.

The River Douglas widens as it moves towards the confluence with the Ribble, and this makes the going easier. Even so, emerging into the vast expanse of the estuary feels like a relief – but in fact you're far from over the worst. At this point in its course, the Ribble is so close to the Irish Sea, it IS the Irish Sea. The waves can be high, the winds notorious. There are strong cross-currents and underwater obstructions. You round the Astland Lamp, avoiding a potentially treacherous shortcut, to head for Savick Brook, a natural watercourse that has been canalised to provide the link between river and canal. Coming from the river, the entrance is overgrown and easy to miss, but once you've found it, the contrast is dramatic: from open water to a narrow, overgrown ditch that wriggles about like a worm on a fishing line. It's all too easy to lose concentration and get stuck on the many sharp bends – as many do. There are locks along the way, culminating in a short three-lock staircase, which you have to navigate backwards because there's a hairpin bend on the approach that is so sharp there's no room to turn to go up the normal way. You may feel this approach to the Lancaster Canal is undignified, given everything you've had to go through to get to it. But at least you've survived to tell the tale.

Visit

Access

For booking passage on the Ribble Link, maps and navigational advice:

canalrivertrust.org.uk/enjoy-the-waterways/canal-and-river-network/ribble-link

In the area

Savick Brook has been incorporated into the Guild Wheel, a multi-use path circling Preston, and sections can be walked:

lancashirewalks.com/page70.htm

A flotilla of narrowboats make their way across the Ribble estuary, so close to the Irish Sea they are almost at sea.

⚙(43)⚙ The Rochdale 9

Urban waterways have an atmosphere of their own, which it's worth experiencing for the different perspective they lend to the towns and cities they pass through.

Many boaters shy clear of them because they don't dovetail with the common image of the waterways as placid ribbons of water winding through the countryside. It's a great shame, because canals and rivers in cities offer a different sort of cruising experience. They are frequently more spacious and open than you'd expect: they're places where people come to play and have fun.

Places like the park-lined Great Ouse as it passes through Bedford, the Regents Canal around Victoria Park in London or the Nene at Peterborough.

Sometimes though – there's no denying it – waterways in towns can feel sinister and threatening. The cobbled and vaulted

'Dark Arches' taking the River Aire under the station in Leeds are so menacing you could use them as a set for a Jack the Ripper movie. You wouldn't want to get stuck on a dark night in parts of the canal system around Birmingham either.

However, the extraordinary and unique stretch of the cut in Manchester, where a flight of locks starts the Rochdale Canal on its long climb across the Pennines, is the only length of canal we know that combines these two elements in such a short distance. At one and the same time the flight is a confirmation of Manchester's reputation as the best place in the country to have a good night out, and a testimony to

The Rochdale 9 flight confirms Manchester's reputation as a great place for a night out. But there's another side of the coin too...

The North

some of the worst aspects of urban life in contemporary Britain.

The Rochdale 9 – as the locks are known by boaters – is around the corner from Castlefield Basin in the heart of the city, an attractive and easy-going area of bars and restaurants. Next to the first lock of the flight is a wisteria-clad two-storey lock cottage, as pretty as it is unexpected. It seems to bode well, but soon you pass under the low Deansgate Bridge where there are spiders as big as birds, and where platoons of pigeons wait under the girders ready to use you as a toilet bowl as you pass. Nevertheless, it's all fun and games along the banks. There's Manchester's Comedy Store and, further on, the site of the now demolished Haçienda nightclub, HQ of Tony Wilson's Factory Records where Joy Division and The Smiths made their name. Beyond that, the canal runs adjacent to Canal Street, Manchester's 'gay village', which today is more of a general haunt of the city's young, regardless of their sexuality. It can get quite wild along the towpath here at certain times, so much so there was a spate of drownings as alcohol-fuelled partygoers used the lock platforms as a shortcut from one bar to the next.

The Rochdale 9 is a notoriously difficult flight to navigate. The locks are stiff and heavy, the beams often shortened so you have to open them by a system of chains worked by a windlass. But the main problem is that there are no by-weirs to drain excess water around them. Consequently, after heavy rainfall water floods off the Pennines and comes bucketing over the gates, turning them into waterfalls. At best, the fierce flow makes it difficult to use the locks; at

Visit

In the area
For details of the many other places to visit in the city:
| visitmanchester.com

The Lock Keepers Cottage in Castlefield can be rented through Airbnb:
| tinyurl.com/2p897fr8

worst, it poses a serious sinking threat to boats if they get sucked into the whirlpools beneath.

The towpath disappears after Canal Street; the canal narrows and buildings rise around you claustrophobically. Suddenly, just a step or two from the Hilton Hotel, the canal plunges under Piccadilly into the underbelly of Manchester and what is the most unpleasant part of the flight. At the infamous underground Lock 85, hypodermics crunch underfoot and homeless street-sleepers stinking of meths shout aggressively as you pass. But what can you do? It used to be much worse here back in the day, and though it's much improved and Manchester City Council and the police periodically attempt to clean the place up, they're like Canute trying to hold back the tide. Pretty murals and community support officers aren't going to solve what is essentially a social problem. We've already forced these people underground. What are we going to do with them now?

And I wonder if we as boaters would want it anyway. For us the cut is a playground, not a home. All we're looking for is a challenge and the Rochdale 9 certainly presents one.

44 Saltaire

Looking at the huge Salts Mill, adjacent to the Leeds & Liverpool Canal near Shipley in Yorkshire, you think of William Blake's 'dark, Satanic Mills' immortalised in his best known poem-turned-hymn-turned-unofficial-national-anthem: 'Jerusalem'. Yet nothing could be further from the truth.

The mill here, built by textile magnate and philanthropist Sir Titus Salt, was intended as a rebuke to those exploitative industrialists who treated their workers as little more than slaves. Salts Mill was a template for something better.

This display of Victorian benevolence wasn't just do-goodism. Salts Mill was in the vanguard of efficient mass production. At its high point, 3,000 mill workers produced 29km (18 miles) of worsted cloth a day on 1,200 looms. The massive, imposing bulk of this

Sir Titus Salt built his mill and model village to be away from the crowded slums of Bradford. He planned workers should have a chance of staying healthy.

monumental factory dominates Saltaire, now a World Heritage site; and it's the reason the place exists at all. Saltaire was a company town, you see. A product of that paternalistic Victorian capitalism that believed workers would be more productive if decently housed, schooled and provided with sanitary and recreation facilities. Not to mention exposed to the teachings of scripture and deprived of the temptations of the demon drink.

The name Saltaire is a compound of Salt's name and the nearby River Aire. Salt's Big Idea was to build his mill and model village beyond the wretched slums and horrific factories of Bradford, in a place where the air was clean and workers had a chance of staying healthy. This was in 1853, at a time when Bradford was the wool capital of the world and a byword for squalor, ill-health and short lives. Karl Marx's friend and compatriot Friedrich Engels had toured the industrial centres of the north-west and found desperate living and working conditions. His reports pricked the Christian consciences of some of those profiting from such conditions and helped fuel a social reform movement that campaigned for an end to child labour, limits on working hours and improvements to health and safety.

Saltaire looks much the same now as it ever did: a small grid of streets speckled with parks and filled with terraces of tidy, handsome houses. A fine church survives, along with the Institute, which originally housed a reading room, recreation and social facilities. There was a hospital and almshouses and a park, complete with bandstand and boathouse.

The scale of the mill – now open to the public – is breathtaking. One floor tells the story of Saltaire and the mill, including moving accounts and records of some of the women and children who worked there. The looms long since silent, another floor houses the largest permanent collection by local artist David Hockney.

Visit

In the area

For information about the town, including a heritage trail, other walks, and events including the annual Saltaire Festival in September, which takes place over ten days:
| visitbradford.com/saltaire.aspx

For details of the mill (Victoria Road, Saltaire, BD18 3LA, satnav BD17 7EF and follow signs. Tel: 01274 531163), including exhibitions and its cafes, including Salts Diner (Tel: 01274 530533), which we can recommend:
| saltsmill.org.uk

Today the Mill houses an exhibition on its history along with a permanent display of works by internationally renowned artist, local boy David Hockney. It's also got a good restaurant.

(45) The Springs Branch

Skipton, an attractive Yorkshire market town on the Leeds & Liverpool Canal, bills itself as 'the gateway to the Dales', but it's got an attraction or two of its own up its sleeve, including one of the most picturesque and intriguing bits of waterway on the entire system.

Still navigable – just – the Springs Branch, which veers off from the main canal in the centre of town, takes you on a scenic detour around the back of Skipton's Norman castle, looking and feeling for all the world like a moat. After leaving the main canal, it passes a series of old wharves before wriggling its way through what can only be described as a ravine skirting the sheer rock face beneath the castle perched 30 metres (100ft) above.

Only 483 metres (0.3 miles) in length, this diminutive arm is also called the Thanet Canal after the Earl of Thanet, a former owner of the castle, who dug it out so that limestone could be transported by water from his nearby

quarries. The stone was dropped over the edge of the ravine into waiting boats from a horse tramway by way of chutes, one of which can still be seen today.

For many years, the branch was also a feeder for the Leeds & Liverpool Canal main line, taking water from Eller Beck, the stream running next to it. At one point, the towpath runs along an enchanting narrow embankment between the canal and the beck. Today, lengths of the Springs Branch are permanently lined with moored boats that make getting in and out a challenge even for small craft. Back in the 1980s, we cruised down here in our 9-metre (30ft) boat, *Pelikas*, marvelling at the

The Springs Branch makes for a picturesque diversion on foot or short boat from the main line of the Leeds and Liverpool Canal.

sense of entering a forgotten, secret world. If the boat had been any longer, we wouldn't have been able to turn at the end; it was a one-off experience, impossible to repeat in our current 17.5-metre (57ft 6in) boat.

You can take a boat trip to experience this beguiling backwater, or you can follow the towpath on foot. Crane your neck upwards to admire views of the castle towering above you before the path leads you into pretty Skipton Woods. If you visit the castle – well worth doing in its own right – you get an entirely different but equally impressive view looking down on the water from a great height. The castle stands at the top of the High Street and dates back almost 1,000 years. Six massive 14th-century round towers survive, but it was largely rebuilt in the 17th century after being besieged for three years during the Civil War. Cromwell allowed it to be restored – but only in such a way that it could never again be used for military purposes.

Visit

In the area
Skipton has twice won a *Sunday Times* award as one of the best places in the country to live. It's also won a trophy as the most courteous place in Britain, and has been rated by official statistics as the happiest place to live in the UK. It's not hard to see why it attracts the accolades. It's absurdly pretty, with an elegant marketplace and clusters of stone cottages wherever you look, and it's replete with good shops, pubs, restaurants and tearooms. More information from:
| welcometoskipton.com

If you fancy one of the most scenic train journeys in England – if not the world – you can join the Settle–Carlisle Railway from Skipton station. The line has been described as 'the only mountain railway in the world built for express trains'. For timetable and fares, see:
| settle-carlisle.co.uk

For opening hours and current admission prices at Skipton Castle, see:
| skiptoncastle.co.uk

For boat trips:
| penninecruisers.com

(46) Standedge Tunnel

Standedge Tunnel cuts deep through the millstone grit of the Pennines, carrying the Huddersfield Narrow Canal (HNC) underground for 5.2km (3.25 miles) between Marsden in West Yorkshire and Diggle on the edge of Saddleworth Moor.

It's a stunning achievement, a masterpiece of early engineering. Built over 16 years between 1795 and 1811, it's Britain's deepest, highest and longest canal tunnel. Some sections are brick-lined but much is bare rock, hewn by hand by navvies working under candlelight using just pickaxes, shovels and basic explosives. Two thousand five hundred were employed on the project; at least 50 of them died before it was finished.

Waterways tunnels are many and varied. Some barely merit the name and are little more than long bridge holes; but the bigger ones need headlights, a steady hand on the tiller and a stout resistance to claustrophobia. There are arguments about which presents the greatest difficulty to boaters, but there's no doubting that Standedge is a strong contender. It always posed tough challenges, even when new, and as a result it struggled to compete with its rival, the broad-gauge Rochdale Canal, which offered a quicker and more convenient trans-Pennine route. The last commercial boat passed through Standedge in 1921 and it was officially closed 20 years later. By the early 1970s, the whole of the HNC was derelict, long stretches filled in, built over or clogged with weeds and rubbish.

Standedge Tunnel was not only disused but dangerous. No one could imagine boats would ever use it again.

So when in 1974 a group of enthusiasts formed the Huddersfield Narrow Canal Society with the wildly ambitious intention of restoring the canal, most people thought they were bonkers. The project involved reinstating not just Standedge, but 74 locks, too – not to mention rebuilding parts of the canal from scratch through Stalybridge, where factories and a sports centre had been built on the original course, obliterating signs it had ever been there. At a time when the society only had £40 in its funds, it was estimated the restoration would cost £19 million. It is less a wonder, more a miracle, that in 2001, after 27 years of work against seemingly impossible odds, the full length of the canal reopened to navigation, including its magnificent centrepiece, the Standedge Tunnel. In the end, the restoration cost nowhere near the original estimate. The final bill was nearer £45 million.

In its early days after reopening, you couldn't navigate your boat through the tunnel yourself. It had to be measured up and cleared for passage by the Canal & River Trust before being swaddled in thick rubber protective sheeting and towed through in a small convoy by an electric tug. Boaters weren't even allowed to stay onboard their craft but had to travel in a glass-topped passenger vessel, nervously listening to their towed boats bumping and grinding along the tunnel walls and hoping that they would emerge at the other end in one piece. It was an odd experience then: unnerving and tedious, mostly the latter. Halfway through, you lost the will to live. Believe it: three hours is a long time stuck in a hole in the ground.

On one of our trips, the journey was enlivened when the tug towing the convoy died on us and there was a tense half hour while the crew tinkered with the engine to try to get it going. Luckily, the canal tunnel is one of three that run parallel through the hillside. One is a disused railway tunnel operating as a support route for the canal, allowing a C&RT engineer to arrive out of the Batcave to rescue us.

Visit

Access

You can steer your own boat through the tunnel now, but you have to have a Canal & River Trust chaperone on board and book at least three working days ahead. Boats must not exceed maximum dimensions. Those without their own boat can book on the same site for either short or all-the-way-through trips with commentary:

canalrivertrust.org.uk/places-to-visit/standedge-tunnel-and-visitor-centre

Facilities

At Tunnel End at Marsden there's a visitor centre and the dog-friendly Watersedge Cafe. You can even get married in a beautiful adjoining warehouse, if that floats your boat:

canalrivertrust.org.uk/places-to-visit/standedge-tunnel-and-visitor-centre/the-watersedge-coffee-house

(47) Wardle Canal

This is going to be a short one, because it IS short. The Wardle Canal, that is. In fact, the Wardle Green Branch of the Trent & Mersey Canal, to give it its original name, is the shortest canal in the UK. It lies at Middlewich in Cheshire and begins at the junction of the Trent & Mersey and terminates all of 46.9 metres (154ft) further on at a lock officially named – what else? – Wardle Lock.

Now, we wouldn't advocate making a special trip to visit this canal, which you could walk up and down comfortably in less than five minutes. However, if you happened to be strolling around the not unpleasant old salt town of Middlewich – perhaps pottering up the towpath looking at the locks that pass through the place, maybe attracted there by its (much recommended) annual Folk and Boat Festival, which draws crowds of up to 30,000 people every June – you might find yourself at the junction of the Trent & Mersey. And there you can't help but notice the name of the Wardle canal and the date 1829 carved into a worn sandstone tablet set into a low bridge over what appears at first glance to be an arm off the main canal. You might wonder what that's all about.

Chaos on the Wardle Canal in the 1970s as a hire boat leaving the lock struggles to avoid the bow of a former working boat adapted for camping. Camping boats were a common sight then and for many enthusiasts it was their first taste of canals.

The North

Wardle lock from the other side; Maureen Shaw's cottage is on the right-hand side.

The answer to this is the same as it is for so many oddities you find on the cut. As former US President Bill Clinton might have said, 'It's the money, stupid.' For the Wardle Canal isn't an arm to anywhere. It's actually the link between the Trent & Mersey and a branch of the Shropshire Union canal, which leads to its mainline 16km (10 miles) away. In other words, this was the meeting point between two canal companies that were bitter competitors. By building this 'canal', the Trent & Mersey company – the older of the two – could levy punitive tolls on boat traffic, ensuring it made money from craft passing between the two.

Over the years we've been cruising, Wardle Lock has increasingly become known as Maureen's Lock after Maureen Shaw, who lived in the adjacent cottage until her death in 2012 when she was getting on for 80. She was an old working boatwoman and in her later years she'd become the unofficial lock-keeper, in the tradition of other strong, elderly women who lived in lock cottages. Another was Irene Pain at Bourton Lock on the Oxford canal. Both were brusque, no-nonsense women who didn't suffer fools on boats gladly – though both seemed to have a soft spot for us. We think it was because our engine was quiet and we were careful not to attract a lambasting from them by crashing against the gates.

A memorial plaque celebrating Maureen's life was raised by public subscription and installed at her lock.

Visit

For the Middlewich Folk and Boat Festival, details of dates, headline acts and tickets:
| middlewichfabfestival.co.uk

(48) Wigan Pier

Judging by its name, you might expect this to be a classic English seaside pier, complete with amusement arcades, kiss-me-quick hats and everyone sucking a stick of rock.

But Wigan is landlocked on the Leeds & Liverpool Canal, a good 30km (20 miles) from the nearest beach. And its famous pier was built to be functional rather than fun: a loading wharf where coal from local collieries was tipped into waiting boats. Look for it today and all you'll find is a couple of tramway rails cutting across a cobbled towpath, supported at their curved ends by scaffolding planks overhanging the cut.

The renown afforded to this modest feature is entirely down to George Orwell's 1930s' polemic *The Road to Wigan Pier*, which chronicles the grim lives of northern industrial workers during the depression years before the Second World War. The idea of calling a Wigan coal jetty a 'pier' was a music hall

Wigan Pier. A music hall joke turned national icon.

joke even before Orwell appropriated it for his own use, making the gag (such as it was) a homage to working-class resilience in the face of grinding poverty.

The area around the pier has been the subject of a number of unsuccessful attempts to develop it as a leisure and tourist destination, most recently when the exhibition *The Way We Were* attracted millions of visitors before it closed. The Wigan Pier nightclub closed too, along with The Orwell, a pub/restaurant located in the former Gibson's Warehouse, built in 1777 and rebuilt, coincidently, in 1984.

Today, a new initiative to develop the Wigan Pier area as a cultural quarter is nearing completion, with a microbrewery, food hall and educational and event space planned as part of a regeneration masterplan for the town centre. This is not such an outlandish idea as it might first seem because Wigan once *was* a cultural centre of international importance. A ten-minute walk from the pier and marked by a blue plaque is the site of Wigan Casino: one of the birthplaces of Northern Soul, where black American music legends like Jackie Wilson and Junior Walker played to capacity crowds. In 1978, the club was voted the greatest disco in the world by the US music magazine *Billboard*– beating New York's last word in disco-cool, Studio 54.

There's much impressive industrial architecture still to be seen by the canal, like the massive Trencherfield cotton mill, now partly residential, where the enormous 2,500hp steam engine that originally powered the looms is still in working order. The equally fine Number 1 Terminal Warehouse, straddling the canal and supported by a symmetrical pair of arched, covered loading bays, was derelict in the mid-1970s and is one of the success stories of earlier restorations. Hopefully, this long overdue latest renaissance will achieve what the others didn't. Wigan deserves it.

Plans are underway to transform the Wigan Pier area as part of a £190 million regeneration plan for the town centre. There is much impressive industrial architecture bordering the canal.

Visit

In the area

Literally around the corner from the pier is the junction where the canal divides. In one direction, the 21 locks of the Wigan flight take it up the main line on the start of its long journey to the summit of the Pennines; in the other, a short walk along the towpath brings you to the Wigan 'flashes', extensive lakes formed as a result of mining subsidence, now a nature reserve and home to many species of birds and dragonflies.

Cream tea and chippy cruises in a wide-beam boat from the pier:
| kittywake.co.uk

At the time of writing, the steam engine at Trencherfield Mill (Wallgate, Wigan, WN3 4BF) is closed to the public, but is expected to reopen soon:
| visitmanchester.com/things-to-see-and-do/trencherfield-mill-engine-p102991

49 Worsley Delph

This is where it all began. Before canal mania gripped the nation and the Industrial Revolution got underway, one Francis Egerton, Duke of Bridgewater and major landowner, pondered the rust-coloured waters seeping from his mines in search of a solution to his problem.

He needed to move coal from where the mines were sited at Worsley to the mighty cotton mills of Manchester, which were desperate for the stuff. Heartbroken after being jilted by the love of his life, his despair gave impetus to a visionary project he had first conceived while he'd been in France on his Grand Tour. There, he had seen the Canal Royal de Languedoc – the astonishing artificial waterway linking the Mediterranean and the Atlantic. Known today as the Canal du Midi, it was already almost 85 years old when he saw it, but nevertheless it was the inspiration for him to build a canal of his own – the Bridgewater Canal.

So, in one sense, we have a broken heart to thank for the birth of the

A sign erected in 1961 marks the 200th anniversary of the opening of the Bridgewater Canal.

waterways as we know them: the spark that ignited the modern world. Fresh-hewn coal was extracted from an extensive network of underground canals on specially built craft, christened 'starvationer' boats because of the distinctive ribbing of their hulls. So efficient was this new transport system that His Grace couldn't sell his coal fast enough. He made himself a fortune and the price of coal in Manchester halved.

Though plagued by busy roads on all sides, Worsley today is a tranquil beauty spot and locals have battled hard to keep it that way, fighting off a string of development proposals that would have destroyed its unique character. It is at a junction where the canal changes direction and joins with a short arm coming from the Delph itself, forming a wide pool with ochre-coloured water, the residue of iron ore leaching from the mines. There is a pretty bridge spanning the arm, and the handsome half-timbered Packet House where fast passenger boats once departed for Manchester. Opposite is Worsley Green, which has all the appearance of a traditional village green, but which until the beginning of the 20th century was an industrial area, occupied by boatbuilders and the trades associated

Pretty Worsley Basin, characterised by the black and white half-timbered house from which faster 'packet' boats departed.

with it.

Until recently, the Delph itself was something of a mess though. The point at which the old mines emerged into daylight had become overgrown with vegetation, blocked off by wire grilles and further sullied by an inaccessible rusted bridge built out of girders, which at some stage must have been erected to give access to the site. Where the importance of the site was recognised at all, it was by a tarnished plaque erected in 1961 by the long defunct Worsley Urban District Council. Now, after a £5.5 million facelift – a joint endeavour by the National Lottery Heritage Fund, Salford Council and the Bridgewater Canal Company – it's unrecognisable. The site has been cleaned up: a new island has been built and a towering steel structure erected on it in the shape of a spinning top, an interpretation of the crane that was originally used to excavate rocks from the mine. There's a new viewing platform

and striking new bronze artworks are dotted around the site to represent its history: a Davy lamp, a pickaxe and representations of newspapers and the Act of Parliament that launched the canal. The art may not be everybody's cup of tea, we grant you. But a site this important had to be recognised somehow.

Visit

Access
For details of how to get there, events, maps and history trails etc:
| est1761.org

Guided tours of the Delph:
| bridgewatercanalguidedtours.com

In the area
Those interested can walk the 8km (5 miles) up the towpath to the Barton Swing Aqueduct (see Wonder 30).

(50) Roving Bridges

They're a bit like those drawings by MC Escher. You know who I mean: that Dutch graphic artist who used to compose pictures of imaginary castles in which he played with perspective. People walk up staircases to infinity in a way that appears impossible. That's because what the drawings depict IS impossible. They are visual tricks that play mind games with our two-dimensional view of a three-dimensional world.

But that's what crossover bridges can feel like sometimes. Their purpose is to allow a horse towing a boat to cross the canal. But here's the rub. They were

Functional and practical but also graceful.

built not just so the horse could cross the bridge, but so that when the towpath changes from one side of the canal to the other they could cross it without having to be unharnessed. Think about that for a moment; think about the challenges it poses. The horse has to cross the canal bridge but it has to go under it too. How can that be done? Like an Escher drawing, it's impossible, surely. The rope would get tangled in the bridge.

But actually it isn't impossible, and the way the bridges cunningly twist and turn to achieve their purpose creates some of the most flowing and graceful stone engineering to be seen anywhere in the country, let alone on the canals. They are sometimes called roving bridges, and they do seem to snake around without any fixed destination, more wandering than roving. You find them all over the country but the best examples by far are on the Macclesfield Canal, which connects the Trent & Mersey at Kidsgrove in the Potteries to the Peak

Forest Canal at Marple, on the very edge of Greater Manchester.

Foden Bank Bridge, number 43, in Macclesfield itself is one; Morris Bridge, number 76, in Congleton is another. A third is Clarke Lane Bridge, number 29, half a mile south of Bollington, where a couple of majestic spinning mills tower above the canal, a reminder of when cotton was king in these parts.

Our favourite, though, is Junction Bridge, Number 1, in Marple. Perhaps because it lies on a T-junction, its archway framing the lawn and frontage of a delightful stone-built cottage; or perhaps it's because it's at the head of the 16 locks that compose the Marple lock flight, one of the steepest in the country and one of the prettiest, too. Either way, there's something in its flowing lines

The aqueduct at the bottom of the locks that takes the Peak Forest Canal over the River Goyt is impressive, too, another contender as a Wonder in its own right. Marple station is half an hour from Manchester Piccadilly with regular trains throughout the day.

There are some lovely walks, a series of which, first published by the late Gordon Mills, are available free: marple.website/walks-around-marple.html

and graceful curves that make it as much a work of art as an example of industrial architecture. Like the Escher drawings, there's something not quite real about it – as if it's located in a different world. Except that, of course, it's in Canal World and very real indeed.

The listed Bridge 77 on the Macclesfield Canal at Lamberts Lane, Congleton. Found at points where the towpath changes sides, roving bridges were designed so that horse-drawn boats could continue underneath without having to unharness. Even when you know why they were built, you still have to think twice to figure out how they worked.

(51) Tow Rope Grooves

They're all over the place: on the edges of low-slung humpback bridges and on mooring bollards; on lock walls and sometimes on the paddle gear that controls the flow of water into them. They are the deep lateral grooves gouged into stone, brickwork and iron by the abrasive effect of countless thousands of tow ropes used by horse-drawn canal boats before the advent of engine power.

Grooves on a bridge on the Stratford Canal.

These humble indentations can easily go unnoticed and ignored, yet nothing more instantaneously transports you back to an age when these newly dug ditches were the motorways of their time, busy with streams of narrowboats so heavily laden they were only inches from sinking. The grooves are both commonplace and mysterious, miraculously dissolving the centuries between then and now. As goods of all sorts were being hauled from one end of the country to the other by water, it's a testament to the pure volume of traffic on the canals that the ropes literally left their mark – one that has, astonishingly, survived until the present. You could understand it on stone or brickwork, which is soft. But so destructive were the tow ropes, canal companies erected cast-iron protectors at vulnerable points. Yet even these wore away and showed grooves over the years. Touch the cavities and explore them as you might a sculpture; close your eyes and you can almost feel the moisture and the towpath grit the ropes have deposited. Though the men and women who crewed the boats are all long dead, their boats broken up, rotted and sunk, these evocative reminders of the Canal Age stand like monuments, an enduring reminder of their lives.

The evocative power of these almost insignificant details of the canals have always had the potency to touch us. Not so the eminent waterways author and publisher Charles Hadfield, co-founder of the Inland Waterways Association (see Wonder 1), whom Steve visited in the 1980s at the modern house where he lived in Gloucestershire. Hadfield was in his 70s then, Steve in his 30s and surprised that an historian of Hadfield's eminence wasn't living anywhere more, well … more traditional, somewhere thatched and built of natural stone. He was even more surprised when Hadfield reacted to Steve's confession that he found these tow rope grooves charming with an amusement that touched on derision. Hadfield explained that his interest in canals wasn't because they were vestiges of the past, but because in the past they were at the sharp end of technological advance. Or putting it another way, it was Hadfield who was acting the part of a young man and Steve behaving like a septuagenarian.

The IWA is among the most successful restoration groups of post-war years. But my, Hadfield was no friend of his co-founder Robert Aickman, who, with author Tom Rolt, is generally credited with taking the lead role in the association's early years until his bloody-minded inflexibility led to

Built to protect the softer stone of a bridge, this cast iron guard has nevertheless been almost eroded itself by towropes.

both Hadfield and Rolt resigning. Steve asked Hadfield what he thought about Aickman. Hadfield shook his head. 'Messianic,' he said.

(52) Hobbit Houses

Well, what's this then? A little Hobbit House in the bridge? A bolthole for Bilbo Baggins? Or maybe a refuge for destitute rabbits? Perhaps a holiday home for a wise old owl who wants a break from living so high up in the Hundred Acre Wood?

No, nothing as mundane as any of this. This little door hides the equipment required to drain the canal of its very lifeblood, and sometimes to prevent it from bleeding to death, too. Behind it are what are called 'stop planks' – large beams of wood the size of railway sleepers. They notch into grooves at bridges and aqueducts, which you can see if you look closely, and they allow sections of the canal to be shut off and drained for repair, or sometimes if there's been a breach and it's an emergency, to prevent it from draining

Stop planks are essential pieces of equipment for maintaining canals; they are kept in a variety of places. These sit under a specially constructed 'chalet' to protect them from rain.

Above: Stop planks in use while repairs are in progress. Some have already been inserted into position; others wait to be dropped if water levels rise. Right: No, sadly no Hobbits behind this door, but they may take up residence anytime soon as wooden stop planks are phased out.

completely, avoiding the loss of millions of gallons of water. Stop planks are stored in all manner of places along the canals. Some are in specially built brick shelters, some in attractive open-ended wooden sheds; some in less appealing concrete bunkers or beneath corrugated iron covers. One way or another, they may soon be a thing of the past. Wood is expensive, and sleepers are stolen for gardens or even just vandalised for the hell of it. Nowadays, waterways staff have taken to using aluminium stop planks, which they can carry about with them and are lighter to use. So who knows? Maybe Hobbits will soon relocate to the vacant bridge holes.

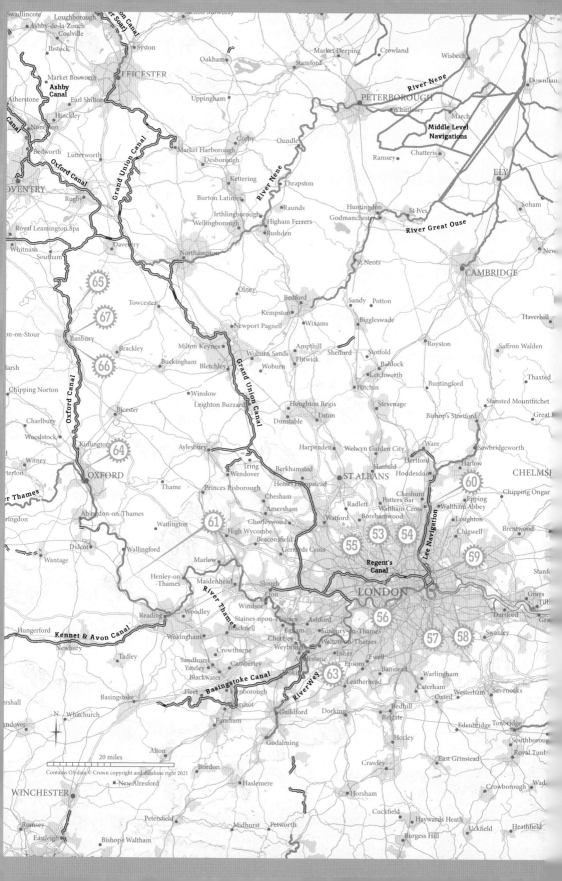

The South

Little Venice

Blow-Up Bridge (Macclesfield Bridge), Regent's Canal

53

Passing under this unusually elegant three-arched bridge across the canal near the zoo in London's Regent's Park, you might notice something puzzling.

The tow rope grooves (see Wonder 51) etched into its fluted, cast-iron Doric columns by countless horse-drawn boats can be seen not just facing the canal, as you would normally expect, but also on the towpath side. Why? It doesn't make any sense unless generations of distracted horses had somehow pulled boats from the water and dragged them along the towpath before depositing them back in the cut again.

The story that explains this is one of the most dramatic in canal history. In the early hours of 2 October 1874, a convoy of five boats, pulled by a steam

The original columns reused having survived the blast.

tug and laden with an assortment of cargoes, was bound for the Midlands. Third in the convoy was Tilbury, steered by Charles Baxton of Loughborough, Steve's birthplace. It was carrying sugar, coffee and nuts, along with several barrels of petrol and some 5 tons of gunpowder. A few minutes before 5am, just as Tilbury passed under Macclesfield Bridge, the load exploded, '...with a roar and a blast which awakened more than half the metropolis from its slumbers', as the Illustrated London News reported at the time. 'It was as swift, as devastating, as irresistible as a bolt from heaven. It suggested to many minds the end of all things... People ran out in their night-gear into the streets, and in frantic terror sought means of succour and escape...' According to The Morning Post: '...the sensation produced was as that of an earthquake. Houses were shaken to their foundations ... the effect was that of apparent immediate annihilation.'

The blast blew the boat to smithereens, killing the three-man crew on board. It sunk the next boat in the convoy and reduced the bridge to rubble, its supporting columns sent flying. The impact shattered windows up to 5km (3 miles) away and left nearby houses in ruins. It lifted roofs and stripped plaster off walls. Ceilings collapsed, doors were torn off their hinges, furniture wrecked and '... smashed to atoms'. There were even rumours of dangerous animals roaming wild in the capital, having escaped from the nearby zoo.

During the inquiry that followed, it was generally agreed to be a miracle that London had got away without greater devastation and loss of life. There was much soul-searching and hand-wringing in newspaper columns and Parliament over the extraordinary lack of controls on transporting hazardous cargoes through densely populated cities. Just a year later, following the public outcry, the Explosives Act of 1875 was passed, putting new safety measures in place designed to prevent similar accidents happening again.

The bridge was rebuilt exactly as it had been. The original columns, which had survived intact, were reused in the new structure, but rotated 180 degrees, so that the old tow rope grooves faced the towpath rather than the water. In time, new tow rope grooves made new marks

Visit

Access

The best way of seeing the bridge is by taking what must be the most rewarding waterways walk in London, one that takes in two more of our Wonders. Start at Little Venice (see Wonder 55) by taking a Tube, not to Warwick Avenue, as the guidebooks recommend, but to Paddington Station, where there is a walkway that brings you out to the Paddington Arm of the canal. The sudden contrast between the bustle of one and the calm of the other is startling.

In the area

After exploring the arm, you can walk to Blow-up Bridge, and on to Camden Market (see Wonder 54) and beyond to the Thames if you want:

canalrivertrust.org.uk/enjoy-the-waterways/walking/walking-routes/little-venice-to-camden-walk

on the water side, too, which is why to this day you can see them on both. And ever since, the new bridge has been known among boatmen by a nickname it still carries today among those of us on the cut: Blow-up Bridge.

A tranquil scene which belies the tragic incident that brought panic to London in 1874.

54 Camden Lock

Camden Lock is not so much a place as a time warp. If you were part of the counterculture of the 1960s you'll feel at home here, a place where flower power, psychedelia and kaftans have never gone out of fashion.

In this last bastion of hippiedom, you can indulge in some gentle nostalgia for a time when it seemed peace and love reigned and you could solve the world's problems, picking up a statue of the Buddha while you were at it. Today, melting into a miasma of shops, market stalls and patchouli oil, it's clear that a whole new generation who weren't even born at the time – dammit, whose *parents* weren't even born at the time – are here to enjoy that same vibe.

The lock itself – official name Hampstead Road Lock – is on the Regent's Canal in London, and it's actually two locks, the only twinned pair in the city, designed to conserve

Camden Market spills out to the water's edge of the Regents Canal, attracting thousands of visitors and tourists.

water. It's always busy and the crush of onlookers on the towpath is so great that, as a boater, you have to use a key to get through a restraining fence in order to operate the lock beams and paddle gear, which could otherwise be hazardous with so many pubs and bars close to the deep water.

What few realise is that, in a different guise, this was once part of the huge Camden Goods Depot, the first freight transport hub in the country, a place where rail, road and canal converged in a massive complex. It was completed by Robert Stephenson in 1839 on a 10ha (25-acre) site as the freight terminus of his London and Birmingham Railway, the first intercity railway to reach London. Sited close to the canal so as to have access to London's docks, where seagoing ships arrived and departed from across the globe, it was a complicated nexus of train tracks, goods yards and locomotive sheds, one of which today is the famous Roundhouse music venue. On the canal side there were stables, horse tunnels and a covered canal basin. Part of this is still visible in the shape of The Interchange, an imposing red-brick warehouse alongside the market, with its cast-iron towpath bridge over the entrance to what

The South

was once the basin where narrowboats were loaded and unloaded.

Approaching from Camden Town Tube station along Camden High Street, there's a huge sign emblazoned on a railway bridge announcing Camden Lock – so there's no excuse for missing it. Indeed, you'd surely be out of your head on something if you did. Apart from loud music pouring from the place, the market doubles as a global kitchen, serving street food from across the world. You can smell it a mile off and even if you're not hungry, the tempting aromas from the stalls ensure you soon will be.

The neighbouring Pirate Castle canal-side community centre (thepiratecastle. org) has been providing accessible, water-based activities to local kids and adults for over 50 years; various trip boats ply this stretch of the cut, with regular services between here and Little Venice (see Wonder 55).

Visit

Access

It may seem counter-intuitive to suggest it, but if you are intending to go to Camden Market then make it a Saturday or Sunday, neither too early nor too late. OK, so you'll hit crowds worse than the rush hour at Oxford Circus. But you're coming for the London vibe, aren't you? – and Londoners are not weekend early birds. It's the same with the stalls: some are on holiday time and don't kick off until later. The drawback to this is that at its busiest, Camden Town Tube – the closest to the market – is so overrun it's subject to unannounced closure on safety grounds. So get off at Chalk Farm – the walk is only a couple of minutes longer, a distance hardly worth talking about. There are buses too – just don't even THINK about driving.

TOP TIP 1: Don't expect to find anywhere to sit once you've bought food. Like Londoners, you'll have to develop the Camden Shuffle, which is a way of not just eating on the move, but shopping at the same time too.

TOP TIP 2: Try the Music Boat (5–89 Lower Walkway, Camden Lock Place, NW1 8AF. Tel: 07888 863447), in which you can be poled up the cut in a punt to the sound of some live tunes. Great idea, great experience. For prices and to book a trip: | themusicboat.org

55 Little Venice

Estate agents tend to exaggerate; everyone knows that, don't they? Any window that doesn't look out on a brick wall has an 'unrivalled view'. A house no one but a millionaire could afford is described as 'realistically priced'. One falling down is called 'an investment opportunity'.

It was ever thus. Once upon a time there used to be a meadow overlooking the triangular basin in London where a tiny island marked where an arm of the Regent's Canal at Paddington joined the main line. Families would picnic there on the banks, watching the boats. Then, in the early 19th century, developers began to build houses – rather fine, elegant houses of white stucco in the style of John Nash, who had earlier designed Regent's Park nearby.

Now, we're not talking a big basin here. In fact, Browning's Pool, as it's known (named after the poet, who lived round here), is small, very small indeed. It's not much bigger than a professional football pitch. However, with typical estate agent hyperbole, the area became talked of as 'London's Venice', a term attributed to the poet Byron who was surely drunk or being facetious when he called it that. Either way, the absurdity of this bit of poetic licence caught on because in 1934, when the detective writer Margery Allingham referred to the area in one of her books, she talked of it as Little Venice. And this is when the estate agents really kicked in. They loved the term, and as the price of houses in the area hit stratospheric levels, they loved it even more.

It is a terrific place to visit, with good canal-side pubs, one of them a small theatre. The floating Waterside Cafe (waterside-cafe.co.uk) is in the pool and there is a wide selection of other places to eat along nearby Paddington Arm. The highlight of its waterway year takes place annually on the May Bank Holiday, when huge numbers of colourfully decorated

Boats gather in Browning's Pool for the annual Canalway Cavacade, a cross between a central London carnival and a village fête.

A short tube ride from the centre of London, but Little Venice could be in a different world.

boats, bunting flapping, jam the pool for Canalway Cavalcade, a celebration of everything watery. There's an illuminated narrowboat procession and a boat-handling competition at which we made fools of ourselves one year. There are food and craft stalls, music, beer tents and kids' stuff, too, a cross between a Central London carnival and a village fete. The surrounding area drips with wealth, the sort of place you couldn't afford to live even if you won the lottery. The houses are Regency style, some of them detached with impressive front porticos; others are in terraces with more than a passing resemblance to Buckingham Palace. Some have barred gates, and if you're willing to risk having your nose bitten off by savage guard dogs, you'll sometimes be lucky enough to see through them and glimpse a luxury swimming pool or gym that has been dug out of the basement. It's that sort of place.

Visit

Access

Believe it or not, it is possible as a boater to moor in Little Venice for a derisory sum. You'll have to book and your stay will be limited. Even so, with hotels in the area costing a fortune, it must be the steal of the century given that you moor in Rembrandt Gardens overlooking Browning's Pool itself:
canalrivertrust.org.uk/about-us/where-we-work/london-and-south-east/boating-facilities/pre-booked-visitor-moorings-in-london

There are other moorings in Paddington Basin, the arm off the junction, but be warned, it's like a scene out of *Blade Runner* down there with all the flash contemporary architecture. Space is at a premium here too, like most London mooring spots, which are generally taken up by residential boats; it's first come, first served, and a bit of a lottery to get a place. But then, that's the same right across the city where, triggered by a housing crisis, the canals are so overcrowded they've reached crisis point too.

56 The Thames Tunnel

Does anyone give a second thought to travelling beneath water these days? Apart from our own Channel Tunnel, there are so many foot, road and underground railway tunnels across the world underneath rivers and estuaries that those using them take them for granted. London alone has 23 of them now. Big deal, you might think.

Except that none of them would have been possible but for the breathtakingly bold vision, self-belief and technical genius of Marc Brunel, the French émigré father of the more famous Isambard Kingdom Brunel. His brainchild – the original Thames Tunnel between Rotherhithe and Wapping – was the first underwater tunnel anywhere in the world,

The tunnel soon after its opening: people came from all over the world to admire it.

originally intended to shift produce away from the city's log-jammed docks.

It was a phenomenal achievement, hailed the world over. A crowd of 50,000 attended its opening in 1843 and it became a major tourist attraction; 2 million people from all over the globe visited in its first year, taking home souvenirs ranging from commemorative plates to handkerchiefs. For a period, the tunnel was turned into a fairground, with sword swallowers, acrobats and tightrope walkers. At other times, it became a shopping arcade, a banqueting hall and a ballroom hosting concert parties. But by the 1850s it was better known as 'Hades Hotel', notorious for vice and crime, until it was sold to the fledgling London Underground network in 1869. It's been part of London's transport system ever since.

The stroke of genius that enabled Marc Brunel to succeed where others had failed was in inventing a device that could stop water getting into the tunnel while it was being dug and prevent the roof and walls caving in on his workers. The tunnelling shield he designed has been the model for every major tunnelling project since. It was a ship's worm that gave him the idea. While working in Chatham Dockyard on another project, he observed how the burrowing creature was able to bore through wood very close to water, digest the wood pulp and excrete a solid substance to line the tunnel it had excavated.

Brunel's tunnelling shield was a huge iron framework divided into sections, enabling 36 men to excavate simultaneously in three rows of 12, inching slowly forward while behind them bricklayers lined the newly dug section of the tunnel. Conditions underground were so dreadful that navvies could only work two-hour shifts. Sometimes working only 2.1 metres (7ft) beneath the riverbed, they were either swelteringly hot or shivering with cold. The suffocating airlessness and overpowering stench didn't help either. At a time when the Thames was the biggest open sewer in the world, men regularly collapsed and had to be taken to the surface gasping for air, only to be set to work again once they had recovered. Disease, severe headaches and even temporary blindness were occupational hazards – and there was always the risk of the river bursting in. This happened at least five times, most notably in 1828, when the roof collapsed and Thames water flooded into the tunnel; six men drowned. Isambard Kingdom Brunel – who had been appointed chief engineer on the project aged just 19 – was in the tunnel at the time and was washed unconscious by the floodwater into the shaft, where he was rescued. He was lucky to escape alive. Perhaps it was this experience that made him the boldest, most creative engineering innovator of his time.

Visit

In the area

The Brunel Museum is situated above ground on the south side of the tunnel at Rotherhithe (Railway Avenue, SE16 4LF. Tel: 0207 2313840). Admission includes a guided tour of the tunnel shaft. In a nod to its early days, the tunnel shaft is regularly the setting for the Midnight Apothecary, an underground nightclub, with cabaret performances and a bar. Cocktails are served from the tiny roof-garden bar, where you can toast marshmallows over an open fire and pay tribute to the men who helped shape the London we know today:
| thebrunelmuseum.com

Rotherhithe is on the Thames Path and is a fascinating area to explore:
| tfl.gov.uk/modes/walking/thames-path

Step inside St Mary's church to learn more about its associations with the *Mayflower*, after which the atmospheric local riverside pub is named:
| stmaryrotherhithe.org
| mayflowerpub.co.uk

Other hidden gems include Sands Films Studio (82 St Marychurch Street, SE16 4HZ. Tel: 0207 2312209), which houses a picture library and an unconventional community cinema featuring an eclectic programme. It also has a film and television costume collection:
| sandsfilms.co.uk

Maritime Greenwich

Canaletto painted it. Pepys was a frequent visitor. Nelson lay in state there. Before Christopher Wren and Inigo Jones laid the foundation stones of their sublime buildings, it was the site of Placentia, a favourite royal palace where both Henry VIII and Elizabeth I were born.

Viewed from the north bank of the Thames, maritime Greenwich looks much as it did when Canaletto first put brush to canvas. You can see it for yourself by just walking through the foot tunnel under the river. The perfectly proportioned symmetry of the Old Royal Naval College frames the classical elegance of the earlier Queen's House, leading the eye up the steep hill crowned by the Royal Observatory.

Nestled in that loop of the river opposite the Isle of Dogs – familiar from the opening titles of *EastEnders* – Maritime Greenwich, a World Heritage Site, has long been one of London's top tourist destinations. The centrepiece is the Old Royal Naval College, originally

the Royal Hospital for Seamen, with its grand quadrants, glorious chapel and magnificent Painted Hall. Now home to Greenwich University and the Trinity Laban Conservatoire, in summer you may catch a few tantalising notes from musicians practising, wafting through open windows. You may even stumble across a film set: these buildings have a long list of credits in many movies, including standing in for the Paris barricades in *Les Misérables*.

The Queen's House is a gorgeous

gem of a place. Inigo Jones's startlingly modern 1616 design was the first classical building in the UK. It's now a picture gallery housing treasures including the famous Armada Portrait of Elizabeth I. Next door, the National Maritime Museum tells the story of Britain's illustrious and sometimes dark naval and seafaring history over a period when Britannia really did rule the waves.

Greenwich is also where time and tide converge. Longitude; the Harrison clocks; Greenwich Mean Time; astronomy – it's all here at the Royal Observatory, including the Prime Meridian of the World, where someone is guaranteed to be taking a selfie with one foot planted firmly in the western hemisphere, the other in the east. After dark, a laser beam sometimes marks the meridian line in the night sky.

At low tide, you can go mudlarking along the shoreline. Rising tides lap the foundations of the Trafalgar Tavern – where Dickens, Wilkie Collins and Thackeray came to dine. Topping it all, the masts and rigging of *Cutty Sark*, the famous tea clipper permanently dry-docked in Greenwich, tower above the tourist fray.

Climb up through Greenwich Park, the oldest of London's royal parks, for what is the finest view of London, the skyscrapers of modern Canary Wharf a backdrop to the baroque splendour of Wren's masterpiece. The unmistakable dome of St Paul's, his other masterpiece, is clearly visible to the west. In keeping with all that Maritime Greenwich stands for, although you can visit by train, the best way to arrive is by boat and a regular Thames Clipper service makes this a no-brainer.

Visit

- -

Access
For Thames Clippers:
| thamesclippers.com/plan-your-journey/find-your-pier/greenwich-pier

In the area
Start your visit with the Old Royal Naval College (SE10 9NN. Tel: 0208 2694799):
| ornc.org

For details on visiting the *Cutty Sark*, National Maritime Museum, Queen's House and Royal Observatory:
| rmg.co.uk

Greenwich Market, established in 1737 and still trading from its original covered hall (though the goods on offer have changed radically), is a treasure trove for flea market fans:
| greenwichmarket.london

For information about the Greenwich foot tunnel:
| visitgreenwich.org.uk/things-to-do/greenwich-foot-tunnel-p1373551

58 The Thames Barrier

It looks like a distant cousin of the Sydney Opera House, with its row of parabolic hoods in shimmering silver creating a mesmerising vision across the Thames at Woolwich. They could be the giant helmets of an advancing army, ghosts of the many armed men who've attempted invasion up the Thames Estuary, from rampaging 9th-century Vikings to the 17th-century Dutch navy intent on scuppering the English fleet to gain a trade advantage.

In fact, it's the main flood defence protecting London. When raised, its movable gates form an impregnable steel wall the height of a five-storey building, able to hold back surge tides that would otherwise deluge large parts of the city, destroying, among so much else, the Houses of Parliament, Tower Bridge and Buckingham Palace. Since its opening in 1982 it has had to be closed more than 200 times, and as the climate changes, the need for it becomes increasingly critical.

It's pretty serious stuff. The lives of almost 1.5 million Londoners and

The Barrier from the air at high tide; look carefully and you can see that it's closed for testing.

property worth £321 billion are at stake, not to mention heritage sites, world-class museums and art galleries; and countless schools, hospitals and churches, along with the entire London Underground system, power stations and the infrastructure that provides the city's water supply. The consequences of it failing don't bear thinking about.

Fourteen people drowned when London last flooded badly, in 1928; but it was the catastrophic North Sea storm surge floods of 1953, which claimed 307 lives and wreaked devastation across eastern England, that were the catalyst for improving the capital's flood defences.

In normal conditions, the barrier's ten rotating steel gates lie flat on the riverbed, allowing shipping clear passage. Weather, tide and tidal surge forecasts are constantly monitored, along with river levels – all feeding into a complex calculation used to decide if the barrier needs to be closed. Ultimately, it's up to the Duty Controller at the time to make the all-important call.

Open or closed, it's an engineering triumph and an awesome sight. One

The late afternoon sun reflects dramatically off the polished steel of the Barrier's distinctive hoods.

of the best ways to see it up close is to take a trip on one of the Thames Clipper services to Woolwich, during which you actually get to go through it. Nothing beats the view from the water, especially when late afternoon sun reflects off the polished steel of the barrier's hoods. Next to it on the south bank is an informative visitor centre, where you can book a place to watch when the barrier goes through its once-monthly testing.

With regular monitoring and maintenance, it is predicted the barrier in its current incarnation is set to be effective until 2070, but already long-term plans to meet London's changing flood defence needs are in place. Rising sea levels mean higher tides, and the defences will have to be adapted accordingly; a new barrier may have to be built sooner than expected. In the meantime, the existing one works with little fanfare but reassuring reliability.

Visit

Access
For more information on how it works, forecast closures and visiting:
| gov.uk/guidance/the-thames-barrier and visitgreenwich.org.uk/things-to-do/thames-barrier-information-centre-p1368561

For Thames Clippers timetables and services:
| thamesclippers.com

59 Three Mills Island

We talk a lot about renewable energy these days – green power that can wean us off our addiction to fossil fuels and help us save the planet from irreversible climate change. Sun, wind and water are driving new technologies like solar panels and wind farms. Yet we largely ignore one mighty natural resource whose power our forebears harnessed almost 1,000 years ago: the power of the tide.

Three Mills Island in Bromley-by-Bow is tucked away in the heart of London's East End – not far from the northern entrance to the Blackwall Tunnel, close to the Bow Back Rivers, a series of forgotten, interconnected semi-tidal waterways that underwent a massive restoration and clean-up for the 2012 London Olympics. Here, you'll find one of the city's hidden gems: the world's largest surviving tidal mill, the House Mill. It's a remarkable industrial relic, one of an unexpectedly splendid complex of Georgian buildings, which includes a second mill, the Clock Mill, and the Miller's House.

There have been mills on this site since the Domesday Book and though the Grade I listed House Mill was only built in 1776, it was erected on the foundations of a much earlier building. Millers made use of the strong flow in the river by holding back the twice-daily tides in a 23ha (57-acre) mill pond. When the tide ebbed, they opened sluice gates to release the stored water, which powered the water wheels. These could operate for up to eight hours at a stretch and as a result the mills became major grain millers for London, grinding flour for the bakers of Stratford-atte-Bow, who supplied the burgeoning City of London market and whose bread was a byword for quality. Later, the mills here ground gunpowder that helped defeat the Spanish Armada. Later still, they reverted to grinding grain once more, though this time to make gin when the demand for it had reached epidemic proportions.

In 1878, there were seven water wheels at Three Mills – four in the House Mill and three in the Clock Mill – driving 14 pairs of millstones. Back then, the island would have resounded to the thunderous roar of water, drowning out the shouts of carpenters and the hammering of coopers making barrels – not to mention

Tucked away in London's East End lies one of London's unexplored gems.

the snuffling and grunting of pigs kept to feed on the edible distillery waste.

German bombers in the Second World War ended milling at the House Mill in 1941 and it narrowly escaped demolition in the 1970s when its owners wanted to turn it into a car park; luckily, the Passmore Edwards Museum Trust (now the House Mill Trust) stepped in to save it and its future was secured. The Miller's House, badly damaged in the Blitz and demolished in the 1950s, was rebuilt in the 1990s to its original design, using many of the original bricks and other materials recovered from the site. It now houses a visitor centre. The Clock Mill continued to operate until 1952, but today is part of 3 Mills film and TV studio complex, where an impressive list of movies and TV series have been filmed, including the original *Big Brother* and *Killing Eve*, as well as work by Hollywood A-listers Wes Anderson, Tim Burton and British Oscar winner and Olympic opening ceremony director Danny Boyle. Three Mills is an urban secret that demands to be seen. But for an island nation that once exploited the immense energy of the sea, surely a revival of tidal power is a no-brainer?

Visit

Access

The following sites are a ten-minute walk from Bromley-by-Bow Tube, though if you must drive, there's parking at the Tesco Superstore just off the Blackwall Tunnel Northern Approach on the A12. Best of luck there.

Three Mills Island borders London's Queen Elizabeth Olympic Park and is linked to London's Olympic waterways and to the Grand Union Canal through Limehouse Cut. Those with their own boats can navigate some of these themselves, booking essential:
| canalrivertrust.org.uk/places-to-visit/ three-mills-and-queen-elizabeth- olympic-park

In the area

There are boat tours around the Olympic Park:
| leeandstortboats.co.uk

The House Mill runs guided tours and hosts concerts, art exhibitions and a range of classes. The Miller's House (Three Mill Lane, E3 3DU. Tel: 0208 9804626) provides a visitor information and education centre, as well as a small cafe. There's also an adventure playground for kids, the Wild Kingdom:
| housemill.org.uk

For walkers/art lovers, there's The Line – London's first dedicated public art walk following the Greenwich Meridian from the O2 to Queen Elizabeth Olympic Park (see Wonder 28):
| the-line.org

60 The Royal Gunpowder Mills

The River Lea puts a lot of people off, and not just because it can't make up its mind whether it's called the Lea or the Lee or whether it's a river or actually a canal. London is what discourages most boaters from going there, because unless you approach from the sea up the Thames Estuary, getting to it means passing through the city and mixing it for mooring space with the many 'liveaboards' who've taken to the water to avoid the city's ever rising property prices.

And it's true: sometimes, trudging past the rows of boats lining the towpath, you wonder at the scale of the problem and what it's led to. Aren't Britain's canals and rivers supposed to be sanctuaries of solitude? Aren't they meant to be placid oases amid the clamour of the urban badlands?

Well, actually, the River Lea soon IS that, and before long you realise you're cruising along a thread that links a

Built for war, but today the Gunpowder Mills site is a haven of peace and quiet.

'necklace' of reservoirs stretching from the Walthamstow wetlands in the south to Ware in the north. This is Lee Valley Regional Park, a 42km-long (26-mile), 4,000ha (10,000-acre) park with sports facilities and wildlife havens, created by a unique Act of Parliament to be a green 'lung' for London, Hertfordshire and Essex. It is an extraordinary waterways corridor. The reservoirs provide the capital with most of its water, but they have become an outstanding sanctuary for birds. We travelled along it once accompanied for an hour by a tern, which dived behind us time and time again, attracted by the fish being disturbed by our propeller. The river takes you past some intriguing locations, the most unmissable being the Royal Gunpowder Mills at Waltham Abbey, which used to be one of only three places in the country making military explosives, and is today the only one that survives virtually intact.

It's a 71ha (175-acre) complex, which was in production for more than 300 years and had its own canal system, built to move unstable explosives around the

The South

A five-mile canal network enabled the safe transport of highly volatile explosive materials around the extensive Royal Gunpowder Mills site.

site in powder barges and punts, several of which still survive on the canal bed. Today, it's an industrial museum where, if you're so inclined, you can explore the armoury and learn all about the history of explosives and be amazed by the high proportion of women involved in their manufacture, especially during periods of war. Alternatively, you can do what we did and wander aimlessly around the site, enjoying its remarkable and haunting ambience, the still waters and derelict locks lending the picturesque ruins a curious charm, a cross between exploring Roman ruins and taking a woodland walk. For safety reasons, the individual processes of making gunpowder needed to be kept separate, which explains why the site is so spread out and why you feel a sense of isolation walking around it. The buildings were not only distanced from each other, but in many cases separated by earth bunds,

constructed to prevent an explosion on one part of the site taking everything else with it. It lends the place a sense of remoteness. You may be near London, but you could be a million miles away.

Visit

For all you need to know about the Gunpowder Mills (Beaulieu Drive, Waltham Abbey, EN9 1JY. Tel: 01992 707370):
| royalgunpowdermills.com

In the area
Lee Valley Park is the setting for a huge variety of activities, from birdwatching to angling to white-water rafting. There are walks and cycle routes aplenty, as well as historic places and gardens to explore:
| visitleevalley.org.uk

61 The River Thames between Goring and Windsor

The Thames is many rivers in one, with as many different identities as the countryside it flows through. It's a river of stories, dreams and imagination. Of power, politics and industry. Majestic, mythical and magical, it's a river of pleasure and leisure, high days and holidays. Sport and splendour. Pomp and pageantry, a waterway of ancient, arcane tradition (see Wonder 62). Not least, it's a playground for the rich and famous, the hoi polloi and everyone else in between.

But between Goring and Windsor there is one sublime stretch of water that seems to capture its spirit, a kind of Arcadia where the Thames is most quintessentially itself. You're left with fleeting impressions and memories: the vivid flash of a kingfisher; the slow circular swoop of a heron; the rhythmic beat of a swan's wings and the skidding wake of its webbed feet as it lands on the water. Here, a riverbank picnic, children in the sunshine plunging into sinuous reeds to cool off, the quiet punctuated by their excited shouts of sudden laughter. There, oars lazily slapping the water, passing expansive Edwardian villas with their magnificent boat houses. The deep, deep green of thick beech woods sweeping down to the water's edge.

This reach of the river is studded with gems that are part of our cultural landscape: Cliveden, where the Astors partied and the Profumo scandal played out; Pangbourne, where the plans of *Three Men in a Boat* (not forgetting Montmorency, the dog) to camp out ended hilariously; Cookham, where Stanley Spencer painted his vision of Christ giving a sermon on the river; Maidenhead, where on certain Edwardian summer weekends Boulters Lock was so jammed with punts that you could barely see water between them; Peter Freebody's boatyard at Hurley, famous for its highly varnished wooden slipper boats and Thames launches, their hulls the colour of raw honey; Henley, home to the famous regatta; Windsor, seat of monarchs for a thousand years; Runnymede, where the Magna Carta was signed ... the list goes on and on. Even

Henley, home of the famous regatta.

The South

prosaic Reading manages to present a regal aspect to the river.

One October morning, as the sun slowly burned off the haze rising from the river, we saw an apparition emerge out of the mist on the far bank. Scarcely able to believe our eyes, we recognised the unmistakable wizard's hat and staff of Gandalf from *Lord of the Rings*, complete with long robes and flowing white beard. He was carrying a protest banner: 'Don't frack the Shires'. Gandalf turned out to be an environmental activist and retired actor walking the length of the Thames to Westminster to deliver a petition to the PM. He accepted the offer of a lift on our boat, and we spent a congenial day together. We tied up at Goring that evening, and in the local pub no one batted an eyelid when he entered in full regalia. It was all in a day's life on the river.

Visit

In the area

For Cliveden (Cliveden Road, Taplow, SL1 8NS (main entrance)), where there are unmatchable views over the river and lovely riverside walks:
| nationaltrust.org.uk/cliveden

Stanley Spencer's tiny but exquisite gallery in his home village of Cookham (High Street, SL6 9SJ. Tel: 01628 531092):
| stanleyspencer.org.uk

Peter Freebody's is a working boatyard and access is restricted to customers, though there are boatyard visits by prior arrangement only (Tel: 01628 824382). For some appreciation of the work it does or, better still, if money's no object, charter the 12-metre (40ft) Edwardian saloon launch *Genevieve*, with driver, restored by them:
| vintagethamescharters.com
| peterfreebody.com

Idyllic summer cruising at Goring Lock.

62 Swan-upping

'Swan-upping' is the colourful annual ritual of marking swans on the River Thames – a flamboyant custom that started in the 12th century and is still going strong today. It's a wonderful bit of English pageantry that takes place over three days in July along the 127km (79-mile) stretch of the River Thames between Sunbury-on-Thames in Surrey and Abingdon in Oxfordshire.

We stumbled across it one year cruising through Reading, and we virtually had to learn a new language to understand what was happening. A flotilla of

Skiffs surround swans and cygnets; today this flamboyant 12th-century ritual has become a valuable scientific tool.

skiffs rowed by 'uppers' and sporting traditional pennants were accompanied by a 'randan', a slightly longer boat. This was rowed by a couple of oarsmen and a sculler carrying the Queen's Swan Marker in red livery, a feather wedged jauntily in his cap. It turns out that the Queen, among her numerous other titles, is the Seigneur of the Swans. She's probably Lord of the Dance, too.

This ceremony began as a demonstration of royal prerogative at a time when the Crown claimed the ownership of every swan in the country, and when swans were one of the luxury foods of Europe – the Beluga caviar of their day. Swans' feathers were valued as writing implements, too, considered more durable than quills from geese. However, over the years, various monarchs granted limited rights to own swans to others, in particular a couple of livery companies – trades associations descended from medieval guilds. Swan-upping was essentially for their benefit: to sort out which swan belonged to which of them.

Today, oarsmen rowing for the Worshipful Company of Dyers (who, as their name suggests, dyed cloth) wear bright blue. Those in the Worshipful Company of Vintners – wine importers – don't bother rowing themselves. Don't ask us why, maybe they're too grand for it, maybe too drunk? One way or another, members of another livery company, the Watermen and Lightermen, who wear white tops, do the grunt work for them. The Queen's rowers wear resplendent scarlet uniforms – what else?

Once they spot 'a game' – one of the many collective nouns for a gathering of swans – the cry of 'All Up!' rings out across the water and the skiffs surround the birds in a triangular formation, trapping them. The cry is the source of

Visit

For more on the history of swan-upping, its modern role in conservation, the dates it will next be happening and the times and locations where you can see the spectacle first hand:
| royal.uk/swans

the term 'swan-upping', and the first of the day every morning is music to the ears of the Vintners, since they're not allowed to open the champagne until they hear it. We have read that one morning, back in the mists of time, they had to wait for all of three hours to get the corks popping – which must have been a taxing experience for them since it's still spoken of today with some anguish.

Until 1996, the bills (for goodness' sake, don't call them 'beaks') of birds belonging to the Dyers were marked with one nick, whereas those of the Vintners merited two. The sovereign's birds were left unmarked, of course. Why wouldn't they be? Now, as then, every unmarked swan in the country officially belongs to the Queen anyhow.

Like many traditional ceremonies, swan-upping has adapted itself to the present and today the birds are all marked with stainless-steel rings on their right leg, containing a British Trust for Ornithology identification number. Indeed, the ceremony has become a valuable scientific census of swans during which their health can be checked and the number of cygnets on the river monitored.

The Wey Navigation

In 1812, the year of Napoleon's defeat by Russia commemorated in Tchaikovsky's famous overture, William Stevens took a job as lock-keeper on the 24km (15-mile) River Wey near Woking, a waterway his family would eventually come to own.

Fast-forward 150 years and in 1964 one of his descendants, Harry Stevens, gave it to the National Trust. Like many bequests of this sort, it was less generous than it first seemed. The navigation had once been a lucrative industrial superhighway between Surrey and London, the A3 of its day. But by then it was near derelict. It hadn't made a penny in years.

We weren't overly impressed with the NT's stewardship of the Stratford Canal when they were custodians (see Wonder 24), but any misgivings we may have harboured from the past evaporated the first time we left the Thames for the Wey Navigation and passed through the maze of backwaters around Weybridge. After 5km (3 miles) it joins with the Basingstoke Canal, where the M25 crosses it at Byfleet. After that, though, the Wey just gets prettier and prettier, meandering in haunting stillness past the ruins of Newark Priory, through serene and enchanting water meadows, breathtaking in their beauty. This is testament to the NT's conservancy, because although you're scarcely aware of it, the navigation passes through some of the most heavily populated parts of the south-east commuter belt, and over the years it's bought odd pockets of land

to protect it from encroaching suburbia. The Royal Horticultural Society's splendid gardens at Wisley – just a short walk from The Anchor at Pyrford, and both well worth a visit – has done its bit too; and where its extensive gardens border the river, it has restored parts of the original watercourse, creating a series of valuable wildlife habitats.

It's free to walk the canal but you need a special licence to cruise it, both are worth doing because there's a lot to see. The triple-arched cast-iron Victorian bridge crossing the Wey may not be the original that gave Weybridge its name, but it's still an elegant example of its type. In the town itself is the house where the author EM Forster wrote most of his

The Royal Horticultural Society's showpiece gardens at Wisley, a pleasant walk from The Anchor at Pyrford where there are good moorings.

The South

major novels, and further up towards Godalming – the limit of navigation and the most southerly point of the navigable canal system – are the latticed windows of what was once the summer house of Pyrford Place, where the poet John Donne lived for four years after his imprisonment for eloping with the 16-year-old daughter of his boss. The Wey also passes through historic Guildford, lapping the banks of the low sandstone escarpment – the 'guilden sands' – from which the town takes its name.

But the star of any trip up the navigation is the Wey itself, which has been so channelled, dredged and straightened over the years that it's sometimes difficult to say whether you're on a river or a canal. Either way, it's beautiful and one of the oldest navigations in the country, so old that much of the material used to reconstruct London after the Great Fire of 1666 was carried along it, including the Guilford stone that Sir Christopher Wren used for St Paul's Cathedral.

At Guns Mouth the navigation veers off along what used to be the Wey &

Visit

- -

Access

For more information on the Wey Navigation, check the NT website, where application forms for licensing can also be downloaded. Alternatively, they can be purchased on entrance from the Thames at Thames Lock:
| nationaltrust.org.uk/river-wey-and-godalming-navigationsand-dapdune-wharf

Facilities

The Anchor pub (Pyrford Lock, Wisley, GU23 6QW. Tel: 01932 342507):
| anchorpyrford.co.uk

In the area

RHS Garden Wisley (GU23 6QB. Tel: 01483 224234):
| rhs.org.uk/gardens/wisley

Arun Junction Canal towards Portsmouth and the sea by way of Chichester, where the old canal basin has been developed with new housing. The canal is currently unnavigable but work by the Wey & Arun Canal Trust has succeeded in restoring short lengths with the ultimate aim of reopening the entire canal.

The afternoon sun catches the 'golden sands' that give Guildford its name.

Port Meadow and Oxford

Even though it's a walk from the centre, Port Meadow – where the Thames sweeps languorously around the flood plains of the city – encapsulates Oxford in a way that even its colleges don't. There's something about it reminiscent of *Brideshead Revisited,* that evocative novel by Evelyn Waugh that looks back nostalgically to an age of English aristocracy and privilege.

On hot summer mornings, cows cool themselves knee-deep in the water; in the afternoons, undergraduates lounge timelessly on the grass, picnicking from wicker hampers with companions, or sit cross-legged in existential isolation, reading from books too heavy for them to hold. A rowing boat of giggling friends passes, fracturing the calm afternoon with its splashing oars. An eight slips by soundlessly, cutting the water so cleanly it barely leaves a wake.

Port Meadow is an ancient area of grazing land, which is said never to have yielded to the plough. Today, it's common land bordered by the river on one side and the 'dreaming spires' on the other. Stretching from Wolvercote Common in the north, it's said the freemen of the city were bequeathed the right to graze

On sunny days on the river, everywhere's a swimming pool.

their animals on the land by Alfred the Great for their help in defending the city he founded in the 10th century against marauding Danes – a story that might have greater credibility if Alfred hadn't died in the 9th century. But that's Oxford for you: a city of myth, tradition and privilege; a city where it's said some of the best brains in the country have been educated. Boris Johnson, for example...

Rivers have been central to Oxford's evolution. It grew up around the confluence of the Cherwell – pronounced Charwell – and the Thames, which in these parts was often called the Isis until the jihadists of the Islamic State of Iraq and Syria purloined the name for themselves, which took the shine off it somewhat. As it suggests, the city's name came about because there was a ford where you could get oxen from one bank to the other. Girded by rivers and later penetrated by the Oxford Canal, Oxford is an island in itself. But it's an island of islands, too, threaded by mill streams, rivulets and tributaries weaving through the city like a bloodstream and incorporating places that have insinuated themselves into the city's culture. Places like the elegant Magdalen Bridge over the River Cherwell, where as part of May Day morning celebrations students traditionally used to jump drunkenly into the water, until so many of them injured themselves they had to put a stop to it. As we say, some of the best brains in the country...

Even the workaday Oxford Canal has carved an intellectual place for itself as it arrives surreptitiously in the city by a secret, back-door route through Jericho, home of the Oxford University Press and academics whose long gardens stretch

Horses and cattle graze on Port Meadow against the backdrop of the 'dreaming spires'.

down to the water's edge. The canal stops dead suddenly. Sadly, a basin that used to mark its terminus has long since been filled in and is now a car park for Nuffield College. Despite the explosion of canal restoration throughout the country, the college adamantly refuses to develop it in any way sympathetic to its history. The car park is just too lucrative, it admits shamelessly. That's Oxford for you, too.

Visit

Facilities
Two historic riverside pubs are:
The Trout Inn at Wolvercote (195 Godstow Road, Oxford, OX2 8PN. Tel: 01865 510930):
| thetroutoxford.co.uk

The Perch at Binsey, with its garden overlooking Port Meadow (Binsey Lane, Oxford, OX2 0NG. Tel: 01865 728891). Customer moorings are available:
| the-perch.co.uk

The long-established Salter's Steamers in Oxford (Tel: 01865 243421) rents punts as well as offering river trips via Port Meadow, some with a picnic lunch:
| salterssteamers.co.uk

65 Cropredy Festival

For one weekend every year, the normally peaceful village of Cropredy on the Oxford Canal near Banbury is transformed into party central when tens of thousands of music fans descend for the annual Fairport festival.

Crowds in flamboyant shirts, skirts and floral headdresses throng the lanes and take over the pretty churchyard, which becomes an extension to the bar of the thatched Red Lion opposite. They jam the bridge over the canal, while the road leading to the festival site is lined with stalls selling everything a festival-goer could possibly need, from tie-dyed T-shirts to flashing fluorescent collars for their dogs. Long queues form outside the Bridge Stores and it's touch and go whether the pubs will run out of beer, even though they've been preparing for this weekend since last year's festival ended. The Canoe Club serves up heart-stopping breakfasts in a marquee by the canal, and the Old Coal Wharf arts centre becomes a crafts and antiques market, adding to the general gaiety of the occasion by serving afternoon teas. It's all quintessentially English. It's also the only music festival you can turn up to by boat.

Fairport's Cropredy Convention, to give it its official name, started almost by accident when two of the pioneering folk rock band's members lived in Cropredy in the 1970s. Glastonbury it ain't, but part of its attraction is that it started small and it's stayed that way. Performances take place on a single stage, playing to a 20,000-strong crowd spread out across a gently sloping field forming a natural amphitheatre. The music leans heavily towards its folk roots but always with an eclectic twist that can sometimes be surprising. There's the usual festival food and gallons of real ale, with a generous sprinkling of New Age craft stalls.

Even if there are the odd one or two people who have indulged in more drugs than are good for them, there's no air of paranoia about the place, just the general good humour of people having a good time. The pastoral setting is perfect, and there's a truly spine-tingling moment when, by tradition, the band plays the Fairport classic 'Meet on the Ledge' to end the festival.

The first time we went, in the 1980s, we were able to turn up in our boat the day the festival started and find a mooring place with no trouble – which you certainly couldn't do today. At the end of the evening, we boaters partied on ... until an anguished cry went up as a wooden boat belonging to one of our number suddenly began to sink. Everyone sprang into action, some baling out the boat while others got the distraught owners' belongings to safety on the towpath. Luckily for him, one of the people there was the artist and musician Ian Staples, who at the time restored wooden boats for a living. He just happened to have with him a tub of 'Charlie' – that thick mixture

Visit

Fairport's Cropredy Convention, billed as the country's friendliest festival, usually takes place from Thursday afternoon through to Saturday midnight on the second weekend of August. Tickets, camping and glamping places can be booked on their website, which also has information about the upcoming line-up and FAQs:
| fairportconvention.com

The festival is a genuine community event involving the whole village, so even without tickets, you can soak up the atmosphere at the Fairport Fringe, with free live music at both village pubs, the Brasenose and the Red Lion.

It's an easy walk from the canal to the festival site, but if you're thinking of going by boat, you'll need to plan well ahead to find a mooring.

of tar and horse manure traditionally used in wooden boat repair – and he successfully set to work by torchlight, fixing the leak. His quick thinking that night saved one very grateful young man from homelessness.

Flags, food and fun: typical festival fare – except Cropredy has its own unique ambience which has to be experienced to be understood.

66 Southern Oxford (and Llangollen) Lift Bridges

There are lift bridges of different sorts all over the country, but the ones that have come to epitomise the image of canal lift bridges are those on the southern Oxford and Llangollen canals. They are of different designs, but both have shades of medieval castle drawbridges about them. Coming across one on a boat, you'll be faced either with a charming sight enhancing the natural beauty of its rural setting ... or a pig of a device designed to test your strength and patience to the limit. It all depends on whether it's open or closed.

These 18th-century relics punctuate the landscape with their tilting decks, black-and-white wooden hand rails, and balance beams set at a rakish angle. When the canal was built, money was tight, and they were a cheap alternative to brick bridges. In the down position, they allow farmers access to their fields; in the raised position, they allow boats to pass underneath. However, they're not robust enough for contemporary agricultural machinery and many are rarely used by farmers now so are fixed permanently open. In which case, on a boat, you can simply relax and admire them as you pass.

Approaching one that's down is a totally different matter though. It's like arriving at a roadblock and it should set off alarm bells. Boat crews need to be on full alert. Very soon, someone is going to have to leap off the boat for a spell of hard work to get it open. On the Llangollen Canal this is a relatively simple matter, since the mechanism to lift them is worked by a windlass of the sort you use in locks. On the Oxford Canal, however, you have to haul them

up manually. Just how difficult can such a simple operation be, you might ask? The answer, trust us, is that sometimes it can be very difficult indeed. You can heave them with all your might, pulling on the chains that hang from the balance beams until you're dangling in the air. You can keep tugging them until your insides are coming out; you can swing on them; you can do acrobatics on the chain. But sometimes the damned things still won't budge. Then you just have to run up the white flag and admit defeat, accept that this is all too much for one person and enlist help from other

A classic Llangollen lift bridge between Trevor and Llangollen itself. It has been left open to favour the passage of boats.

indolent members of your crew, who've been watching your whole performance with growing amusement but without any sign of lifting a finger to assist.

So have pity on single-handed boaters, for whom lift bridges pose particular problems, especially when they're padlocked shut, as they sometimes can be. They are daunting to negotiate and, travelling alone, some are downright dangerous. The one in Banbury on the Oxford, for instance, used to be potentially lethal: messing around on it was too great a temptation for generations of kids who didn't fully understand the implications of dropping it on to a passing boat, or worse, on to the legs of their friends. Tragically, the latter eventually happened and the bridge had to be redesigned so that now it can only be operated with a windlass, like those on the Llangollen Canal. Some lift bridges that carry considerable road traffic – like the one at Thrupp on the Oxford, or at Wrenbury on the Llangollen – have been completely mechanised and are worked electronically. Hardly traditional, but a good deal more convenient.

Visit

Thrupp and Wrenbury are both renowned canal settlements. Thrupp is a thriving canal village with a vibrant canal club, which means there are always a lot of boats around. The lift bridge lies on a 90-degree turn, near an attractive row of original stone cottages that face the canal.

Facilities

Annie's Tea Rooms (Canal Yard, Canal Road, Thrupp, OX5 1JZ. Tel: 07425 621742) is nearby:
| anniestearoom.co.uk

There are two good canal-side pubs to choose from, both serving food:

The Boat (Canal Road, Thrupp, OX5 1JY. Tel: 01865 374279):
| theboatinnthrupp.co.uk

The Jolly Boatman (216 Banbury Road, Thrupp, OX5 1JU. Tel: 01865 377800):
| jollyboatman.com

At Wrenbury Mill on the Llangollen is the Dusty Miller (Cholmondeley Road, Wrenbury, CW5 8HG. Tel: 01270 780537), directly opposite the lift bridge and a boatyard:
| robinsonsbrewery.com/pubs/dusty-
| miller-wrenbury/

At Marbury, an hour's walk away, is The Swan (Wrenbury Road, Marbury, SY13 4LS. Tel: 01948 522860), from where you can press on for a delightful amble to St Michael's Church, overlooking the beautiful Little Mere:
| swanatmarbury.co.uk

A cow makes its way to the water's edge to drink near Bridge 141, Boundary Bridge on the Oxford Canal.

67 Tooley's Boatyard

Tooley's Boatyard in Banbury is a revered place of pilgrimage for anyone interested in Britain's inland waterways. This is because in the summer of 1939, an idealistic engineer called Tom Rolt set off from the place on a honeymoon cruise with his wife Angela after their boat *Cressy* had been adapted for life afloat, one of the very earliest pleasure craft. Sadly, the marriage didn't last long; however, the honeymoon inspired Rolt's *Narrow Boat*, a book that has never been out of print since it was first published as a 'War Economy Standard Edition' in 1944.

It is impossible to overstate the book's importance to Britain's inland waterways. It's not exaggerating to say that without it, the extensive network of rivers and canals we know today simply wouldn't exist in any recognisable form. *Narrow Boat* touched a chord in the British psyche. It's overly sentimental. Regressive, maybe. At times reactionary.

Steve (right) and the late John Coombes (left) take a tea break in the dock. Today, Tooley's is totally enclosed but in the past the moveable wooden framework in the picture would have been covered with tarpaulin to provide shelter for those working underneath.

Even so, after years of war, the British public was looking for a reason why they had been fighting, and they found it as much in the certainties of their traditional industrial heritage as they did in the futuristic modernity of the 1951 Festival of Britain.

After reading the book, a young London literary agent called Robert Aickman contacted Rolt and the result was the Inland Waterways Association (see Wonder 1), arguably the most successful of post-war pressure groups. Today, though it's still influential, it's a more conventional organisation than in its heyday, when it pioneered radical strategies of direct action, celebrity supporters and public promotion, all of which are commonplace for campaigning groups now.

When we first arrived in Banbury, Bert Tooley, who was involved in the conversion of *Cressy*, was still living at the dock in a caravan, the last of his family to be associated with it. We weren't intending to stay, but needing to get back home we left our boat there and in the odd way life works, Banbury has been our home mooring ever since. The boatyard and dock were already 200 years old then, and over the years we've stood shoulder to shoulder with those fighting to preserve it against some insufferable development plans, including one to turn it into a hamburger restaurant with tables in its listed dock.

Today, thanks to the backing of some big hitters, the survival of Tooley's is assured. They're an amiable crew who run the place and – notwithstanding boat work in the dock, which still continues – they're generally happy to show you around. The blacksmith's forge and carpenter's shop date from when they built wooden boats here and are well worth a look.

Banbury's new shopping centre dwarfs Tooley's, which nevertheless still continues to function as a working dock. The bridge across the canal leads to Banbury Museum.

Visit

Banbury today is very different from when fine ladies rode frisky horses to the Cross. Even so, in its market squares and narrow streets it still has the feel of a sleepy Oxfordshire town, though the view from the canal is of a modern shopping centre dominated by a mall, hotel and cine complex. Tucked away inside the mall is Tooley's boatyard and dry dock (c/o Banbury Museum, Spiceball Park Road, Banbury, OX16 2PQ. Tel: 01295 272917), barely visible except from the towpath opposite:
| tooleysboatyard.co.uk

There's a cafe there that's not a bad place from which to look at it:
| pavementcoffeeco.com

The main entrance to the dock is over the other side of the lift bridge, directly in front of you. It's a busy boatyard where all types of work are undertaken, so it's best to arrange a visit in advance. There are regular boat trips from there during the summer. The dock is open to the public during Banbury Canal Day, which takes place every year in October.

68 Mikron Theatre Company

Ideas are funny things. Most of them have disappeared by the following morning when you wake with a hangover. Or maybe when you wake to discover that that tremendous project you'd dreamed about for making millions was just a nonsense notion of selling fresh air.

However, some ideas change the world – or at least a little bit of it. Mike Lucas had an idea after he'd puzzled about how to bring live theatre to places with no access to it. He was an actor who'd appeared in TV comedies like *The Liver Birds* and dramas like *Doctor Who*. He'd also been the first director/manager at the University of Kent's Gulbenkian Theatre and something of a canal lover, too, after he and his wife, Sarah, had taken a couple of holidays on the cut during the 1960s.

In 1972, it occurred to him that he could combine the two and take a narrowboat around the country with a small group of actors in the manner of Shakespearean travelling players, performing in local pubs and village halls. There were a number of drawbacks to the idea though, not the least being that Sarah had just fallen pregnant. Added to which, they didn't really know all that much about canals either, especially their condition at the time, when you could scarcely depend on them to get you anywhere, let alone get you to places to a tight schedule of the sort a theatre group would need to keep to complete a tour. Oh, and there was one other tiny problem they were faced with

Mike Lucas, his wife Sarah and son Sam, with members of their travelling theatre company in 1973.

The converted working boat Tyseley takes Mikron shows all round the country by water.

as well. They didn't have a boat or the money to buy one...

It seems wondrous that from this shaky start the Mikron Theatre Company should have got off the ground at all, let alone survived so successfully that in 2022 it celebrated its 50th anniversary. Mikron – the 'Mik' pronounced as in Mick Jagger – is the Greek word for small; and for five decades this diminutive group has done annual tours with a constantly evolving repertoire that began promoting the waterways, their stories and history, and has since blossomed out across a variety of subject matter.

In the process, this constantly changing band of actors, which at any one time never numbered more than four, has originated more than 65 shows, composed over 390 songs and performed more than 5,000 times to audiences estimated at getting on for half a million strong. Moreover, it's managed all this while surviving sickness and injury, grant cuts, engine failure and the sort of personality clashes common to any theatre group. To do this in a stationary location would have been impressive enough, but to do it on the move on

boats, on a waterways system that by its very nature is unreliable and subject to regular and unpredictable stoppages, is nothing less than miraculous.

But Mikron kept calm and carried on and over time it managed to inveigle itself into the culture of the waterways to such an extent that during the Covid-19 epidemic a £40K appeal to cover its costs when it couldn't perform achieved its target in just two weeks. But perhaps what speaks most for the company is that it's created in its wake new generations of travelling theatre groups, performing musicians and artists, an impressive legacy of which anyone would be proud.

For information on what the company is performing, when and where:
| mikron.org.uk

Performances are invariably in pubs, so wherever you choose to see them you're in for a good night out.

Another waterways-based company well worth checking out is Alarum, specialising in women's contribution to the waterways:
| alarumproductions.org.uk

(69) Tim and Pru

They're household names, so much so that their Christian names are enough to identify them. Tim and Pru – married actors Timothy West and Prunella Scales – have acquired National Treasure status. As a couple, they have also done as much as anyone in recent years to popularise Britain's inland waterways and inspire thousands of people to get to know the canals better.

Great Canal Journeys, the Channel 4 series they presented from 2014 until 2019, followed their waterways travels all over the world. But its heart was always in Britain, on the canal and river network they know best and where they feel most at home. The programme proved an unexpectedly big hit with viewers, its popularity surprising even its makers, with its focus on slow travel and gradually getting to know the real Tim and Pru en route.

Other celebrities and actors have fronted shows about canals, but what makes Tim and Pru different is their authentic love of boating. They weren't just parachuted on to a narrowboat to provide suitably famous faces for the cameras. As Pru put it in the introduction to the very first programme, they are 'canal nuts' who have been pottering about on boats since 1976 and have had a boat of their own for decades. They have also been active from the start in

Prunella Scales and Timothy West fell in love with canals as young actors.

They aren't celebrities grafted onto a TV programme: they are genuine enthusiasts who share their lifelong passion with a huge audience, inspiring many to venture onto a boat for the first time.

supporting canal restoration, and as passionate backers of the Kennet & Avon Canal restoration they were even invited to be the first boat for 42 years to travel its whole length when it reopened in 1990.

The joy it brings them shines through in every episode. Even the pain of Pru's gradually failing memory seems soothed while on the water. As she puts it herself, it doesn't stop her remembering how to open a lock gate. And as Tim says, expressing an experience familiar to anyone who has spent any time on a canal boat, it helps that you are compelled to live in the moment, to notice all the small things that usually get lost in the hubbub of a busy life. The two of them capture the essence of the appeal of the waterways: the tranquillity and seclusion; the chance to slow down, to escape the stresses and hectic pace of modern life and get close to nature. Their programmes demonstrate the therapeutic combination of strenuous activity and relaxation, the delight of

seeing both new and familiar places from a completely different perspective and the easy camaraderie with others you meet on passing boats.

Like us, they have kept their boat on the Oxford Canal for many years and our paths have crossed occasionally. Once was in the dry dock at Tooley's (see Wonder 67), transformed into a theatre on Banbury Canal Day for a performance of *Idle Women of the Wartime Waterways* by the Alarum Theatre Company. Tim and Pru were just members of the audience like us, there to support fellow boaters in a place that's special to us all.

All episodes of *Great Canal Journeys* are available on Channel 4's on-demand service All 4: | channel4.com.

In 2019, Dame Sheila Hancock and Gyles Brandreth took up the mantle as presenters, after Tim and Pru decided it was time to bow out.

NORTH SEA

The Wash

LINCOLN

NORWICH

PETERBOROUGH

CAMBRIDGE

CHELMSFORD

ST ALBANS

LONDON

CANTERBURY

River Trent
River Ancholme
River Witham Navigation
River Welland
River Nene
River Great Ouse
River Thames
River Wey
River Lea Navigation
Regent's Canal
Grand Union Canal
Basingstoke Canal
Middle Level Navigations

The Broads

Immingham · Grimsby · Cleethorpes
Brigg
Scunthorpe
Gainsborough
Market Rasen · Louth · Mablethorpe
Wragby
Horncastle · Spilsby · Skegness
North Hykeham · Woodhall Spa · Wainfleet All Saints
Newark-on-Trent · Sleaford · Heckington · Boston
Grantham · Bourne · Spalding · Long Sutton
Melton Mowbray · Market Deeping · Crowland · Wisbech
Oakham · Stamford · Whittlesey · March · Chatteris
Uppingham · Corby · Oundle · Ramsey · ELY · Soham
Kettering · Thrapston · Huntingdon · St Ives · Mildenhall · Newmarket
Desborough · Raunds · Godmanchester · St Neots
Harborough · Irthlingborough · Higham Ferrers · Rushden
Wellingborough · Olney · Bedford · Sandy · Potton · Biggleswade
Kempston · Newport Pagnell · Wixams · Shefford · Royston · Saffron Walden
Bletchley · Woburn Sands · Woburn · Ampthill · Flitwick · Baldock · Buntingford · Thaxted
Milton Keynes · Leighton Buzzard · Houghton Regis · Letchworth · Hitchin · Stansted Mountfitchet
Winslow · Dunstable · Luton · Stevenage · Bishop's Stortford · Great Dunmow
Tring · Wendover · Harpenden · Welwyn Garden City · Sawbridgeworth · Braintree · Coggeshall
Princes Risborough · Berkhamsted · Hatfield · Hoddesdon · Harlow · Witham
Chesham · Hemel Hempstead · Potters Bar · Cheshunt · Epping · Chipping Ongar · Maldon
High Wycombe · Amersham · Radlett · Waltham Cross · Loughton · Brentwood · Wickford
Beaconsfield · Chorleywood · Gerrards Cross · Watford · Borehamwood · Chigwell · Billericay · Rayleigh · Rochford
Marlow · Maidenhead · Staines-upon-Thames · Ashford · Dartford · Grays · Tilbury · Gravesend · Basildon · Stanford-le-Hope · Leigh-on-Sea · Southend-on-Sea
Slough · Bracknell · Chertsey · Weybridge · Esher · Sutton · Epsom · Swanley · Rochester · Sheerness · Minster · Queenborough · Herne Bay · Broadstairs
Woking · Aldershot · Guildford · Dorking · Redhill · Reigate · Sevenoaks · Tonbridge · Maidstone · Sittingbourne · Faversham · Whitstable · Margate · Ramsgate
Farnham · Godalming · Horley · Crawley · Caterham · Oxted · Westerham · West Malling · Goudhurst · Canterbury · Sandwich · Deal

Hunstanton · Wells-next-the-Sea · Sheringham · Cromer · Caister-on-Sea
Holt · North Walsham · Stalham · Great Yarmouth · Gorleston
Fakenham · Aylsham · Reepham · Lowestoft
Dereham · Swaffham · Hingham · Wymondham · Loddon · Beccles
King's Lynn · Downham Market · Watton · Attleborough · Bungay · Harleston · Halesworth · Southwold
Brandon · Thetford · Diss · Eye · Framlingham · Saxmundham · Leiston · Aldeburgh
Bury St Edmunds · Stowmarket · Needham Market · Wickham Market · Woodbridge
Haverhill · Clare · Acton · Sudbury · Hadleigh · Ipswich · Kesgrave · Felixstowe
Halstead · Colchester · Manningtree · Harwich · Walton-on-the-Naze · Frinton-on-Sea
Wivenhoe · Brightlingsea · Clacton-on-Sea · West Mersea
South Woodham Ferrers · Southminster

20 miles

Contains OS data © Crown copyright and database right 2021

N

The East

Bridge of Sighs

⚙️ ⑦⓪ The Broads

Anyone who knows anything about boats or boating has heard of the Broads, yet surprisingly few have explored this 200km (125-mile) network of lock-free navigable waters. The reason's simple: the Norfolk and Suffolk Broads – holiday destinations for decades – are not easily accessible from the rest of the country's waterways, which means boatowners can only get to them from the sea at Great Yarmouth or Lowestoft. It would be a reckless inland boatowner who attempted either.

Renting a boat on the Broads is easy and the rewards for spending time travelling them are legion. The Broads Authority, incorporating the waterways in both counties, was established through an Act of Parliament in 1988, effectively recognising its status as a national park.

The Ted Ellis Trust reserve at Wheatfen where you can see how the broads looked half a millennium ago.

There are seven lovely tidal rivers and about three dozen actual broads – that is, shallow lakes formed by flooded medieval peat workings hundreds of years ago. On the Broads, you get to experience the best East Anglia has to offer: huge skies, stunning scenery and unparalleled wildlife, the Broads being home to more than a quarter of the rarest species in the UK. There are many other delights to be enjoyed, too, from Norfolk's trademark round-tower medieval churches to its ancient stone bridges, from its historic sailing boats to its ruined and restored windmills, which aren't windmills at all, but windpumps, built to control water levels. In addition, it has an excellent selection of waterside hotels, hostelries, shops and cafes. The truth is, we could write another book of 101 Wonders on this area alone.

There's easy cycling and a comprehensive network of walking trails and footpaths, but aficionados would claim that the only way to see the Broads properly is by boat. They're all but invisible by car from the road and often the sole clue to their existence is the surreal sight of a distant sail apparently making a stately progress across a field.

The Broads were formed in the Middle Ages and country people from that time would still recognise most of the area today because there has been so little development over the centuries. However, with the current level of global warming, a visitor from today might very well not recognise the area in even a few decades' time because the whole region lies only just above sea level. So, check out this magical water-world while you can...

Most people hire powered cruisers of one sort or another to explore the Broads, though for the more traditionally inclined, there are yards offering vintage sailing boats, such as Hunter's at Womack Water, Ludham. Either way, ensure the boat you hire comes with a dinghy or canoe so you can search out the hidden gems of the area, which are often unreachable in anything bigger. The whispering golden reed beds of the Upper Thurne, for instance; the gorgeous tree-lined River Bure above Wroxham and Coltishall; the mysterious shallows of Surlingham Broad on the Yare, and the Royal Society for the Protection of Birds and Norfolk Wildlife Trust reserves that spangle the area. There's also the amazing Ted Ellis Trust reserve at Wheatfen, where you can see what the Broads looked like half a millennium ago.

Thurne Mill — actually a windpump. It was bought and restored by Ronald 'Bob' Morse in the 1930s and has become a landmark of the Broads.

Visit

In the area

Hunter's Yard (Horsefen Road, Ludham, NR29 5QG. Tel: 01692 678263):
| huntersyard.co.uk

The RSPB in the Broads:
| rspb.org.uk/our-work/conservation/
| landscape-scale-conservation/sites/
| the-broads/

Norfolk Wildlife Trust reserves:
| norfolkwildlifetrust.org.uk

The Ted Ellis Trust:
| wheatfen.org

Nearby Norwich is a good base for a visit with its stunning cathedral, its medieval streets, its famous market and its wealth of museums, theatres, pubs and restaurants:
| visitnorwich.co.uk

Other centres for the Broads are Wroxham, Beccles on the Waveney, Potter Heigham on the Thurne, and Oulton Broad on the edge of Lowestoft. All of these offer a range of craft from family-sized cruisers to kayaks:
| www.visitthebroads.co.uk

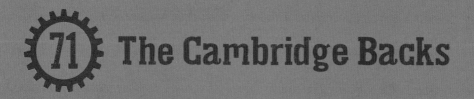

71 The Cambridge Backs

Rivers and canals often allow you to see 'back-door Britain', a more intimate view than the public facade towns and cities present to the world. Cambridge is no exception – but this is a backdoor like no other.

The River Cam flows along the rear of half a dozen of the most illustrious Cambridge colleges. Known as the Backs, beautifully manicured lawns sweep down to the water's edge and cattle still graze freely in college grounds, as they have for centuries. Ancient trees shade sunny expanses of grass, and gracing these perfect gardens are some of the most magnificent buildings in England, from King's College Chapel to the Bridge of Sighs, named after the one in Venice.

Although it's a Grade I historic park, there's no public right of way, so you have to be a Cambridge student to get unfettered access to the grounds. But hey! what does it matter? The best way to see the Backs is from the water anyway. Cambridge is famous for punting – and punts give you an unparalleled view of some of its world-

renowned colleges: Magdalene, St John's and Trinity where you can see the famous Wren Library with its collection of priceless books, kept above ground level in case the Cam floods.

In the summer months, punts crowd the river like colliding dodgems as novices play pinball-punting alongside professionally-chauffeured boats. The guys poling these stick to the centre channel where, in the days of horse-drawn barges, a cobbled causeway was laid so that horses could wade through the water hauling boats laden with provisions for the colleges.

Visit

Among the many companies offering the Backs by punt are Scudamores, who claim to have introduced punting to Cambridge in 1910, and Punt Cambridge. It's worth shopping around for price.
| scudamores.com
| puntcambridge.co.uk

Powered craft are only allowed along this section of the river from Jesus Lock in the quieter months between October and March. If you're thinking of taking a trip you'll need a Canal and River Trust Gold licence and an Anglian pass as well as permission from the Cam Conservators, who must be notified in advance of your plans. They produce a useful boaters' handbook.
| canalrivertrust.org.uk/enjoy-the-waterways/boating/buy-your-boat-licence/gold-licences
| visitanglianwaterways.org/anglian-pass-ways-to-pay
| camconservancy.org/boating

72 Denver Sluice

Despite its industrial functionalism, Denver Sluice, halfway between Ely and King's Lynn where the River Great Ouse exits to The Wash, is a surprisingly pretty place to visit on a summer afternoon, either by boat or car.

The river is impressively wide at this point, lined by attractive grassy banks, tailor-made for soaking up the sun. Those of a less sedentary bent will find much to occupy them just wandering around, getting to grips with the place by means of a number of strategically sited information boards. There are nice pubs as well, in Denver village, a five minute drive away.

OK, visually the Sluice is no Pontcysyllte Aqueduct (see Wonder 86). There's no historical edifice to get the cameras clicking, there's no breathtaking bridge across a wide valley. In fact, Denver Sluice isn't a single edifice at all,

The navigation lock at Denver. This allows passage between the Nene and the Ouse river systems. On the left is the 'Big Eye', a navigation lock for commercial vessels, now sealed off. On the right is the current navigation lock, one of a series of 'Little Eyes.'

but a complex – an intricate network of sluices, interconnecting rivers and relief channels, the wonder of which lies not in what is obviously apparent, but in the critical importance of what it all does and the ingeniousness of how it does it. Despite its fame, the Pontcysyllte is just a water feeder that takes holiday boats across the River Dee; Denver Sluice, by comparison, exists to prevent a large part of the eastern English flatlands from flooding, a role that year after year protects many thousands of acres of valuable agricultural land and potentially hundreds of lives.

It does this in two ways: first by acting as a defence against high surge tides forced upstream from the sea, and second by managing water flowing downstream from the river and its tributaries during periods of exceptional rainfall. It controls this by blocking off the natural flow, containing the water in relief channels until it can be allowed to flow away harmlessly. A separate system, not involving Denver, protects the upper river and cities like Bedford and Cambridge by diverting excess rainfall to the Ouse Washes, the largest area of washland (grazing pasture that floods in the winter) in the UK. Situated ten

The AG Wright head sluice, soon after it was opened in 1964, part of an £11 million flood protection scheme.

miles southeast of March, these are an internationally important nature reserve and wildlife sanctuary managed by the Royal Society for the Protection of Birds.

If Denver Sluice has a single defining feature, it's probably the AG Wright Sluice – the Head Sluice, as it's called – built following floods in 1947, which, though not as notorious as the 1953 floods, were still devastating and turned East Anglia into a huge inland sea. It looks vaguely like the Brandenburg Gate in Berlin, but whereas the Brandenburg Gate is all fancy columns and Prussian imperial frippery, the AG Wright Sluice consists of four brutalist pillars, one of them a tower that could easily pass as a lookout post at a prison camp. Even so, it does have a certain raw architectural style to it, which we're not alone in finding compelling. And where it scores over Brandenburg is that it really is a fully operational gate. Well, actually three gates. Huge guillotines, which, depending on conditions, can be lifted to release water downriver.

Visit

More information on the sluice:
| explorewestnorfolk.co.uk/venues/
| denver-sluice-83

More about birdwatching on the Ouse Washes:
| rspb.org.uk/reserves-and-events/
| reserves-a-z/ouse-washes

The Bell Inn (2 Ely Road, Denver, PE38 0DW), serves pub grub. Regular Irish music nights:
| the-bell-inn-inn.business.site

Recommended is the Blackstone Engine Bar (95 Sluice Rd, Denver, PE38 0DZ. Tel: 07518 099686), a microbrewery in the former workshop of the Denver Mill complex, open Thursday to Sunday.

73 Ely

Travelling the waterways of the east country, we have found ourselves returning time and time again to Ely – the city that once stood on an island in what is now the Fens. We were seduced by its irresistible charisma. There was something about it that got under our skin, something that – cliché aside – put us under its spell. We both agreed that it's one of the most beguiling cities in the country.

Situated on the banks of the Great Ouse in Cambridgeshire, in the middle of what was essentially a swampy marsh, Ely grew up on the site of a wealthy abbey. Its virtually unassailable location gave it military importance and after the Norman Conquest it was the final redoubt of the Anglo-Saxons under their leader, Hereward the Wake. In the 17th century, it was the home of Oliver Cromwell, who became England's first republican leader after the Civil War and the execution of Charles I.

As a visitor, there's so much to see in Ely, and a bonus is that there aren't uncomfortable amounts of tourists around so you can walk on the pavements or stroll up the riverside in relative comfort. Its Norman cathedral – the Ship of the Fens as it's known, since its

towers stand out above the flatlands like the masts of a boat – is spectacular, some say the most beautiful of the English cathedrals. Take the Octagon Tower tour if you possibly can, preferably the last one of the day when the choir is practising before evensong. It's magical. From the cathedral there's a rewarding walk to the waterfront via a park built around the site of the old castle mound. This leads through Jubilee Gardens to the old quay beyond. Strolling along it, you'll find restaurants and bars and an antiques centre where dozens of dealers ply their trade. Nearby is the Babylon Gallery, a former brewery warehouse, now a contemporary arts centre. There are, of course, river trips available. Oliver Cromwell's house at the top end of town is a must-see too and is also home to Ely Tourist Information Centre. Bought by the council in 1988, it has been restored to its half-timbered splendour as it would have been during the eight years Crowell lived there.

The biggest attraction of Ely, however, is Ely itself: a city packed with independent shops, friendly pubs and intriguing cafes. A circular 'Eel Trail' is named after the fish, which were once so important to

St Ives Bridge with its distinctive chapel.

the economy in these parts that they were used as a currency. It's marked by bronze plaques set in the pavement and is a good way of seeing the place. However, if you want to explore further afield, there are attractions nearby.

The Ely Country Park, a little way out of town bordering the river, has walking and cycle trails and a children's playground. Burwell Museum and Windmill is only a 20-minute drive away, Wicken Fen (see Wonder 76) about the same. Prickwillow Engine Museum on the River Lark (see Wonder 77) is only ten minutes or so by car.

Our favourite, though, is Houghton Meadow, just outside of St Ives, half an hour's drive and six hours' cruising away. There are beautiful moorings from where you can do a circular walk into town, through a couple of splendid villages – Hemingford Abbots and Hemingford Grey – and across the 15th-century St Ives bridge, one of only a handful in the country that have chapels on them. Walk up the opposite side of the river to the National Trust's Houghton Mill, crossing back to return to your starting point.

Visit

Access
Ely railway station has hourly services to Cambridge and Birmingham New Street.

In the area
For info on what to do:
| visitely.org.uk

To book an Ely Cathedral Octagon Tower tour:
| elycathedral.org/events/octagon-
| tower-tours

Oliver Cromwell's House (29 St Mary's Street, Ely, CB7 4HF. Tel: 01353 662062):
| olivercromwellshouse.co.uk

Houghton Mill (Mill Lane, Houghton, PE28 2AZ. Tel: 01480 301494):
| nationaltrust.org.uk/houghton-mill-
| and-waterclose-meadows

Burwell Museum (Mill Close, Burwell, CB25 0HL. Tel: 01638 605544):
| burwellmuseum.org.uk

Prickwillow Engine Museum (Main Street, Prickwillow, Ely, CB7 4UN. Tel: 01353 688360):
| prickwillowmuseum.com

Ely Cathedral, the Ship of the Fens, dominates the city and its surrounding flatlands.

74 The Glory Hole, Lincoln

It's a singular experience, arresting and unexpected. One minute you're cruising through Brayford Pool, where the River Witham widens to form a natural pool that is now Lincoln's marina but was once a Roman inland port; the next, you take a turn or two round by Marks & Spencer and you're in a narrow channel that narrows even further until you find yourself passing underneath a bridge below a busy 21st-century shopping street. So far, so ordinary. Unremarkable, in fact. Except that above you is a row of Tudor black-and-white half-timbered shops complete with garret windows, like something out of a film set.

This is actually High Bridge, which carries the High Street in Lincoln across the River Witham. It was built around 1160 and it's the only surviving example in Britain of a medieval bridge with buildings still standing on it. However, for years the river passing underneath – through a gap so narrow it's almost a tunnel – has been known among boating folk as the Glory Hole. No one knows why. Perhaps it's because if you look carefully, you can see a couple of carved angels in the upper storeys of the building. Perhaps it's because in the right light it's said you can see beams of sunlight like the light radiating from

Christ's halo. Maybe it's because at one time it boasted a chapel dedicated to the Middle Ages' most popular celebrity saint, Thomas Becket, the Archbishop of Canterbury who famously got himself mixed up with politics until his old mate Henry II got rid of the 'troublesome priest' by having him murdered.

The classic row of half-timbered shops you see straddling the bridge today date from around 1550, so are relatively modern. They now house a baker's and a suitably quaint cafe where you can enjoy morning coffee or afternoon tea soaking up the ambience.

It can be a tight squeeze for some boats to get through the low, uneven arch of the Glory Hole. Not to mention getting past the dozens of swans that invariably congregate underneath it, reluctant to make way for intruders. Travelling out of the city eastwards through the Glory Hole, the river leads to Boston and The Wash (see Wonder 78), a shortcut to the Fens. In the other direction, the Romans built England's oldest navigable canal, the Foss Dyke, to connect to the River Trent. These days, this links to the rest of the 4,828km (3,000-mile) network of England's inland waterways.

Lincoln is a rewarding city with so much going for it you need a week to see the half of it. Its sublime cathedral, consecrated in 1091, stands at the summit of the aptly named Steep Hill, which more than repays the climb, peppered as it is with small craft and antique shops and some lovely cafes and pubs. Influential Victorian art critic John Ruskin declared the cathedral 'the most precious piece of architecture in the British Isles ... worth any two other

Visit

In the area
General information, including mooring details:
| visitlincoln.com

More information about the cathedral:
| lincolncathedral.com

For the castle:
| lincolncastle.com

Above: the Glory Hole. Left: Steep Hill (and it is!) leading to the cathedral and castle.

cathedrals we have'. It houses one of only four original, signed copies of the Magna Carta. The neighbouring castle commands the surrounding flat countryside, with stunning views best enjoyed by walking the walls. It also has a Victorian prison and an unusual prisoners' chapel, designed so that prisoners couldn't see each other, though they could all see the minister preaching to them.

⚙ (75) Reed Cutters

So many of the traditional industries of East Anglia have disappeared. Sheep farming, and the textile manufacturing that was associated with it, made the area so wealthy that it was once the richest part of the country.

During the Industrial Revolution, though, the focus of manufacturing shifted north and, as a result, rearing sheep in the east country dwindled to nothing – as, later, did shoemaking, another defunct local trade. Farming still survives today, as anyone who travels in a boat through the industrial prairies of the Fenlands can testify; but herring, which every year brought thousands of 'Herring Lassies' down from Scotland for seasonal processing work, had virtually disappeared by the 1960s, when the great shoals along the east coast had

Traditional reed cutters can harvest up to two tonnes of rush a day using a three feet long scythe-shaped blade attached to a six-foot-handle.

been all but fished out. It was the same with eel fishing. These creatures, with their extraordinary lifestyle beginning in the Sargasso Sea 6,000km (3,700 miles) away, were once a staple food, so common that the Domesday Book records 52,000 being caught in a single year in the Great Ouse alone. In East Anglia, there were so many they were sometimes used as a local currency. Ely – the Isle of Eels – was named after them (see Wonder 73). They were slipping towards extinction at the turn of the last century, and despite environmental protection, the question nowadays is less whether the small amount of eel fishing that is still done can survive, and more if eels as a species can.

Against this background, you wouldn't have given the old craft of reed cutting a shout. Reed cutting, we hear you say. How can that ever have been important? Well, in the days when reeds were the only affordable and easily available roofing material, and when they were woven into mats for floor covering, cutting reeds in East Anglia was a key local industry. We thought we were lucky glimpsing a single eel adjacent to the quayside at St Ives a few years back, but this was nothing compared to us spotting reed cutters further up the Great Ouse. It

On the Great Ouse, reed cutter Felicity Irons balances bundles of freshly cut English freshwater bulrushes across her punt, 'helped' by Molly the dog.

was almost as if we were photobombing a Constable painting. There, amid the quiet seclusion of the river, were a couple of punts making stately progress along the bank. Men and women were leaning over the sides, harvesting the rushes with traditional long-handled billhooks, piling them on the boats as if constructing aquatic haystacks.

The leader of this crew was Felicity Irons, who makes a good living for herself and her company weaving medieval matting for use in high-end locations such as New York's Metropolitan Museum of Art and the Globe Theatre in London. Unsurprisingly, a big customer is the National Trust. She also makes smaller curios – baskets and the like – which she sells through Ralph Lauren shops. This sort of stuff doesn't come cheap, though, as we can attest personally, having paid a fortune for a small example of her work about the size of a business card.

At the time, we thought Felicity must surely have been the only reed cutter left in East Anglia, but we've subsequently discovered that there are nine of them in North Norfolk alone and more yet on the Broads (see Wonder 70). Even so, there still aren't enough of them, for such is the contemporary demand for reeds that roofers, who much prefer the English variety, are instead being forced to import inferior product from abroad.

Visit

For more information, see Felicity's website. Weekend weaving workshops available:
| rushmatters.co.uk

The North Norfolk Reed Cutters Association also has information about the Broads Reed and Sedge Cutters Association (BRASCA):
| norfolkreed.co.uk

⚙ 76 Wicken Fen

The landscape of the East Anglian Fens tells the story of people's age-old battle to reclaim land from water and gain the upper hand over the sea. It's a landscape of dykes, ditches and drains, criss-crossed by lodes – artificial waterways that look as if they've always been there.

Very few places have escaped reclamation but Wicken Fen is one of them, a rare remnant of never-drained wetland, which survives like a glimpse of a lost world. It's one of Europe's last remaining and most important areas of its type, and it's also the National Trust's oldest nature reserve, in their care since 1899 thanks to Charles Rothschild, of all people. It turns out this scion of the banking dynasty was also a passionate

A rare vestige of natural wetland, Wicken Fen is a naturalist's paradise, boasting more than 9,000 species of plants and wildlife.

early environmentalist who was later to found the Society for the Promotion of Nature Reserves, an organisation dedicated to protecting the country's prime wildlife habitats. He bought a couple of acres of the fen for £10 and donated them to the National Trust.

The National Trust likes to describe Wicken as England's best-known fen. That said, we didn't know about it until we were deep into an exploration by water of Cambridgeshire fenland. Of course, we should have heard of it, but the Fens are remote, not to everyone's taste. Some might say bleak – forbidding, even: sparsely populated, with such huge skies it constantly reminds you of how small and insignificant you are against the cosmos. The countryside is flat, flatter than anything you've ever seen – scoured by bitter winds straight from the Russian steppes.

Yet this landscape can get under your skin. It's unlike anywhere else. It has its own austere beauty. And no doubt about it, Wicken Fen is seductive. Originally used by locals for peat digging and harvesting sedge – that grass that isn't a grass, used for weaving, baskets, mats and even boats in early pre-industrial England – Wicken Fen became popular with naturalists in Victorian times. Charles Darwin was among them – he collected beetles here as a young man in the 1820s, and it's still home to more than 9,000 species of plants and wildlife.

There's a raised boardwalk and grass tracks (known locally as droves), giving visitors easy access to flowering meadows, sedges and reed beds, where sightings of rare animals and birds such as hen harriers, bitterns and water voles (see Wonder 79) are not uncommon. You can also see herds of Highland cattle and konik ponies, descended directly from the tarpan, a feral European forest horse that was hunted to extinction in Neolithic times. These were introduced to graze the fen to allow indigenous grassland plants to become established.

There's cycle hire, and in the summer the National Trust runs boat trips on Wicken Lode in its small open electric boat *Mayfly*. There are nature trails, bird hides and the Docky Hut cafe. And there

Visit

Access

Wicken Fen is 14.5km (9 miles) by road from Ely and 27km (17 miles) from Cambridge. Admission is free but there is a charge for parking (NT members free). For more details – including a series of self-guided walks – and to plan a visit: nationaltrust.org.uk/wicken-fen-nature-reserve and wicken.org.uk

There are also facilities for wild camping in four open-fronted log shelters raised off the ground among the trees: details on the National Trust website above.

are two remarkable buildings that stand out in these flat surroundings: Wicken Fen's iconic windpump, looking like everyone's idea of a traditional windmill with its black wooden tower and white sails; and Fen Cottage, an original dwelling that has survived and been restored using traditional methods and materials. Inside, you'll find a typical 1930s' fenman's workshop, showing how its occupants would have harvested sedge and reed, collected alder buckthorn (used for making gunpowder), and dug peat, as well as wildfowling, eel catching and willow working.

For our money, no book better evokes the spirit of the Fens than Graham Swift's superb 1983 novel *Waterland*. With the lightest of touches, it manages to weave the history of how the Fens were drained – and much, much more – into a compelling depiction of life there for successive generations. Haunting and moving.

⚙(77) Tributaries of the Great Ouse

One of the aspects of the waterways that most captivated us when we first started boating was that you were able to escape contemporary life. A narrowboat wasn't a Tardis, but it was about the closest you could get to time travel in real life. A narrowboat could transport you to a world you could hardly believe still existed in the present day, let alone on an island as heavily populated as ours.

In some places, you could go days without seeing another boat. The towpaths too were virtually deserted; many of them had crumbled away to nothing and were impassable. There was a solitude to boating then that was otherworldly, yet paradoxically that connected you more intensely to the landscape through which you passed.

Today, it's very different. The canals are busier, which is not to say they're busy in any sense you might understand from roads. You might have to wait for a lock now and then, but you won't get trapped in traffic jams or find yourself travelling in speeding queues of traffic like you do on motorways. Sometimes, though, you do feel the presence of

A narrowboat makes its way along the Great Ouse disturbing the solitude with its wake. The main river is hardly busy; its tributaries are criminally underused.

Dawn breaks over the River Wissey, wisps of September mists still hanging above the water.

others more than you might want. Sometimes it's just more difficult to get away from it all in the way you used to.

However, there are exceptions, and the Great Ouse and its tributaries remain one of them. Although it can be busy on the main river around Ely (see Wonder 73) and on the Cam as you get towards Cambridge (see Wonder 71), the Wissey, the Little Ouse and the Lark are criminally underused. Yet all three are delightful waterways, flanked by willows and ancient water meadows and carpeted in season with lawns of yellow water lilies where dragonflies the size of small birds dive-bomb you from out of the sun.

The only trace of the industrial world is on the Wissey around Wissington – a village that doesn't exist any longer – where the river suddenly breaks up into a baffling confusion of ponds and lakes beneath the smoking chimneys of a huge British Sugar plc beet-processing plant. The Prickwillow Engine Museum on the River Lark reminds us how different it all was in the past, and how water

management has always been critical on the Fens.

Moira was at first reluctant to visit the east country by boat; she had expected it to be flat, bleak and featureless, so it took a while for Steve, who was at university in Norwich and knew it well, to persuade her to visit. She was immediately smitten, particularly by the Great Ouse and the tributaries; and we were both taken by the numbers of great crested grebes that have repopulated these rivers after being hunted almost to extinction in the 19th century when their magnificent head plumes were used to decorate women's hats (see Wonder 80).

Visit

Prickwillow Engine Museum (Main Street, Prickwillow, Ely, CB7 4UN. Tel: 01353 688360). Opening times are limited; check before visiting: | prickwillowmuseum.com

⚙️(78) The Wash

If you look at a map of this sceptred isle, you can't help but notice that there's a large chunk of it missing on the east coast, south of Skegness in Lincolnshire. It's as if someone's taken a bite out of it and what should be land is water. This is The Wash.

It is open sea, 24km (15 miles) long and 20km (12 miles) wide, not far short of 520sq km (200sq miles) of saltwater. If you head due east from here across the North Sea, you won't make landfall until you hit the Frisian Islands 400-odd km (250-odd miles) away off the coast of the Netherlands.

So, you may well ask, what's all this talk of salty stuff doing in a book about inland waterways? The Wash is not an inland waterway. It's not even an inland sea. But whatever you call it, it's certainly not to be recommended for flat-bottomed narrowboats, which couldn't be less suited to briny boating. They lack the keel needed to keep them steady in even a gentle sea. They pitch in a way that is terrifying. They roll alarmingly.

Nonetheless, every year, a few dozen or so reckless narrowboaters fail to heed the warnings and decide to take this handy but hazardous shortcut from Boston to Wisbech. We should know – we are among their number. It's an adventure, yes; but more practically, it means you can travel between Lincolnshire and Cambridgeshire by water in a day, instead of the week or more it would otherwise take you using the inland waterways.

If you're tempted, don't even think about taking this trip without a pilot. You may as well just call out the lifeboats before you set off. We went in a convoy of three after weeks of waiting for the right conditions. The pilots decide the day for the crossing and their word is law. However, any delay gives you the opportunity to explore Boston, a fascinating and much underrated town, with the tower of its famous parish church, the Stump, dominating not just the surrounding countryside but The Wash too, where sailors still use it for navigating. Boston is inextricably linked to the Pilgrim Fathers, some of whom were imprisoned in the town's Guildhall, where you can still see the cells in which they were incarcerated. Later émigrés went on to found a settlement in present-day Massachusetts, where they named

Wisbech, with its elegant waterside frontage.

The East

their new town after their old one. Some are buried here, having made their mark on both sides of the Atlantic.

You can't get between Boston and Wisbech on one tide, and so not long after you've navigated the Witham, past the marker buoys that guide you to the open sea, you have to run yourself up on a beach to wait for the next tide to give you enough water to navigate into the River Nene. The wait can be a long one, with only a colony of vile-smelling seals and noisy low-flying RAF fighter planes on training exercises to keep you company. On the water again, there's soon no land in sight except the distant, hazy outline of the coast. There's the odd small fishing boat, far-off tankers, and service ships laying cables to nearby wind farms. Apart from that, it's just you, seagulls and weather conditions that even with the best preparation in the world can still sometimes cut up rough.

There's no respite even on the Nene where professional pilot boats zap up and down the river like F1 cars on the home straight, leaving behind them waves that can be higher than the ones you've experienced on the sea, so that arriving at Wisbech Yacht Harbour is a welcome respite after what is a long but exhilarating day's boating.

Visit

Access

Hire-boat companies don't allow it, so to cross The Wash independently you need your own boat or you have to make friends with someone who will take you as crew. Details of pilots can be obtained from the lock-keeper at Boston Sluice. Alternatively, the *Boston Belle* runs sea trips from Boston in the summer months to see the seals. Full details including current timetables:
| bostonbelle.co.uk

In the area

Don't be tempted to just treat Wisbech as a stop-off point. Like Boston, there's a lot to see. It has a couple of beautifully elegant streets north and south of the river, collectively called the Brinks, little changed from Georgian times when they were built.

On North Brink is Peckover House and Garden (PE13 1JR. Tel: 01945 583463), once the home of a family of wealthy Quaker bankers, now in the hands of the National Trust (pre-booking for the house essential; no booking required for the garden):
| nationaltrust.org.uk/peckover

On South Brink (No 7, PE13 1JB. Tel: 01945 476358) is the birthplace and museum dedicated to the life of locally born Octavia Hill, a founder of the National Trust:
| octaviahill.org

(79) Water Voles

Water voles are lovable little creatures, though plagued with being frequently confused with the more common brown rat. The most famous of all water voles is Ratty in *Wind in the Willows*, though his name is not helpful to the cause.

The fact is water voles *are* similar to rats. However, it's not *that* difficult to tell the difference. Water voles have blunt, rounded faces compared to the pointed faces of rats, and they have small hidden ears rather than the obvious pink ones sported by rats. More of a giveaway for those wandering quietly up the towpath, however, is that if disturbed, water voles will dive, making a distinctive plop in the water.

Once seen, the water vole is never forgotten. Their chestnut-coloured fur, their chubby faces, snub noses and bright, inquisitive eyes make them appealing. And if you're lucky enough to catch one feeding, sitting on its hind legs using its tiny paws to hold the vegetarian delicacies it enjoys nibbling, you'll wonder why manufacturers don't produce replicas of them as cuddly toys.

There was a time when they were such common inhabitants of Britain's waterways that you couldn't travel far on a boat without spotting the distinctive

Once seen, never forgotten. Especially if you're lucky enough to see them feeding, which they have to do often, needing to eat 80 per cent of their body weight a day.

Once a commonplace sight on the waterway as they crossed from one bank to another, their numbers dropped 90 per cent during the 1990s. Today they are Britain's fastest declining mammal.

V-shaped wake of one cutting across the water in front of you, from one bank to the other. While always a welcome sight, it was also completely unremarkable.

But oh, how things have changed! In the space of 30 years, this once ubiquitous little creature has become an endangered species, thanks to changes in farming methods, waterways management, and – more than anything else – the deadly impact of the female American mink. The water vole is a tempting morsel to a wide range of predators, including owls and herons, but a breeding female mink can wipe out a whole colony of voles single-handed, mink being the only predators that can get into the burrows where water voles live.

As a result, their population dropped by almost 90 per cent in the 1990s, and according to The Wildlife Trusts they're the UK's fastest declining mammal. So rare have sightings become that a few years ago, while exploring the Cromford Canal in Derbyshire, Steve stumbled on a bevy of 20 or so photographers hanging about waiting for the appearance of a

local celebrity – who turned out not to be the soap star he expected, but a newly resident water vole. The Cromford Canal (see Wonder 12) is still one of the best places to spot them.

However, things are looking up. Wildlife conservationists are working flat out to ensure this dramatic decline is reversed and water voles have started to make something of a comeback. If you want to help, you can even adopt one for a modest sum. Ratty, the *Wind in the Willows* water vole, is still a fixture in our collective childhood memory, embodying not just the spirit of the riverbank but the unparalleled joy of boating. As he says, 'there is *nothing* – absolutely nothing – half so much worth doing as simply messing about in boats.'

For more information on water voles, including when and where to see them and how to adopt one:
| wildlifetrusts.org/wildlife-explorer/
| mammals/water-vole
| watervole.org.uk

(80) Water Birds

Feeding the ducks: it's a childhood ritual unchanged for generations – except that now we're advised to feed them sweetcorn, oats, rice or even frozen peas rather than the traditional bread. Whatever you dispense, communing with water birds in their natural habitat is part of the joy of messing about on canals and rivers. Waterways can be a birdwatcher's paradise, where you can spot anything from the familiar and domestic to the rare and exotic.

Take mallards, so commonplace they go almost unremarked, but who doesn't love watching a cluster of yellow fluffballs paddling furiously to keep up with mum on a sunny spring day? Or seeing a swan

A heron takes flight on the Shropshire Union canal. These once shy birds have become less timorous of late.

literally taking her cygnets under her wing, or giving them a piggyback as she swims, the young birds nestling in the shelter of her raised wing feathers? If you have a boat with a side hatch, as we do, you soon get used to swans sticking their heads through demanding breakfast, and sometimes stealing it too if they can get to your plate, nipping your fingers with their serrated bills if you attempt to stop them.

In spring, you can see gaggles of greylags and Canada geese with a long trail of goslings swimming behind them like an infant school outing. And you won't go far without spotting a soot-black coot with its cry as startling as its white markings, like a Norman helmet across its forehead; or a lone moorhen with its perpetually bobbing head and distinctive red beak and straw-thin legs, making a home of a half-submerged twig.

Then there are the solitary herons standing sentinel on the bank, so still they could be mistaken for the plastic lookalikes sold in garden centres to adorn ponds. At one time, you could never get close to them in a boat; they would take off before you reached them, launching themselves skywards and swooping in a looping arc to land in exactly the same spot once you'd passed. Now, with so many boats on the cut, they seem undisturbed by passing craft and more often than not sit it out while you go by. Common terns actually use boats to feed. We were followed by one for miles one year travelling up the River Lea, and watched transfixed it as it dived repeatedly for the fish disturbed by our propeller.

The champion divers of the waterways, though, are the aristocratic-looking great crested grebe and their zebra-striped young, the signature bird of the Great Ouse and its tributaries in Cambridgeshire (see Wonder 77). They dive for so long, surfacing so far away from where they started, you think they must have drowned. Grebes have a flamboyant mating ritual involving much ostentatious head shaking. They also have an extraordinary plumage and were hunted almost to extinction in the 19th century for women's hats; indeed, the RSPB was established specifically to protect them. Today, thankfully, they are commonplace.

More elusive are kingfishers, their dazzling plumage almost always glimpsed at a distance on the wing, making you wonder if you've really seen one or just imagined it. Occasionally, you'll spot a cormorant perched on top of a wooden post, stretching its wings wide to dry like some immense Gothic bat. At twilight, swallows glide across the water, skimming so close to boats it sometimes seems inevitable that they'll collide – though of course they never do.

Our favourite water bird, though, has

Waterways and their surrounding areas are havens for water birds, and some feature hides conveniently close to the towpath. There's one next to the Crinan Canal in Scotland overlooking Moine Mhor, the Great Moss:
| wildaboutargyll.co.uk/visit/inveraray-knapdale-kilmartin-and-crinan/trips/moine-mhor-national-nature-reserve/

Another, built by the Lincolnshire Wildlife Trust at Fiskerton Fen adjacent to the River Witham, is shaped like an Iron Age roundhouse:
| lincstrust.org.uk/nature-reserves/fiskerton-fen

Slimbridge Wetland Centre, set up by naturalist, conservationist and early canal pioneer Peter Scott to protect wildlife, particularly migrating waterfowl, is sited a short walk from the Gloucester & Sharpness Canal:
| wwt.org.uk/wetland-centres/slimbridge/

There are three public hides on the Tring Reservoirs on the summit of the Grand Union, one of the best birdwatching spots in southern England:
| hertswildlifetrust.org.uk

to be the flashy male mandarin duck, one of which we christened Mandy when his extravagant, jewel-like plumage brightened up one wet Welsh winter afloat in Llangollen. Mandy kept us company through the dark days, convincing us we had developed a special relationship with him, until, walking by the nearby River Dee one day, we came across a colony – dozens of Mandys who had obviously been taking it in turns to visit our boat. Or maybe not. Maybe the one that sought our companionship really was one particular bird, and we were as special to him as he was to us. Well, either that or he was keeping this source of food to himself...

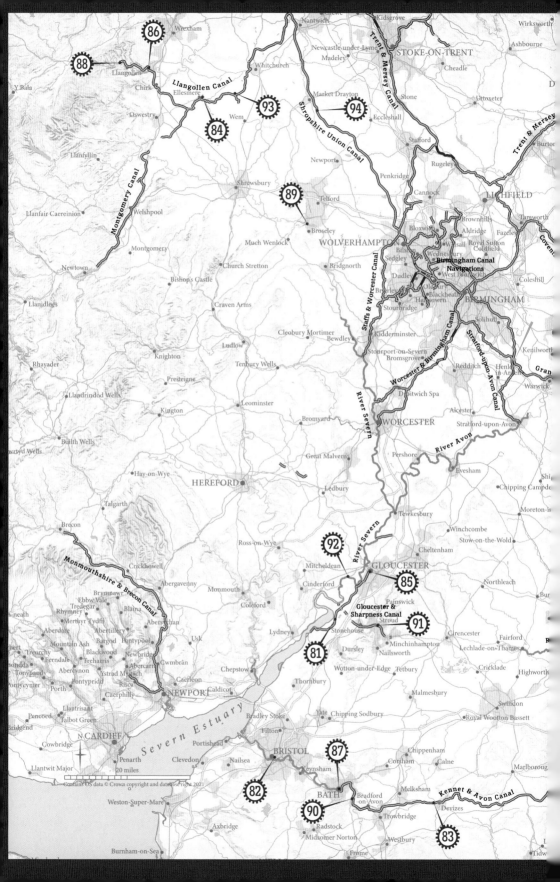

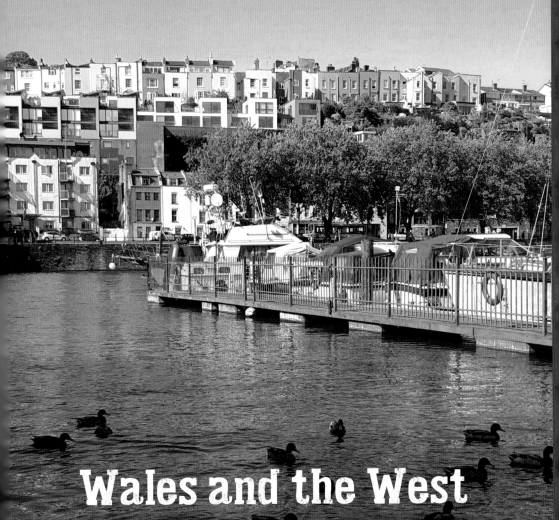

Wales and the West

Bristol Floating Harbour

81 Bridge-keepers' Cottages, Gloucester & Sharpness Canal

It's enough to make you do a double take. They're incongruous, splendid but completely out of place. They've been likened to miniature Greek temples, the sort of thing you'd expect to find under a blazing sun near the glittering wine-dark Aegean – not beside a workaday canal cutting its way through the Gloucestershire countryside in unpredictable British weather.

These surprising oddities are bridge-keepers' cottages, built in the mid-19th century in a style unique to the Gloucester & Sharpness Canal. They are essentially modest bungalows with imposing but completely over-the-top facades, the main feature of which are pediments supported by – of all things! – fluted Doric columns. Why they were built in this style remains a mystery, but all this flummery must have added significantly to the cost of construction.

There are eight of them in total, built as homes for company employees who had to be available to operate the bridges 24 hours a day so that ships could catch the tides at Sharpness, thus maintaining Gloucester's competitive edge over its commercial rival Bristol. The bridge-keepers were kept on after commercial traffic ended, but the cottages are now in private hands and still add a touch of classical elegance to this unusual canal. From the site of one of the most charming of them at Splatt Bridge, you can walk into Frampton on Severn, a lovely linear village that claims to have

the biggest village green in England, 800 metres (0.5 mile) long. A couple of well-placed pubs on the edge may prove irresistible – as they did to us while we were dawdling along the canal one summer, waiting for optimum conditions to cross from Sharpness to Bristol via the Severn Estuary.

The Gloucester & Sharpness Canal was built in 1827 to bypass a dangerous, winding stretch of the tidal River Severn, which, as ships became bigger and cargoes got heavier, was an increasing obstacle to this busy trade route. It was designed specifically as a ship canal and at the time it was the broadest and deepest in the world. It still feels different to other English canals, wider and straighter, altogether more functional. At Sharpness, where a lock opens to the estuary, it's exposed and bleak, wide and wild. The estuary has one of the highest tidal ranges in the world; when it cuts up rough here it's bad, very bad. Steve once stood on the lock gates in a storm when it would have sunk a narrowboat in seconds. It's not officially recommended for narrowboats, but safe passage is feasible for craft equipped for what is essentially a short sea journey. However, it's crucial to travel with a pilot who knows when it's safe to venture out, and this may involve long waits for the right weather.

About 0.8km (0.5 miles) from Sharpness Docks, on the narrow bank between the canal and the River Severn, barely separated from it, lies Purton Hulks – the largest ships' graveyard in mainland Britain. This is where, following a riverbank collapse in 1909, boats were deliberately beached and sunk so as to shore up the banks and protect the canal. Nearly a hundred wooden, iron and concrete hulks now lie here, layer upon layer, their skeletons exposed daily by the tides.

A study in blue. Splatt Bridge and the bridgekeeper's cottage at Frampton on Severn which claims to have the biggest village green in England.

Visit

Access
For Severn Estuary pilots:
| gloucesterpilots.co.uk

In the area
Slimbridge Wildfowl and Wetland Trust is 0.8km (0.5 mile) north-west of the canal at Patch Bridge (Bowditch, GL2 7BT. Tel: 01453 891900) and shouldn't be missed by anyone with even the most peripheral interest in birds, conservation or the environment:
| wwt.org.uk/wetland-centres/
| slimbridge

Saul Junction, halfway along the canal, is an unusual waterways crossroads; here, the Gloucester & Sharpness Canal is intersected by the Stroudwater Navigation, part of the Cotswold Canals currently under restoration, which originally linked the River Thames with the River Severn (see Wonder 91). A heritage centre run by the Cotswold Canals Trust provides more information, refreshments and boat trips:
| cotswoldcanals.com

82 Bristol Floating Harbour

Can there be a more exciting way to arrive in any city than by boat? And of all the destinations in Britain you can reach that way, Bristol is right up there with the best of them – especially if you've come up the steep-sided Avon Gorge from Avonmouth, where you arrive at the Floating Harbour under Isambard Kingdom Brunel's awe-inspiring suspension bridge at Clifton, its two huge abutments dramatically bestriding the river high above you like guardians of the city.

The Floating Harbour is effectively a vast artificial lake, its 28ha (70 acres) of water easily absorbing leviathans like Brunel's famous steamship, the *Great Britain*, the world's first great ocean liner, which was built in a shipyard in the

Isambard Kingdom Brunel's SS Great Britain. For nine years between 1845–1854 she was the largest passenger ship in the world.

harbour and is now permanently moored here. Ice-cream-tinted houses seem to tumble down the hill opposite, vibrantly reflected in the water. Strolling around the harbourside, you could think yourself in continental Europe – Amsterdam, perhaps – as you cross pretty footbridges and pass houseboats and smart Dutch barges overflowing with cats, bicycles and well-tended deck gardens. Cafes and restaurants spill out on to pavements that skirt the water; the illustrious Arnolfini gallery – once a tea warehouse – perches on the bank, and a waterbus darts handily between landing stages at key points in the city.

But why is it called the 'Floating Harbour'? The name sounds senseless. Boats float in harbours, OK. But how can a harbour itself float?

The Bristol Channel has the second highest tidal range in the world: the difference between high and low water can be as much as 12.3 metres (40ft). In the past, ships could easily get up the river to the city on a high tide, but once the tide went down they keeled over. (The phrase 'shipshape and Bristol fashion' is said to stem from this, since vessels needed to ensure everything was safely stowed away and tied down to avoid damage when the ship tipped.)

The Floating Harbour was the ingenious solution to this problem. By 1809, engineer William Jessop had dammed the tidal River Avon to create a pool deep enough for ocean-going ships, developing a way of keeping the water level constant. On one side, a huge lock gives access from the Severn Estuary and Bristol Channel beyond; on the other, a second lock takes smaller boats towards Bath and the Kennet & Avon Canal.

For centuries, Bristol was one of the UK's busiest and most important ports. Like Liverpool (see Wonder 40), it derived much of its vast wealth from its key role in the triangular transatlantic slave trade. So perhaps there was some poetic justice when at the height of the Black Lives Matter protests that swept the world in the summer of 2020, a statue of notorious Bristol slave trader Edward Colston was toppled from its plinth in the city and dumped into the Floating Harbour.

The harbour closed to commercial traffic in 1975, though today it buzzes with activity of a quite different kind. It's a centre of Bristol nightlife, and leisure craft ply the water. There are museums and an annual Bristol Harbour Festival with tall ships. Pubs and bars galore vie for your attention. Mooring one winter in Bristol, our local was the Nova Scotia. Legend has it that its ornate mahogany bar was originally to have graced an ocean liner. True or not, it served cider so powerful that when they saw us quaffing it, fellow customers were amazed: 'How can you drink that stuff ... and yet stay normal?' one asked.

Visit

Access

What better way to see the Floating Harbour than from the water? Bristol's hop-on, hop-off ferry service operates from seven harbourside landing stages. You can use the waterbus service to get from A to B or take a full tour. It also runs a private hire water taxi service, and sometimes offers trips through the big lock and up the Avon Gorge under the Clifton Suspension Bridge. For full details of services, timetables and prices:
| bristolferry.com

For details of more regular sailings up the Avon Gorge:
| bristolpacket.co.uk/boat-trips/avon-gorge-cruise-public-trip

Or if you fancy the experience in a replica of *Matthew*, the ship in which John Cabot famously sailed to Newfoundland from Bristol in 1497:
| matthew.co.uk

Whichever boat you choose, all Avon Gorge trips are dependent on the tide.

In the area

For general information on what to see and do in Bristol:
| visitbristol.co.uk

For information on visiting the SS *Great Britain* and the two museums and historic dockyard connected to it:
| ssgreatbritain.org

For details of what's on at the Arnolfini arts centre (16 Narrow Quay, Bristol, BS1 4QA. Tel: 0117 9172300), including exhibitions and films:
| arnolfini.org.uk

For details of the annual Harbour Festival:
| bristolharbourfestival.co.uk

For the Nova Scotia (1 Nova Scotia Place, Bristol, BS1 6XJ. Tel: 07794 781189):
| pubheritage.camra.org.uk/pubs/8127

83 Caen Hill Lock Flight

To most casual observers, canal boating seems a pretty leisurely pursuit, chugging along at walking pace through peaceful countryside with just an occasional burst of activity at locks to liven things up. It seems great for a holiday, a perfect way to wind down from the stress of work and family life. All this is true. Except that every now and again you come across flights of locks that are cussed to navigate. The flight of 29 locks on the Kennet & Avon Canal at Caen Hill near Devizes is one of them.

There's no getting round it, Caen Hill is a daunting obstacle. The locks in the main part of the flight charge up the hill one after the other in an undeviating straight line, the repeating pattern of their black-and-white balance beams receding into what seems infinity. For anyone wanting to get to Bath or Bristol by inland waterway, Caen Hill is far and away the biggest impediment. It's one of the longest continuous lock flights in the country, rising 72 metres (237ft) over just 3.2km (2 miles); and, depending how fit your crew is, it can take up to six gruelling hours to get through it. Fortunately, walkers can enjoy the locks from the towpath while expending a good deal less time and energy. Enormous and unusually shaped side ponds beside the locks conserve precious water while providing an important wildlife habitat.

This phenomenal feat of engineering was built by waterways visionary John Rennie in 1810, at the tail end of that manic period in the late-18th and early-19th centuries when canals were king.

The 16 locks that form the steepest part are now a Scheduled Ancient Monument, in the same heritage league as nearby Stonehenge. This seems entirely fitting when you realise that as recently as the 1980s, the flight was a complete ruin – and not of the picturesque, romantic kind either. Dewatered and

Intimidating or what? The flight charges relentlessly up the hill in a way that promises hard work for boat crews.

completely derelict, the locks had all but disintegrated, and the idea that they might ever see a boat again seemed fanciful, to say the least.

When we started boating in the 1970s, the whole of the Kennet & Avon Canal was closed, and had been since 1950. We never dreamed we would one day be able to cruise its entire length, though Steve kept donating such large sums to the K&A Trust, which restored it, that he thinks he owns part of it now. Their unshakeable faith and sheer bloody-mindedness paid off and was proved more than justified when the Queen reopened the canal to boats in 1990. These days, an estimated 1,500–2,000 boats travel through Caen Hill locks annually, on what is one of Britain's most popular cruising routes. In a curious twist, old lock gates removed from Caen Hill were donated to the Glastonbury Festival some years ago to build a mock bullring. Olé! How's that for recycling?

Visit

Facilities
At the top of the flight is the Caen Hill Cafe (Tel: 01380 724880).

In the area
The wharf at Devizes is where you'll find the museum of the Kennet & Avon Canal Trust (Tel: 01380 721279, katrust. org.uk), who also run boat trips:
| katrust.org.uk

For self-drive day-boat hire:
| whitehorsenarrowboats.co.uk

If you're travelling by car and have come this far, it's only a 40-minute drive along the A346 to Crofton Pumping Station (Crofton, Nr Marlborough, SN8 3DW. Tel: 01672 870300), which only narrowly missed being one of our Wonders in its own right. On a boat, it's a day's cruising. The pump house contains a still-working Boulton & Watt steam engine dating from 1812, which makes it the oldest working beam engine in the world still in its original location:
| croftonbeamengines.org

Only from the air can you get any sense of the pure scale of the flight and its associated side ponds, built to conserve water.

84 The Ellesmere Lake District

Everyone knows the Lake District, don't they? The one immortalised by William Wordsworth and brooded over by England's highest mountains, its paths painstakingly plotted for generations of walkers by Alfred Wainwright. But there's another English lake district, more modest, less celebrated, and on an altogether smaller scale – but definitely a waterways wonder.

We're talking about the little-known Ellesmere Lake District in Shropshire, through which the Llangollen Canal threads on its way to Wales.

What makes this area special is the extraordinary proximity of the canal to some of the lakes – known as meres. Blakemere is separated from the cut by only a narrow strip of towpath so that the two seem to merge; on the other hand you could almost miss the larger Colemere, below the canal on the opposite side, hidden by woodland. England's only known colony of the

A short arm connects the main canal to Ellesmere Basin where this simple warehouse has become a feature of the waterway.

critically endangered least water-lily grows here, protected by a host of conservation organisations led by the Royal Botanic Gardens at Kew. It also attracts insect life and birds in abundance – waders like snipe and curlew, and insects like brown hawker dragonflies and blue damselflies.

There are nine Shropshire meres in all, glacial lakes formed at the end of the last ice age. The Mere, against which the small but beguiling town of Ellesmere butts, is the largest of these and in summer it feels like a holiday resort. You can buy an ice cream from one of the vans parked along the esplanade, or rent a rowing boat, or take a stroll around pretty Cremorne Gardens, where giant redwoods grow. Those of a more ornithological bent can observe herons nesting in the trees on Moscow Island opposite the Boathouse visitor centre, where you can watch via a webcam as these elegant birds build nests, incubate eggs and feed their hungry chicks.

The canal transformed Ellesmere from a sleepy backwater to big hitter of the Canal Age, for in 1792, at what was then the Royal Oak, a momentous

Wales and the West

meeting was held for potential investors in the Ellesmere Canal, planned to link the rivers Severn and Mersey. It raised an astonishing £1 million in six hours – the equivalent of nearly £60 million at today's prices. The meeting is commemorated in a plaque outside what is now the Ellesmere Hotel, and though the link between the rivers was never established, the importance of the name that Ellesmere bequeathed to the venture still lives on in the town of Ellesmere Port on the River Mersey (See Wonder 35).

A short arm connects Ellesmere to the Llangollen Canal, the stately canal-side Beech House at the junction originally the offices for civil engineer Thomas Telford while he was working on the canal. At the end of the arm, a red brick warehouse stands alongside the canal basin. It's seen better days but it testifies to the canal company's pride at its ability to ship goods across the country.

Less well-known than those immortalised by the poets, the 'meres' of the Ellesmere Lake District bordering the Llangollen Canal are still hauntingly beautiful. They host a profusion of flora, fauna and insect life.

Visit

In the area

There are some good and easy walks in the area, including a circular walk around Colemere – the only mere you can circuit completely on foot:

shropshiresgreatoutdoors.co.uk/route/discover-shropshire-family-friendly-colemere-collywobbles/

For a walk around The Mere in Ellesmere:

shropshiresgreatoutdoors.co.uk/route/discover-shropshire-family-friendly-ellesmere-eccentricities/

or a longer walk:

shropshiresgreatoutdoors.co.uk/route/meres-meander-walk-4/

The Boathouse visitor centre is the Ellesmere base of Shropshire Wildlife Trust, with a cafe and restaurant attached:

ellesmere.info/things-to-do/shropshire-wildlife-trust

This is also home to the Ellesmere Heron Watch scheme, which runs annually from February to the end of May:

heronwatch.org.uk

⚙(85) Gloucester Docks

Gloucester on the River Severn is an old inland port, so old it was a port before it was properly a city, so old that it was used by the Romans, centuries before Queen Elizabeth I formalised its status in 1580, allowing it to trade independently rather than have to play second fiddle to its great rival Bristol.

Its problem, though, was that even with the royal stamp of approval, many seagoing ships were reluctant to venture to the city because that meant going too far up the river. This was (and still can be) an unpredictably treacherous waterway: twisting, shifting and shallow, and it's vulnerable to flooding, not to mention its famous 'bores' caused by tides among the highest in the world surging upstream from the Bristol Channel (see Wonder 92).

Eventually, to get round all the obstacles, in 1827 they built what is today called the Gloucester & Sharpness

Canal, a more direct and reliable route to skirt the tricky part of the river. In its day, this was the broadest and deepest ship canal in the world and as a result, Gloucester prospered. The dock complex became one of the busiest in the country, a key trans-shipment point for timber from the Baltic and corn to feed the expanding Midlands' towns of the Industrial Revolution. In the 1840s, new quays were built, docks constructed and additional warehouses erected, many of them built over high vaulted basements supported by cast-iron pillars.

The docks and its warehouses, some seven storeys high, are a rewarding place to visit today and though the brigs, schooners and barques that once traded from here have long since disappeared from the scene, there is always a selection of interesting craft to see, either contemporary boats passing through or historic craft clustered around the recently renovated National Waterways Museum, which is housed in a listed grain store and shouldn't be missed. From here, you can take a trip boat and get on to the water yourself. There are cafes, restaurants and shops nearby, too; and in the former Custom

House is the Soldiers of Gloucestershire Museum, dedicated to the history and exploits of the county's military. And if you want a break from watery attractions, you can always stroll to Gloucester's splendid 12th-century cathedral, which is only a short distance away.

For us, though, it's the docks that are Gloucester's tour de force. The brick warehouses that overlook the basins are brutally imposing, yet at the same time they're dignified and stately, and have an unexpected elegance about them. Our top tip is to seek out the Mariners chapel. Built in the mid-19th century by public subscription to minister to sailors, dockworkers and émigrés bound for the New World, this modest building in white stone hidden among the towering warehouses has a tranquil and comforting simplicity to it, both inside and out. It's still a working church with regular services, continuing a tradition stretching back to those days when sailors and passengers facing the perils of the sea would have prayed for a safe passage before setting sail.

Visit

In the area

General information about the city:
| visitgloucester.co.uk

For National Waterways Museum, Gloucester (Llanthony Warehouse, The Docks, GL1 2EH. Tel: 01452 318212), including details of boat trips on the *Queen Boadicea II*, a Dunkirk 'little ship' see:
| canalrivertrust.org.uk/places-to-visit/national-waterways-museum-gloucester

Soldiers of Gloucestershire museum (Back Badge Square, Gloucester Docks, GL1 2HE. Tel: 01452 522682):
| soldiersofglos.com

For the Mariners chapel (The Docks, GL1 2EN. Tel: 01452 540307):
| marinersgloucester.org.uk

Information on Gloucester Cathedral:
| gloucestercathedral.org.uk

Once a busy complex importing grain and timber from the Baltic, today the former dock buildings have been renovated and repurposed so we can appreciate their stately elegance.

⚙(86) Pontcysyllte Aqueduct

Soaring spectacularly on slender tapered columns 38 metres (126ft) over the River Dee below, the Pontcysyllte Aqueduct near Llangollen in Wales is the jewel in the crown of Britain's waterways.

A World Heritage Site since 2009, it's an astonishing feat of Georgian engineering, as dazzling today as it must have been when it was first opened in 1805. The experience of crossing it on a narrowboat is like flying. That's because the iron trough that carries the Llangollen Canal across the valley – just 2.1 metres (7ft) wide – is completely unguarded on one side. As you cross, it's as if you're on the edge of an abyss, a sudden plunge to the distant valley floor below looking all too possible. The other side is more protected, with a narrow towpath and original iron railings, so as a pedestrian there's enough room to walk across freely (and safely). In summer, though, there can be a heavy build-up of traffic both on foot and in boats, and there's usually some poor soul cursed with vertigo who can be found paralysed with indecision at one end or the other.

The aqueduct was Thomas Telford's masterpiece. That's the Thomas Telford whose fingerprints are all over the waterways of Britain: a one-man dynamo of canal construction. And despite what today may seem like primitive technology, the aqueduct still functions exactly as originally built – a testament to Telford's awe-inspiring and unrivalled skills in engineering and use

Narrowboating, walking or canoeing, you'll need a good head for heights however you cross the aqueduct.

It's a simple metal trough on brick piers, but more than two centuries later it is still in use. The aqueduct is fenced off on the towpath side but the only thing preventing boats plunging the sheer drop into the river is the edge of the trough itself.

of materials. Not to mention his vision, confidence and sheer chutzpah. So, the iron trough carries water diverted from the River Dee over the River Dee in an aqueduct still sealed with the original ox blood and lime mortar paste mixture, using Welsh flannel and lead dipped in boiling sugar in the joints. Ingenious or what? And you know something else? It barely leaks. Hardly a drop. Beat that if you can, you 21st-century technocrats.

The aqueduct was originally intended as a key link in the proposed Ellesmere Canal, designed to connect the River Severn at Shrewsbury to the River Mersey. But soon after it was built, the project went pear-shaped. The money ran out and work stopped dead. However, a feeder taking water from the River Dee at Horseshoe Falls (see Wonder 88) at nearby Llangollen for drinking water survived into modern times, and in the 1950s, leisure boats began to make it a destination. Today, the Llangollen Canal, as it's now known, is the country's most popular cruising route.

However, one question remains: how do you pronounce its damn name? It's four syllables: learn it and impress the Welsh. The first 'Pont' is pronounced as it looks, the second is 'cus', the third is 'uth', like someone with a lisp talking about 'us'. The final bit is 'te', as in tent, telly or technology. Put them together.

Pont-cus-uth-te. See, simples.

Visit

For more information, see:
| pontcysyllte-aqueduct.co.uk

Take a boat trip across the Pontcysyllte Aqueduct:
| anglowelsh.co.uk/weve-launched-a-new-trip-boatat-trevorand
| horsedrawnboats.co.uk/aqueduct-trips

There is a visitor information centre at Trevor Basin, on the Llangollen side of the aqueduct:
| canalrivertrust.org.uk/places-to-visit/pontcysyllte-aqueduct-world-heritage-site/trevor-basin-visitor-centre

(87) Pulteney Bridge, Bath

Pulteney Bridge is the beautiful, neoclassical, three-arched bridge that crosses the River Avon at Bath. When she lived in the city, Jane Austen would have crossed it every day on her way from her lodgings in Sydney Place to take the waters at the Pump Room, or drink tea and listen to music in the Assembly Rooms. Both feature in her novels and both are still there today. Indeed, parts of Bath have barely altered since her time.

In a city full of Regency splendour and jaw-dropping Georgian architecture – a city that looks as good today as it did when Ms Austen satirised and sympathised with its inhabitants in equal measure – Pulteney Bridge stands out. It's among the most impressive structures in Bath and since the city is stuffed full of architectural gems competing for your attention, that's certainly saying something. With its unusual elliptical weir cascading over three levels below it like a series of waterfalls, it is arguably the most romantic bridge in the world outside of the Rialto in Venice.

It's one of only four bridges in the world to boast shops lining its full span on both sides, but despite its fame, Pulteney Bridge has an air of discretion about it that is in keeping with the city in which it's located. Tourists have passed over it without knowing they have. It's far too refined to draw unnecessary attention to itself. It's as if it knows that sooner or later you will notice its understated proportions and perfect symmetry. When you finally do, it takes your breath away.

Built of the Bath stone characteristic of the city, it was completed in 1774 to a design by Robert Adam, the Scottish

One of the few bridges in the world with shops along its full span on both sides.

architect whose name is synonymous with neoclassical elegance, and whose work is credited with the classical revival that has had a lasting influence on British architecture and interior design.

Stroll across it and you'll find plenty of specialist shops to pique your interest, as well as cafes and restaurants where you can rest your legs. Some have windows giving on to the river so you can combine browsing with the view as your backdrop. To appreciate it in all its glory, though, Pulteney Bridge is best seen from river level. There are steps from the bridge down to a riverside path, where you get the full wow factor and the best photos.

At one time, you were able to moor for a small charge next to The Rec, Bath Rugby Club's riverside ground overlooking the bridge and the weir. We count ourselves lucky that we were able to do this. We had a spectacular view from our front deck, all the more impressive at night when the whole scene was gloriously floodlit. Better than a hotel room at any price.

The unusual elliptical weir underneath the bridge creates the effect of a triple level waterfall.

Visit

In the area
You're spoilt for choice in this World Heritage Site city when it comes to things to see.

Top of the list has to be the Roman Baths and Thermae Bath Spa, where you can enjoy the wonders of the Bath skyline while soaking in a stunning, naturally heated, open-air rooftop pool:
| romanbaths.co.uk
| thermaebathspa.com

Take the waters at the Pump Room and follow it by (more palatable) tea and cake, accompanied by strings and piano:
| thepumproombath.co.uk

Royal Crescent is also a must, especially No 1, which is open to the public and retains its original furniture and fittings:
| no1royalcrescent.org.uk

There's also the Circus, the Abbey, the Assembly Rooms in Bennett Street, Sydney Gardens and the Jane Austen Centre at Gay Street:
| janeausten.co.uk

Take an open-top boat trip from Pulteney Bridge:
| pulteneycruisers.com

You can also hire a rowing boat, canoe or punt from Bath Boating Station:
| bathboating.co.uk

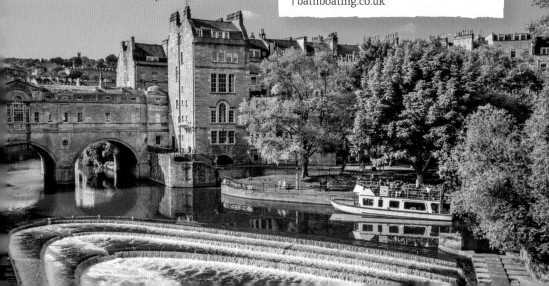

⚙(88) Horseshoe Falls

OK, so if you come here expecting a spectacular waterfall cascading down a wild Welsh mountainside, you'll be a bit, well ... a bit underwhelmed, actually. The name is misleading, to put it mildly. It's not a waterfall at all but an artificially made weir – though don't be fooled: it conceals a cunning triumph of water management.

And it's pretty as well, an almost perfect hemisphere of water gently dropping a couple of feet from the River Dee to form a tranquil pool set among grassy, tree-shaded slopes. A perfect spot for a picnic. But there's more to it. The structure is designed to draw 12 million gallons of water a day from the river to feed the Llangollen Canal and to help supply drinking water to south Cheshire. Without this, there would be no water in this canal or indeed others in the system that feed off it. In fact, it's the main reason the Llangollen Canal – the most popular cruising route in Britain

Tiny St Tysilio church is renowned for its snowdrops, celebrated in an annual service every February.

– has survived as a navigable waterway at all. The 140-metre (460ft) arc of the weir is positioned on a sharp bend in the river above rapids. It diverts water at a regulated rate via a system of sluices through a gauging station into the canal. The plan for the falls was first hatched by canal engineer William Jessop in 1795 and completed in 1808 by waterways titan Thomas Telford, making it one of the first river regulation schemes anywhere in Britain.

We spent two happy winters living on our boat in Llangollen, one of a dozen or so craft on winter moorings there. We were spoilt for choice when it came to hill walks, but Horseshoe Falls was a favourite destination for a gentle afternoon stroll, with plenty of interest along the way. It's a couple of miles along the towpath from Llangollen – unnavigable to powered craft, though a horse-drawn trip boat takes summer visitors there.

You pass the site of the world-famous international Eisteddfod, held in the purpose-built pavilion that you see from the towpath. Soon after is a motor museum and the Chainbridge Hotel, a stopping-off point for refreshments and

You'll be disappointed if you're expecting something spectacular, but Horseshoe Falls is set in idyllic surroundings, ideal for a picnic.

a good spot to see canoeists shooting the rapids on the river below. The hotel is named after the bridge there, a local landmark, and one of the first chain suspension bridges in the world; it connects to Berwyn railway station on the other side, part of Llangollen's justifiably renowned heritage line, where regular steam services run throughout the year.

A little further on, beyond the falls, is the medieval church of St Tysilio's at Llantysilio on the banks of the River Dee. Every year in early February, the graveyard is thickly carpeted with snowdrops. We stumbled across them by chance after a long, wet winter and they seemed so truly miraculous that we were moved to attend the annual snowdrop service there, where you are asked to give a simple commitment to do your bit to protect the environment.

Visit

For general information:
| llangollen.org.uk

For a free downloadable map:
| canalrivertrust.org.uk/places-to-visit/
| llangollen-and-the-horseshoe-falls

Facilities
Chainbridge Hotel (Berwyn, LL20 8BS.
Tel: 01978 860215):
| chainbridgehotel.com

In the area
Horse-drawn boat trips and day-boat hire:
| horsedrawnboats.co.uk

Llangollen railway:
| llangollen-railway.co.uk

The Llangollen International Music Eisteddfod in July is one of the world's great music festivals and competitions, though to time any holiday trip requires significant planning, both for mooring and tickets:
| international-eisteddfod.co.uk.

⚙ (89) Ironbridge

It's like the ads. Ironbridge does exactly what it says on the tin. This enchanting Shropshire town has a bridge over the River Severn. And it's made of iron. But this is not just any old iron bridge. This is the world's first ever iron bridge, built in 1779 by Abraham Darby III, whose grandfather first developed a new process for smelting iron using coke instead of the traditional charcoal – a process that kick-started the Industrial Revolution.

It's no exaggeration to say that the bridge's pioneering design and use of materials heralded a technological revolution. The delicate latticework of its graceful single arch belies its strength and the rudimentary nature of its construction. It may be an icon of civil engineering, but in those days they knew nothing about building iron bridges and it was experimental, held together by preposterous carpentry joints that wouldn't look out of place on a kitchen table.

Held together by a series of carpentry joints, the iron bridge was an experiment in new technology.

Clusters of attractive houses, shops, churches and pubs fan outwards from it, ranged in tiers along the steep sides of the Severn Gorge, the brick and stone set snugly into the vibrant green backdrop of the densely wooded river valley. The tranquil rustic setting gives no hint of the role Ironbridge and the surrounding area played in changing Britain's place in the world, and changing the rest of the world with it.

Nearby Coalbrookdale is where the new coke smelting process first took place. There's a famous 1801 painting in London's Science Museum of the place by night, looking like the gates of hell, the darkness lit by a massive sheet of flame belching into the sky from blast furnaces. In the corner of the canvas is a wan and wasted moon. It seems to capture the moment of Britain's transition from an agrarian to an industrial nation.

Rich in raw materials, the Ironbridge Gorge rapidly transformed itself into an industrial powerhouse. Soon, bricks, decorative tiles and internationally renowned Coalport China were being

Wales and the West

mass-produced nearby using local clay. These easily breakable goods could be more safely transported by water than road, and in 1793, the spectacular 63-metre-high (207ft) Hay Inclined Plane opened, connecting the River Severn to the Shropshire Union and the main canal system using 6-metre (20ft) box-shaped 'tub boats'.

All this is now part of a World Heritage Site complex of ten indoor and open-air museums including Coalbrookdale Museum of Iron, Coalport China Museum, Blists Hill Victorian Town and, of course, the Iron Bridge itself. Every August Bank Holiday Monday there's an entertaining coracle regatta featuring the traditional bowl-shaped craft once a common sight on the river. You can even learn to make one yourself if you fancy it.

We first explored the place one glorious Easter when we couldn't go cruising because our boat had broken down. Paradoxically, we learned more about the importance of canals in our history that weekend than if we'd have been cruising them. What until then had been abstract suddenly became very real. Afterwards, we sprawled on the grass outside the All Nations pub, luxuriating

Visit

Facilities

The All Nations pub (20 Coalport Road, Telford, TF7 5DP. Tel: 01952 585747):
| allnationsinn.co.uk

In the area

Free downloadable walking leaflets at:
| severngorge.org.uk/walking-leaflets

For details of all ten Ironbridge Gorge Museums:
| ironbridge.org.uk

More on the annual coracle regatta:
| ironbridgecoracles.org/the-coracle-
| regatta

in the sudden warmth of unexpected spring sunshine, quenching our thirst with pints of the deceptively light, refreshing beer they brewed then. We came home with a print of the Boy and Swan fountain cast by Coalbrookdale for the Great Exhibition of 1851 and a Coalport teacup and saucer. Lasting reminders of a weekend in a place that changed the world and changed the way we looked at it, too.

90 The Rennie Aqueducts

When it comes to aqueducts, Telford's Pontcysyllte, which carries the Llangollen Canal high over the River Dee (see Wonder 86), is so spectacular it tends to put all others in the shade. Which is a pity, since two of those designed by his contemporary, fellow Scot John Rennie, deserve to be celebrated as masterpieces in their own right.

At one end of the country, the Lune Aqueduct takes the Lancaster Canal 202 metres (664ft) across the River Lune near Lancaster, while in the south-west, the 137-metre (450ft) Dundas Aqueduct conveys the Kennet & Avon Canal over the River Avon near Bath. The similarities in design between the two are striking: both combine beauty and utility with understated neoclassical grace and elegance. In an age when engineering and architecture went hand in hand and both disciplines were considered as much art as science, Rennie's flair for design matched his technical skills. No surprise then that in 2018 a collection of six plans drawn and signed by him for aqueducts on the Lancaster Canal was sold for £4,375 by London auctioneers Bonhams.

The Grade I listed Lune Aqueduct came first, completed in 1797. Built of local sandstone, its five pleasingly curved and balustraded arches are supported on piles of specially imported Russian timbers driven deep into the riverbed. The mortar mix used contained Italian volcanic ash known as *pozzolana* to help it set underwater and increase its durability – a technique

The Dundas Aqueduct carries the Kennet and Avon Canal over the River Avon near Bath.

Wales and the West

used on the canals of Venice. The central arch keystone on one side bears an inscription: 'To Public Prosperity'.

The aqueduct was always behind schedule and the rush to complete it before winter floods set in led to a massive overspend, which had profound implications for the future of the Lancaster Canal. It meant – paradoxically, in the light of the Latin inscription – there was no money available to connect it to the rest of the inland waterways system by another aqueduct that had been planned over the River Ribble. The water connection wasn't achieved until a link was opened in 2002 (see Wonder 42). This avoided the need for an aqueduct by the much cheaper solution of sending boats on a challenging tidal journey across the Ribble Estuary.

Dundas Aqueduct, at the other end of the country on the Kennet & Avon Canal, is judged by many to be Rennie's crowning achievement. Completed in in 1810 in local Bath stone, it shares the harmonious curves of the Lune Aqueduct, with a single central arch spanning the river in the embrace of two smaller arches hugging the bank on either side. It was the first canal structure to be awarded Scheduled Ancient Monument status, and you can understand why, though to see it properly you need to look at it from river level as well as crossing it on foot or by boat. Only this way can you appreciate its full glory. Fortunately, it's well looked after; in the summer of 2021, a specialist team of abseiling stonemasons were suspended on ropes 12 metres (40ft) above the Avon Valley to carry out repairs to its decorative mouldings, reinstating it to its original splendour.

Visit

Access

The Dundas Aqueduct is at the junction of the Kennet & Avon Canal and the derelict Somerset Coal Canal, a short stretch of which is still in water, including Brassknocker Basin (BA2 7JD), where a canal centre is located. Here, there's a car park (charges apply) and boat and bike hire. It's a short walk to the aqueduct and the main Kennet & Avon Canal.

The Kennet & Avon Canal Trust, the charity responsible for saving and restoring the K&A, runs several trip boats crewed by volunteers, including one that visits both the Dundas and Avoncliff aqueducts, embarking at nearby Bradford-on-Avon:
| katrust.org.uk.

Facilities

The Angelfish Restaurant/Café is at the canal centre (Brassknocker Basin. Tel: 01225 723483).

In the area

The Avoncliff Aqueduct – another Rennie creation – is a sort of 'mini-me' version of its better-known neighbour but an interesting place to visit in its own right. From there – only a 1.5km (1-mile) walk or cruise away – is a 14th-century tithe barn (Pound Lane, Bradford-on-Avon, BA15 1LF. Tel: 0370 3331181), which is situated by the canal at Bradford-on-Avon and free to visit:
| english-heritage.org.uk/visit/places/
| bradford-on-avon-tithe-barn/

In Lancaster, the Kingfisher waterbus runs trips to the Lune Aqueduct from outside the Water Witch pub:
| kingfishercruise.co.uk

The Wyre Aqueduct on the Lancaster canal – also known as the Garstang Aqueduct – is on the outskirts of the charming market town of Garstang and another Rennie 'mini-me'. Like the Avoncliff, it's of similar design to its more famous kindred companion, but just smaller.

91 Sapperton Tunnel and the Cotswold Canals

The Cotswolds? Canals? Surely this is a marriage made in heaven? You might be tempted to think that some 18th-century romantic had idly dreamed up the idea of a scenic route by water through one of England's loveliest areas merely for their own pleasure and amusement. But no canal was ever dug without there was money to be made. All of them meant business – and in this case the business was linking the River Severn to the River Thames.

The Cotswold Canals, as they are known today, are two canals that join seamlessly. The first, the Stroudwater Navigation, was opened in 1779, linking the River Severn with the Stroud valley, where the expanding woollen cloth industry was hungry for coal. So profitable was it that there was soon a proposal for a second canal to continue the line to the River Thames, near Lechlade. This involved the ambitious construction of the 3.49km (2.17-mile) Sapperton Tunnel, which in 1789, was not just the longest canal tunnel ever

built, but the largest, too. It was 4.6 metres (15ft) wide to accommodate broad Thames boats, and was 4.7 metres (15ft 4in) high. This meant that boats going through it had an extraordinary 3.1 metres (more than 10ft) clearance between the waterline and the roof – which is cavernous compared to that hole in the ground at Harecastle near Stoke (see Wonder 16), where you virtually graze your head on the roof. It also sported two splendid portals, one a castellated rampart, the second, near the small village of Coates, more elegant altogether, with statue niches, decorative medallions and a couple of Doric columns built to give the appearance of the entrance to a stately home. It was a wonder of its own age, its renown sealed during its construction with a visit by George III.

The Thames & Severn Canal, as it was called, was opened ten years after the Stroudwater, though there was a sad lack of joined-up thinking with regard to the project and the canals were built to different gauges. Cargoes had to be transhipped at Brimscombe near Stroud, which soon became an important inland port. The Thames & Severn closed in 1933, its 15 locks taking it down to the Thames steadily fell into disrepair and the Sapperton Tunnel collapsed and became impassable. The Stroudwater soldiered on until 1954, when traffic along it effectively ceased. In time, parts of the canal were filled in and blocked. Nevertheless, because the canal passes through such attractive countryside there was a powerful incentive to open up the route to leisure boating; and the highly focused and energetic Cotswold

Visit

Check the Cotswold Canals Trust's website for full details of the ongoing restoration programme. You can also learn how you can support their work and find out how to become an active volunteer. The trust runs boat trips from bases at Saul Junction on their boat *Adventure*; from Ebley on their boats *Perseverance* and *Endeavour*; and from Lechlade on their classic Thames launch *Inglesham*. It has information centres at Wallbridge Lock, Saul Junction and Bonds Mill:
| cotswoldcanals.org

For general information on walking, cycling and canoeing the Cotswold Canals:
| cotswoldcanalsconnected.org/visiting

To download walking and cycling maps for the Slow Canal Trail:
| cotswoldcanalsconnected.org/wp-content/uploads/2021/05/Stroud_WALK_CYCLE_A4_LEAFLET.pdf

For farm and food trails:
| cotswoldcanalsconnected.org/wp-content/uploads/2021/05/Stroud_AGRIFOOD_A4_LEAFLET.pdf

A long-distance footpath, the Thames and Severn Way, follows the canal towpath:
| ldwa.org.uk/ldp/members/show_path.php?path_name=Thames+and+Severn+Way

Canal Trust has been working towards re-establishing both canals for full navigation. Taking inspiration from the success of other restoration campaigns, it has already surmounted what looked like impossible obstacles towards its goal of full restoration. Until it's completed, you can enjoy this Area of Outstanding Natural Beauty as a walker or cyclist.

92 The Severn Bore

No, it's not the bloke who always seems to be propping up the bar in that pub near Worcester. The Severn Bore is actually a spectacular natural phenomenon, a tidal surge, a wall of water up to 3 metres high (10ft) in midstream, barrelling up the River Severn at speeds sometimes as high as 20km/h (12mph). At its most powerful, it can leave mayhem in its wake, flooding villages along its route and overtopping the weir at Tewkesbury.

You've heard of ocean surfers riding the Atlantic breakers in Cornwall? Safe to say it's less likely you know about the river surfers chasing the best wave on the Severn Bore. One even made it into the *Guinness Book of Records* when he broke a world record by surfing up the Severn for an incredible 12km (7.6 miles) in 2006. Canoeists are the other foolhardy adventurers who risk life and limb to use the natural force of the

The Bore attracts surfers from all over the world.

bore to go shooting upstream against the current. All this river adventuring started with local legend Colonel 'Mad Jack' Churchill, who in 1955 slipped his 4-metre (14ft) home-made surfboard into the river and became the first person ever to surf a tidal bore.

In the years since, it's become so popular that scores of surfers can converge on the river on days when the biggest bores are expected, so many that Gloucester Harbour Trustees have had to issue official safety guidance for surfers, canoeists and spectators (gloucesterharbourtrustees.org.uk/severnbore). They warn that bore surfing is not to be undertaken lightly. Even with experience, it's testing and potentially dangerous, and there are no lifeguards to pull you out if you get into trouble. It also warns surfers that if they drop off the bore, they can be swept downstream more quickly than they can imagine, in currents stronger than any they will have encountered in the ocean. When the bore arrives, the incoming water fights the outgoing current and produces a turmoil of whirlpools, confusing currents and 'stoppers' – recirculating currents that are a feature of deep water and extremely dangerous since they are difficult to escape.

Severn bores appear on about 130 days of the year, mostly those immediately following a full or new moon. This is because they are governed by tides, and start as tidal waves in mid-ocean, an astonishing 1,126km (700 miles) wide. The bore effect is caused by this mass of moving water being funnelled into an ever narrowing channel as it surges directly from the Atlantic up the Bristol Channel, through the Severn Estuary and into the River Severn itself. The bore wave is the head of a great slab of water 19km (12 miles) long, so powerful it forces the river to reverse its flow. Its size and timing depend on a range of factors including high tide times, barometric pressure, wind speed and direction, and the amount of water flowing down the river.

Visit

The most impressive bores happen around the time of the spring tides in February to March, and August to October, when the tidal range – the difference between high and low water – exceeds 12.5 metres (41ft) at Avonmouth. The biggest of all happen at the time of each spring and autumn equinox. Timetables for the Severn Bore and predictions of bore heights are published each year:
| severn-bore.co.uk

There are lots of places along the riverbank where you can see the Severn Bore. The most popular, with easy road access, are at Over Bridge near Gloucester, Minsterworth and Stonebench, the last of which is within walking distance of the Gloucester & Sharpness Canal. You should choose your viewing position carefully since as the bore passes it can often break violently along the banks, the river level rising instantly, flooding the surrounding area ... and spectators with it.

Spectators watch from the bank as surfers ride the Severn Bore past Newnham.

⚙93⚙ Whixall Moss

There's something primeval about Whixall Moss, one of England's last remaining peat bogs. It's a land that time forgot, an unearthly prehistoric landscape where it's not hard to imagine giant reptiles slithering out of the floating vegetation, or winged creatures swooping from the sky. It feels desolate, a lonely place even when you're in the company of other people. Even on a warm summer's day, its other-worldly atmosphere can send a shiver down your spine.

The Llangollen Canal runs alongside, in a remote, isolated part of rural Shropshire straddling the border with Wales. The spongy heather- and moss-covered bog is criss-crossed by water-filled ditches and is treacherous underfoot, but a network of paths and wooden boardwalks allow easy access from the car park adjacent to Morris Bridge, a characteristic Llangollen lift bridge (see Wonder 66). If you're on a boat it's easy to moor up on the towpath and explore, though when we tried it first years ago, before the place was developed for visitors, we were deterred from venturing far by the ground bouncing precariously under our feet.

The Shropshire Mosses are part of a landscape that was formed 12,000 years ago by retreating glaciers. Lowland

raised bogs – of which Whixall Moss is a prime example – are one of the most endangered habitats on Earth, relics of a time long before humankind began to reshape the natural landscape with agriculture and settlements.

Whixall Moss is a naturalist's paradise and its astonishingly varied wildlife makes it internationally important. Now a National Nature Reserve (NNR), you might spot adders or lizards, and the outflow ditches have become a stronghold of water voles, a common sight when we first started boating, but now vanishingly rare (see Wonder 79). Birdwatchers are in their element, too: an impressive 166 different species have been recorded here, including teal, curlews and shoveler ducks – like mallards but with wide bills.

A host of rare plant life also thrives in these conditions. There are 18 species of bog moss, and insect-eating sundews. Cloudberry and cranberry turn the bog gold and red in autumn. Invertebrates like the raft spider, which walks on water, and window-winged caddisfly mingle with 29 species of dragonfly and damselfly. Some exceptionally rare creatures, such as picture-winged bog craneflies, have been rescued from the verge of extinction thanks to the successful restoration of their natural habitat. This was despoiled by peat cutting, which was first recorded back in the 1570s and only stopped in 1990 when the site was saved for conservation.

If this hadn't happened, there's no doubt Whixall Moss and its neighbouring Bettisfield Moss and Fenn's Moss would have been completely destroyed and the natural wonder we can still enjoy today would have been lost forever.

Visit

For more information:
shropshiresgreatoutdoors.co.uk/site/fenns-whixall-and-bettisfield-mosses-nnr/ and gov.uk/government/publications/shropshires-national-nature-reserves/shropshires-national-nature-reserves

For walks around the Moss:
themeresandmosses.co.uk/visiting-the-mosses/walking-trails/es

Now, Whixall Moss plays a crucial role in the battle against climate change. Peat bogs trap and hold vast stores of carbon; cutting peat releases this carbon into the atmosphere, but restored bogs like Whixall Moss reabsorb the carbon. Really, what's not to like?

The Moss is an environmentalist's paradise: an impressive 166 different bird species have been recorded there.

⚙94 Woodseaves Cutting

The Woodseaves cutting on the Shropshire Union Canal near the border with Staffordshire is spellbinding at any time of the year, but for us it's best in late October when the trees are resplendent in their autumn livery, the towpath carpeted with fallen leaves and the air dank and earthy, evoking a delicious sense of melancholy.

The cutting is deep, its sides sometimes almost vertical; and it is always damp, and very narrow, at points too narrow for boats to pass. In places, luxuriant ferns spring directly out of the bare slate-grey rock, and creepers like twisted ropes dangle from the branches of overhanging trees. Kingfishers are common, their bright turquoise and burnt-orange plumage lending a flash of colour to the sunless scene as they

A boat passes under the striking Bridge 57, which towers above the deep cutting.

weave along the canal. All in all, it's a remarkable place.

Even though it's less than an hour's walk from the Georgian town of Market Drayton, it feels like a different world, more rainforest than English canal. At 2.7km (1.5 miles) long and in places almost 21 metres (70ft) deep, Woodseaves is the longest and deepest cutting on Britain's inland waterways system. It's part of what was originally the Birmingham & Liverpool Junction Canal, Thomas Telford's last major civil engineering project, which wasn't completed until 1835, after his death. Along with the 1.6km (1 mile) Shelmore Embankment, it typifies the epic cuttings and embankments that are the hallmark of his direct method of canal building, aimed at cutting down on locks and keeping canals competing with railways.

There are two dizzyingly high-level bridges to watch out for on the Shropshire Union Canal. One (Bridge 57), over the Woodseaves cutting, carries a road on what looks from the water like an arch in the sky. The other (Bridge 39), over Grub Street Cutting, 11.3km (7 miles) south, is a curious and unmistakable double arch, the

The cutting is always dark and dank, the towpath wet and the walls dripping, evoking a sense of melancholy.

lower one sporting a disused, truncated telegraph pole erected in 1861 when telegrams were the Twitter of their day. The supporting structure was more of an emergency measure, a 'strainer arch' built to reduce the pressure on the bridge from the walls of the cutting.

One guidebook describes these bridges as 'portals to the mysterious caverns of another world'. Certainly, the impression of the cuttings from canal level, whether on a boat, bike or on foot, is more of natural river gorges than man-made artefacts. The cuttings have suffered from repeated landslips over the years and there's always the risk of others, but they're still a monumental achievement. They're also places of rare peace and seclusion, conducive to meditation and enjoyment of the natural world. Should you need refreshment, the Shropshire Union is home to some of the most celebrated pubs on the whole inland waterways, including The Anchor at Bridge 42, close to the Grub Street cutting, a wonder in itself since it has survived almost intact from canal-carrying days.

Visit

Market Drayton burned down in 1651 and was rebuilt with lots of picturesque half-timbered buildings:
| shropshire-guide.co.uk/places/market-drayton

Facilities
For The Anchor (Peggs Lane, Old Lea, High Offley, ST20 0NG. Tel: 01785 284569):
| pubheritage.camra.org.uk/pubs/307

For a walk along the Shropshire Union, taking in Market Drayton, Woodseaves Cutting and the pretty Tyrley Locks:
| waterways.org.uk/waterways/using-the-waterways/activities/tyrley-to-market-drayton

95 Waterways Pubs

Certain things go together naturally. Like fish and chips, love and marriage, Tim and Pru (see Wonder 69). It's the same with waterways and pubs. As the old song goes, you can't have one without the other.

That's because in the past, working boaters depended on pubs, not just for their social life – a chance to meet other boaters and escape the confines of their tiny back cabins – but for stabling the horses that pulled their craft. In return, the pubs depended on trade from the water. It was a symbiotic relationship, as close as that of sharks and pilot fish, as intimate as crabs and sea anemones.

The legacy this has left us with today is that the waterways of Great Britain abound with pubs wherever you go. True, many of them – some wonderful

The Grove Lock near Leighton Buzzard on the Grand Union. Decent beer, food and convenient moorings; what else could you need?

ones – have closed over the years; but there are still so many good ones surviving that we're not going to get sentimental over those that have been lost. Pubs like the long-departed Bird in Hand on the Macclesfield Canal close to where it turns off from the Trent & Mersey near Kidsgrove in Staffordshire. The place was like going into someone's front room; you felt you were imposing. There were wooden settles round the walls and no bar: beer was brought up from the cellar in a chipped blue and white enamel jug by the fearsome lady who ran the place. She was an old music hall star, it was said – though whether this was true or just part of the mythology that seems to adhere to vanished pubs, we couldn't say.

Even so, many of these old-style ale houses still survive, like The Anchor Inn (pubheritage.camra.org.uk/pubs/307) stuck in the middle of a field near Bridge 42 on the Shropshire Union; or The Navigation (barrowuponsoar. org.uk/leisure/Pubs/navigation-inn. html) close to where Steve was brought up in Leicestershire; or the Boat Inn at Ashleworth near Gloucester (temporarily closed as a result of flood damage), which has its own purpose-built jetty now, but where you used to have to run your boat on to the beach of the River Severn and paddle barefoot to get to it. All of these are favourites of ours. But then the same could be said of so many other pubs: The Navigation (navigationinn.co.uk) at Bugsworth Basin near Whaley Bridge on the outskirts of Manchester (see Wonder 32); The Hollybush Inn (hollybushleek.co.uk) on the Caldon Canal in Staffordshire; The Admiral Nelson (admiralnelsonbraunston. co.uk) in Northamptonshire (see Wonder 8); the Malt Shovel Inn (whatpub.com/pubs/DER/119/malt-shovel-inn-shardlow) and the New Inn (thenewinnshardlowpub.co.uk) side by side in Shardlow, Derbyshire; The Greyhound (thegreyhoundlongford.

If you're planning a canal outing on foot, bike or boat, our top tip would be to do some research on your route before you set off so as to take in a pub or two as part of the full waterways experience, though you've no need to go as far as we've done in the past and plan a holiday completely around them. Regulars to the waterways might think about investing in one of the books about canal pubs, available from the net or booksellers. Even old editions can be useful.

co.uk) at Hawkesbury Junction near Coventry; The Swan (swaninnfradley. co.uk) at Fradley near Lichfield … the list goes on and on. They are all lovely pubs and each is very different with its own particular character, so much so that it seems almost discourteous to those we don't mention not to highlight them all.

The Corn Mill at Llangollen with its fine terraces overlooking the River Dee. In winter the sound of the rising river waters can be almost deafening.

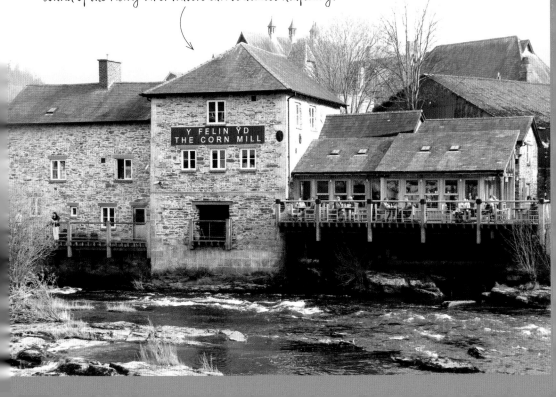

(96) Traditional Boatman's Back Cabin

We've often pondered what a contemporary designer might come up with given a brief to create a living space with kitchen, bedroom, dining area and storage space – all in an area no bigger than a broom cupboard. Yet this is essentially what a traditional boatman's cabin is in a narrowboat. It's Tardis-like. Situated at the back end – or stern – it's only about 2.4 metres (8ft) long and 2.1 metres (6ft 10in) wide.

This 1944 picture of boatwoman Rose Skinner preparing an evening meal shows the cramped living conditions of an authentic back cabin on a working boat.

Yet in this ridiculously tiny space, a boat family of the past had to live their whole lives. Sleeping, eating, cooking and bringing up children. Birth and death and everything in between. The use of space was ingenious. No one invented this layout, it just evolved because it couldn't be bettered. From the back deck – or counter – a step down into the cabin doubles as a coal box; a solid fuel stove like a small Aga immediately to the left is used for both cooking and heating; and a cupboard just beyond becomes a table when folded down (with an aptly named 'crumb drawer' beneath). For sleeping there's a double cross-bed, which folds back into a cupboard – the 'bed 'ole' – during the day, and an adjacent side bed for children can be used as daytime seating. Everything fits together without an inch of space being wasted. And it's all snug: chintz curtains screen the cross-bed and a token 'modesty door' divides the children's bed from the adults', a concession to Victorian morality. Brightly painted roses and castles (see Wonder 27) decorate the doors, and colourful rag rugs grace the floors. Beribboned lace plates and brass bed knobs polished to within an inch of their lives embellish the walls.

Boatmen's cabins in the past were made out of cheap salvaged wood, grained and scumbled to resemble more expensive oak. A side porthole and a dome of glass in the roof known as a 'bullseye' let in just enough daylight to see by, while a hinged oil lamp illuminated the cabin by night.

Our own back cabin is a modern artifice, the result of a collaborative effort between the combined boating brains of Banbury, which relished the challenge

By comparison, reproduction back cabins — ours included — are merely decorative nods to the past.

of recreating the traditional version in a newly built boat. The layout and decor is similar, the dimensions much the same – though try as we might, there was no way we could squeeze ourselves into beds as narrow as the old boaters did, so we had to make ours a foot wider. We often sleep there when friends and family visit, enjoying its claustrophobic cosiness and its duck's-eye view of the canal.

Visit

Many fine original examples of cabins can be seen at boat festivals such as the ones held annually at Braunston in Northamptonshire:
braunstonmarina.co.uk/historic-boat-rally

Canal Cavalcade in Little Venice, London:
waterways.org.uk/support/ways-to-get-involved/events/iwa-canalway-cavalcade

And Rickmansworth on the Grand Union Canal:
rwt.org.uk/festival

Others are on public display in inland waterways museums like those at Ellesmere Port near Chester (see Wonder 35):
canalrivertrust.org.uk/places-to-visit/national-waterways-museum

And Gloucester (see Wonder 85):
canalrivertrust.org.uk/places-to-visit/national-waterways-museum-gloucester

But you're just as likely to come across one by chance as you walk the towpath, and if you express an interest, the proud owner is almost guaranteed to invite you to take a closer look.

Scotland

Caledonian Canal

97 Caledonian Canal

Most waterways have a long history, but none goes back as far as the events that led to the formation of the Caledonian Canal – the most spectacular waterway in the UK and one of the most extraordinary in the entire world.

The Great Glen, through which the Caledonian Canal passes, stretches 96.5km (60 miles) arrow-straight from Inverness in the north-east of Scotland to Fort William in the shadow of Ben Nevis in the south-west Highlands. It was formed 430 million years ago by a collision of continents that left a great gash in the Earth's crust. Later erosion of the land by glaciers formed a necklace of lochs, the most famous being Loch Ness, monstrous in more ways than one in that on misty mornings it can sometimes seem more an inland sea than a lake.

In the 18th century, engineers looked

A holiday barge passes through the staircase of five locks at Fort Augustus, the only sizeable settlement on the canal.

at linking these lochs together, using existing rivers and digging canals where necessary, the intention being to construct a shipping route from the North Sea to the Atlantic Ocean avoiding the dangerous sea journey around Cape Wrath. Another consideration in the minds of those spearheading the project was to create jobs. The crushing of the Jacobite Rising of 1745 had catastrophic social implications for the Highlands, with famines and mass emigration following the Highland Clearances. The project would eventually engage the minds of some of Scotland's finest engineers. James Watt of steam engine fame surveyed a possible route in 1773, John Rennie surveyed it again 20 years later, and ten years after that Thomas Telford surveyed it once more. He was eventually appointed chief engineer, working with his former mentor William Jessop.

Today, you can walk or cycle the Great Glen either self-guided or in a group. It's 127km (79 miles) over the hills and takes between four and seven days, depending on the weather and the state of your legs. From the water, you're spoiled for choice: you can canoe it, either alone or in an arranged party, you can hire a boat and cruise it yourself, or you can take any

On the Caledonian Canal you are never far away from the looming presence of the mountains. Here at Corpach near Fort William, snow-capped and cloud covered, Ben Nevis, Britain's highest peak, is reflected in the placid waters.

one of a number of hotel boats, some more luxurious than others.

Eschewing an entirely indolent journey, we opted for a compromise: a trip where we could go cycling, canoeing, sailing or paddleboarding when the boat stopped; or if we wanted, we could disembark and walk, meeting up with it later. It was a memorable voyage. We boarded just outside Inverness and travelled along the River Ness into the tiny Loch Dochfour, which leads into Loch Ness, at the end of which – 36km (22 miles) later – is Fort Augustus, strung out along a staircase of five locks and the only sizeable settlement you pass. Afterwards, we travelled into Loch Oich, and from there, through sections of canal, into Loch Lochy. Framed by mountains and forests, each part of the cruise had its unique charm, but arriving at Neptune's Staircase (Wonder 101) in the shadow of Ben Nevis, was a fitting grand finale to our trip.

Visit

For walking, cycling, boating – self-cruise, hotel or yacht charter:
| scottishcanals.co.uk/canals/caledonian-canal

For practical information and advice on exploring the Great Glen by boot, boat or bike:
| highland.gov.uk/greatglenway/

98 Crinan Canal

It's often called the most beautiful shortcut in Britain. The 14.5km (9-mile) Crinan Canal in Argyll links the Firth of Clyde to the Atlantic, enabling boats to avoid the much longer and more hazardous sea journey around the Mull of Kintyre.

From its opening in 1809, the canal was used by fishing vessels, but it's most celebrated as the domain of the famous Clyde 'puffers' – those, chunky, cheerful-looking steam-powered cargo ships immortalised by Neil Munro's tales of the fictional *Vital Spark* and its roguish captain, Para Handy, which led to no fewer than three separate BBC adaptations. These boats plied their trade mainly out of Glasgow and were a key supply line carrying goods, people and livestock to and from the Western Isles and the communities along the canal. One local living in the 1940s recalls exchanging cabbages for coal. Another nursed unpleasant memories of the dentist's chair fixed on board for tending the teeth of those who couldn't make it to the mainland.

Though short, the canal passes through an astonishingly varied landscape, from the untamed west coast to the haunting remains of the ancient Scots kingdom of Dalriada, set in the strange peat bogland of Moine Mhor (Great Moss), now a nature reserve. Stretching as far as the eye can see, it's where in the 5th century the Stone of Scone, otherwise known as the Stone of Destiny, was first used to crown Scottish kings. There's a bird hide nearby

where osprey and sea eagles have been spotted. Along the way are attractive white stone cottages and the unique Dunardry rolling bridge, a low bridge that neither swings nor lifts but (when it's restored) rolls back on rails.

It's easy to explore the canal on foot or bike along the well-maintained towpath. Starting at what you might call the 'business end' is Ardrishaig, its workaday plainness in complete contrast to the rest of the canal. Here, thousands of Clydesiders arriving by steamer passed through the turnstiles of the passenger terminal before embarking on a smaller boat for the onward canal journey to Crinan itself. The handsome buildings

The Crinan Canal: domain of the famous Clyde 'puffers'.

still evoke the memory of those holiday crowds who would once have thronged the harbourside during Glasgow Fair fortnight, when the shipyards and factories closed and families headed 'doon the watter' on holiday.

The tourist boom started after Queen Victoria made the trip, accompanied by bagpipers, in 1847. The canal was advertised as the 'Royal Route' and by the late 1850s, over 40,000 passengers passed through Ardrishaig annually.

Even today, the picturesque Crinan Basin at the other end of the canal is a popular tourist destination. What better way to pass an idle summer's afternoon than watching yachts go through the sea lock, while munching on a chunky smoked-salmon sandwich and taking in views of the Western Isles receding to the horizon. If you're lucky, you'll even be treated to a spectacular sunset sinking into the darkening blue sea over Jura and Mull.

The lock and swing bridge at Cairnbaan, near the midway point of the canal.

Visit

Facilities

There was a cafe and tea room at the old steamer terminal in Ardrishaig (Pier Square, PA30 8DZ), which closed. However, according to Scottish Canals, it's currently under offer and hopefully will be open again soon. For the latest news visit:

scottishcanals.co.uk/placemaking/ opportunities/steamer-terminal-cafe-to-let/

About halfway along the canal, at Lock 10, is Polly's Coffee Stop, operating from a mobile van, weekends only.

At Crinan itself, with unparalleled views to the Western Isles, is the harbourside Crinan Hotel (Crinan by Lochgilphead, PA31 8SR, booking essential: Tel: 01546 8326):

crinanhotel.com

There's also the Crinan Coffee Shop next door, serving sandwiches and cakes.

In the area

For more on walking, boating, cycling and canoeing:

scottishcanals.co.uk/canals/crinan-canal/

For boat trips and holidays on the historic puffer *VIC 32*:

savethepuffer.co.uk

For more on Moine Mhor nature reserve border in the canal near Crinan:

wildaboutargyll.co.uk/visit/inveraray-knapdale-kilmartin-and-crinan/trips/moine-mhor-national-nature-reserve/

99 The Falkirk Wheel

The first thing you notice about the Falkirk Wheel is just how big it is. It's the world's first and only rotating boat lift and looks like a giant corkscrew boring sideways into a hill, figures around it reduced to the size of ants. It dominates the landscape. If it had a voice, it would be shouting 'Look at me!'– an attention-seeking, scene-stealing, uncontested supreme wonder of the modern Canal Age.

To call it spectacular really doesn't do it justice. If you're in search of a waterways wow factor, look no further. This is the ultimate 21st-century space-age riff on 18th-century Canal-Age technology. It's the structure that single-handedly put the charisma back into Scottish Canals. Conceived as a Millennium prestige project to restore the navigable link between Edinburgh and Glasgow along the Union and the Forth & Clyde canals,

At its upper level, longer trips from the Wheel take you along the Union Canal under a series of girdered arches and onwards through the psychedelically-lit Roughcastle Tunnel.

it was built to replace a flight of 11 locks that rose more than 35 metres (115ft) up an escarpment. These were dismantled in 1933, when both canals had largely fallen into disuse. Critically, this severed the sea-to-sea link between the east and west coasts.

Located in the heart of Scotland's populous central belt, the Falkirk Wheel is a triumph of engineering, which, in keeping with the great Rennie aqueducts of the Canal Age (see Wonder 90), owes as much to artistic imagination as it does to technology. It's a reminder that Scotland has produced some of the world's most important and innovative engineers. The dramatic design is variously claimed to have been inspired by a Celtic double-headed axe, the propeller of a Clyde-built ship, or the ribcage of a whale – take your pick. The Millennium Link, as it is known, cost £84.5 million to build and was opened by the Queen in 2002.

The two water-filled gondolas that lift and lower boats from one canal to the other can accommodate up to four boats apiece, and they work on the Archimedean principle that floating objects displace their own weight in water. Empty of boats or full, the gondolas are the same weight and counterbalance one another: this means that it takes virtually no energy to operate. The output of just eight household kettles is enough to power this big boy.

There's a visitor centre, picnic areas and pop-up food outlets located in the lower basin area, where trip boats depart hourly. You'd be foolish to miss experiencing being raised and lowered on the wheel. It barely seems to move. No noise, no vibration. Just a feeling of calm as you rise gently above the ground as if in a hot-air balloon. The longer of two trip options takes you a short distance along the canal at the higher level and through the psychedelically lit Roughcastle Tunnel before turning round for the return trip to Planet Earth. There are also plenty of opportunities

Visit

For more information and booking:
| scottishcanals.co.uk/falkirk-wheel

Facilities
Refreshments available on site.

to explore the whole site on foot at your own pace at both levels, and the Kelpies, the other must-see attraction close by (see Wonder 100), are a walk or an easy cycle ride along the towpath.

The ultimate 21st century riff on 18th century canal technology.

(100) The Kelpies

You wouldn't have believed that a couple of sculptures of horses' heads could have had such impact on us. After all, we'd seen pictures of them, we'd seen news items. We'd even seen maquettes of them and that ought to have given us a clue, since even these 'small' artist's models were bigger than us. But then we turned a bend on the Forth & Clyde Canal, and there was the real thing, still a long way off but enormous even from that distance.

Close up, the sculptures were literally gigantic, towering above us at 30 metres (100ft) high, not far short of a ten-storey office block, a couple of humongous edifices built of 30,000 perforated stainless-steel plates on a framework of girders, glinting in the afternoon sunshine.

If it had been size alone, they'd have been impressive enough; but there's something about the way the artist, Andy Scott, has managed to express the strength and dignity of these two creatures that touches an emotional chord. One rears its head to the sky, as if in an effort to burst free of the earth to which it is tethered; the other is more subdued, looking down at us with eyes that express a proud but despondent resignation to its fate.

The sculptures are called the Kelpies, a nod to the water spirits that in Scottish folklore are able to take the form of horses. Beyond this mysticism, they're a celebration of the powerful Clydesdale workhorses that, in their heyday, hauled laden barges along the canal from Glasgow to Edinburgh.

The link between Scotland's two principal cities wasn't made until 1822 when the Edinburgh and Glasgow Union Canal was opened. This connected to the Forth & Clyde Canal at Falkirk by a flight of locks, since replaced by the Falkirk Wheel (see Wonder 99). Not that it mattered a lot. In less than 20 years, a railway was opened to connect the cities, and the canal began its long, slow decline, which was only halted in the 1970s when local councils began to realise they had lost a valuable amenity. Since then, the area

has been transformed by an ambitious regeneration scheme, The Helix, with the Kelpies at its heart.

Today, a short extension and a new lock complete the link to the Firth of Forth. This lock is sited right between the Kelpies, which don't just tower above it but dwarf it completely. We have been through many locks in our time on the cut. Believe us: none is more spectacular than this.

The 30,000 perforated stainless-steel plates used in the sculptures allow them to change through the day as the light alters. Here, at sunset, they seem almost ablaze.

Visit

For more on visiting the Kelpies: | scottishcanals.co.uk/locations/the-kelpies

The Kelpies form the centrepiece of Helix Park in Falkirk (visitor centre. Tel: 01324 590600). For more information, including details of guided tours of the Kelpies, when you can even get inside the sculptures: | thehelix.co.uk

There's a cafe and visitor centre here, too.

Neptune's Staircase

There are a lot of misconceptions about canals, some of them shared by experienced boaters who ought to know better. Like the idea that the Bingley Five Rise (see Wonder 31) in Yorkshire is the highest flight of staircase locks in Britain. It isn't. The awesome eight locks of Neptune's Staircase at the small village of Banavie, near Fort William on the Caledonian Canal (see Wonder 97), rise 1 metre (3ft) higher.

True, the Bingley flight rises more steeply and over a shorter distance. But Neptune's Staircase is on an altogether grander scale, composed as it is of 400 metres (0.25 miles) of continuous masonry, a spectacular series of steps cutting through some of the most outstanding scenery in the whole of Europe, with views to match. There's no doubt that in a head-to-head, though we'd score Bingley high, we'd have to score the Scottish flight higher.

Mind you, before we start to get nationalistic about this, it's as well to remind ourselves that as far as staircase locks go, the French beat both Scots and English, hands down. The flight of locks at Fonseranes, on the Canal du Midi near Béziers, lifts the canal 21.5m (more than 70ft). And they were built in the 1600s, which in canal terms was when we in Britain were living in mud huts

The masts of yachts climbing the staircase stand out as visitors watch the activity in the lock chambers at this popular tourist destination.

Scotland

Two-thirds of the Caledonian Canal comprises natural lochs formed by geological movement; the rest is canalised. It was built to link the North Sea and the Atlantic Ocean, avoiding a perilous sea journey around the northern coast, though by the time the Banavie locks came to be built in 1808, considerations of naval strategy had become an important issue too. By then, Britain was at war with Napoleon's France, and as a result the size of the locks along the whole canal was increased to 54.9 x 12.1 metres (180 x 40ft) to accommodate the 32-gun frigates of the Royal Navy. It made the locks exceptionally heavy to work. Until the 1960s, when they were mechanised, gangs of men had to be employed full time to open gates manually using capstans. It was a back-breaking process and it took half a day to get a boat through, compared to around an hour and a half nowadays.

If you're lucky when you visit, you may see the flight in use. But even if not,

Visit

For more information:
| scottishcanals.co.uk/destinations/
| neptunes-staircase

Facilities

For the Moorings Hotel (Seanivan, Banavie, Fort William, PH33 7LY. Tel: 01397 772797):
| moorings-fortwilliam.co.uk

For bike hire on Scottish canals:
| scottishcanals.co.uk/activities/cycling/
| bike-hire

there are fantastic views of Britain's highest mountain, Ben Nevis; and Loch Linnhe, towards the Firth of Lorne and the Atlantic beyond. And if the weather's bad there's always the startlingly contemporary Moorings Hotel and cafe complex, literally on the waterside, where you can take refuge.

The dramatic Highland setting of the locks is a major part of their appeal.

Index

activism, political 8–9
Adam, Robert 190–1
AG Wright Sluice 159
Aickman, Robert 5, 8, 113, 146
Alarum Theatre Company 149
Anderton Boat Lift 5, 68
Arkwright, Sir Richard 32–3
Ashby Canal 27
Atherstone, towpath art at 64
Avoncliff Aqueduct 197

Banbury 146–7
Bancroft Basin 16–17
barrel-roofed lock cottages 18–19
Barton Swing Aqueduct 5, 70–1
Basingstoke Canal 138
Bath 190–1
The Beatles 91
Bewdley 54
Bingley five rise staircase locks 5, 11, 72–3, 220
Bingley three rise staircase locks 72, 73
Birmingham Canal Navigations (BCN) 20–1
  BCN challenge 22–3
  toll islands 61
Blisworth Tunnel 53
Blow-Up Bridge (aka Macclesfield Bridge) 118–19
boat lifts 37, 68–9, 216–17
boat trips, organised 17, 33, 37, 53, 55, 57, 59, 69, 70, 91, 101, 107, 121, 127, 128, 131, 141, 147, 160, 167, 171, 179, 181, 186, 189, 191, 192, 193, 197, 199, 213, 215
boatman's cabins 208–9
Boston 170–1
Braunston canal village 13, 24–5, 63, 209
bridge-keepers cottages 178–9
Bridgewater Canal 70, 108
Brindley, James 28, 40, 54, 55
Bristol Floating Harbour 180–1
British Waterways Board 27, 57
Broads, the 154–5, 165
Browning's Pool 122, 123
Brunel, Isambard Kingdom 125, 180
Brunel, Marc 124–5
Buckby cans 63
Buckingham Canal 30
Bugsworth Basin 74–5
Burnley Embankment (aka The Straight Mile) 5, 76
Byron, Lord 122

cabin decor, narrowboat 62–3, 208–9
Caen Hill lock flight 5, 6, 182–3
Calder & Hebble Navigation 10
Caldon Canal 13
Caledonian Canal 212–13, 220–1
Cambridge Backs 156–7
Camden lock and market 119, 120–1
Canal & River Trust 61, 65, 102–3
Canal du Midi, France 108, 220
Canalway Cavalcade 123
castles and forts 34–5, 100, 101, 163
Cathedral of the Canals, Braunston 25
Chappell, Reuben 64
Charity Dock 26–7, 63
Chester 78–9, 80

Chesterfield Canal 11, 28–9
churches and cathedrals 25, 34, 45, 71, 85, 86, 125, 155, 160, 161, 163, 187, 193
Clifford, Hon Thomas 58
Clock Warehouse, Shardlow 50
contour canals 46–7
Cosgrove foot tunnel 31
Cotswold Canals 179, 198–9
Coventry Canal 26
Crinan Canal 175
Crofton Pumping Station 183
Cromford & High Peak railway 74, 75
Cromford Canal 74, 173
Cromford Mills and Canal 32–3
Cromwell, Oliver 160, 161
Cropredy (Fairport) Festival 142–3
Cuckoo Way 29
cycle hire and networks 29, 69, 75, 85, 93, 154, 167, 199, 212, 213, 215, 221

Darby III, Abraham 194
Darwin, Charles 167
Denver Sluice 158–9
Devizes Wharf 183
'DIS' markers, Oxford Canal 12–13
Dudley Tunnel 23
Dundas Aqueduct 196, 197

Eastwood 38
Edinburgh & Glasgow Union Canal 216–17, 218–19
Edstone Aqueduct 19
Egerton, Francis 108
Elizabeth I, Queen 35, 126, 186
Ellesmere 80, 184–5
  Lake District 184–5
Ellesmere Port 63, 80–1, 185, 209
Ely 160–1, 164, 169
Engels, Friedrich 98
Erewash Canal 32, 38, 39
Explosives Act (1875) 119

Falkirk Wheel 216–17
festivals 25, 81, 99, 104, 105, 142–3, 181, 193, 209
fishing 38, 164
Forth & Clyde Canal 65, 216–17, 218
Foss Dyke 163
Fotheringhay 34–5
Foxton staircase lock and inclined plane 11, 36–7

galleries and installations 26, 29, 64–5, 81, 91, 93, 127, 128, 135, 160, 180
Galton Bridge 20, 21
Gargrave 82–3
Glasson dock and basin 84
Glory Hole, Lincoln 162–3
Gloucester 63, 209
Gloucester & Sharpness Canal 13, 175, 186
  bridge-keepers cottages 178–9
Gloucester Docks 186–7
Goole towpath art 64
Gormley, Anthony 65
Grade Imill 32–3
Grand Canal, Venice 20
'Grand Cross' scheme 55

Grand Junction Canal 13, 24–5
Grand Trunk Canal 55
Grand Union Canal 11, 13, 24, 49, 175
  Cosgrove to Grafton Regis 30
  Gerard Dalton's sculptures 65
Grand Union Canal Company 42–3
Great Canal Journeys, Channel 4 150, 151
Great Haywood 59
Great Northern Basin 38–9
Great Ouse tributaries 168–9, 175
Greenwich 126–7
Grindley Brook staircase lock 11
Grub Street cutting bridge 204–5

Hadfield, Charles 113
Hardcastle Crags 86, 87
Harecastle Tunnels 40–1
Hatherton Canal 44
Hatton Locks (aka 'stairway to heaven') 11, 42–3
Hawkesbury Junction (aka Sutton Stop) 26, 27
Hebden Bridge 86–7
Henry VIIII, King 31, 126
Heptonstall 86
Hest Bank 88–9
High Bridge, Lincoln 162–3
Hillmorton towpath art 64
'Hobbit houses' 114–15
Hockney, David 99
Horseley Ironworks bridges 24
Horseshoe Falls 189, 192–3
House Mill tidal mill 130–1
Huddersfield Narrow Canal (HNC) 9, 102–3

Illustrated London News 118
Industrial Revolution 5, 55, 74, 86, 164, 186, 194–5
Inland Waterways Association (IWA) 5, 7–9, 113, 146
Iron Trunk Aqueduct 30
Ironbridge 194–5

Jessop, William 30, 181, 192, 212
Johnson, Samuel 45
Junction Bridge, Number I, Marple 111

Kelpie sculptures 64, 218–19
Kennet & Avon Canal 9, 150–1, 181, 182–3, 196, 197

Lancashire Coastal Way 85
Lancaster Canal 84, 85, 88–9, 94, 196, 197
Langley Mill junction 38
Lawrence, D.H. 38–9
Lee Valley Regional Park 132, 133
Leeds & Liverpool Canal 10, 72–3, 76, 90, 94, 96, 98, 100–1, 106
licenses 57, 61, 138, 157
Lichfield Canal 44
  aqueduct 44–5
lift bridges 144–5, 202
Lincoln 162–3
Line towpath art walk 65, 131
Little Venice 119, 122–3, 209
the Liverpool Link 90–1
Liverpool Maritime Mercantile City 90

Llangollen Canal 184, 192
  lift bridge 144–5, 202
  Pontcysyllte Aqueduct 188–9
Llangollen railway 193
lock cottages, barrel-roofed 18–19
lock types 10–11
London and Birmingham Railway 120
Lucas, Mike 148–9
Lune Aqueduct 196–7

Macclesfield Canal 110–11, 206
Manchester Ship Canal 70
Manchester via the Rochdale 9 96–7
Maritime Greenwich 126–7
Market Drayton 204, 205
Marple lock flight 111
Mary, Queen of Scots 34–5, 58
Mikron Theatre Company 148–9
mileposts 12–13
moorings 57, 59, 79, 81, 85, 91, 92, 101,
  122, 132, 146–7, 161, 192
Morecambe Bay 88–9
museums and heritage centres 20–1, 29, 37,
  39, 45, 51, 52, 53, 55, 59, 63, 70, 75, 77,
  81, 83, 91, 103, 125, 127, 131, 133, 160,
  169, 171, 181, 183, 186–7, 195

Naburn Lock 92–3
Napton 46–7
Narrow Boat (T. Rolt) 146
narrow canals 56–7
National Trust 57, 59, 91, 138, 166, 167, 171
Neptune's Staircase 220–1
Norfolk and Suffolk Broads 154–5, 165
Northgate Locks 78
Norwich 155
Norwood Tunnel 29
Nurser, Frank 63

Ornamental Bridge (aka Solman's/
  Samson's Bridge) 31
Orwell, George 106
Owen, Jess 63
Oxford 140–1
Oxford Canal 12, 24, 140–1, 151
  lift bridges 144–5
  summit 46–7
  towpath art 64

Paddington Basin 123
Pain, Irene 105
Peak Forest Canal 9, 33, 74, 111
Pennine Way 82
Peter Freebody's boatyard 135
Plath, Sylvia 86
Pontcysyllte Aqueduct 5, 30, 188–9
Port Meadow 140
pubs, cafes and restaurants 27, 28, 37, 43,
  47, 53, 70, 75, 79, 83, 99, 103, 107, 122,
  125, 139, 141, 143, 145, 155, 158, 163,
  178, 181, 183, 185, 186, 195, 197, 205,
  206–7, 215
Pulteney Bridge 190–1
punting 156–7
Purton Hulks 179

Queen's House, Greenwich 127

reed cutting 164–5
Regent's Canal 118, 120, 122
Rennie, John 84, 182, 212
  aqueducts 196–7
rental, boat 17, 55, 154–5, 157, 171, 181, 183,
  184, 191, 193, 197, 212
Ribble Link 94–5, 197
Richard III, King 34
River Avon 9, 181
River Cam 156–7, 169
River Lee/Lea 132–3
River Ouse 82
River Thames between Goring and Windsor
  134–5
River Weaver 68, 69
Robinson, Cedric 89
the Rochdale 9 96–7
Rochdale Canal 9, 86, 102
Rochdale Summit 87
Rolt, Tom 8, 113, 146
Roman archaeology 78, 79, 163, 186
rose and castle canal boat motif 62–3, 209
Rothschild, Charles 166
roving bridges 110–11
Royal Gunpowder Mills 132–3
Royal Ordnance Depot, Weedon 48–9
Royal Shakespeare Company 17, 57

Salt, Sir Titus 98–9
Saltaire and Salts Mill 98–9
Sandiacre lock cottages 39
Sapperton Tunnel 198, 199
Saul Junction 179
Scales, Prunella 150–1
Scottish Canals 65
Settle-Carlisle Railway 101
Severn Bore 186, 200–1
Shakespeare, William 17, 19, 31
Shardlow inland port 50–1
Shaw, Maureen 105
Shropshire Union Canal 80, 105, 195,
  204–5, 206
Shugborough Hall 59
Skipton 100
slave trade 83, 84, 181
South Stratford Canal 18–19
  split bridges 56–7
Southern Oxford Canal lift bridges 144–5
split bridges, South Stratford 56–7
Springs Branch 100–1
St John's bridge, Cambridge 157
Staffordshire & Worcestershire Canal 54,
  55, 58–9
staircase locks 11, 36–7, 72–3, 78, 95, 220–1
Standedge Tunnel 5, 102–3
Stephenson, Robert 120
Stevens, William 138
Stoke Bruerne 52–3, 63, 209
stop planks 114–15
Stourport-on-Severn inland port 54–5
Stratford Canal 9, 18–19, 56–7, 65, 138
Stratford-upon-Avon 17, 19, 57
Stroudwater Navigation 198, 199
Suchet, David 45
Suffolk and Norfolk Broads 154–5, 165
'Swan-Upping' ritual 136–7

Teddington barge lock 10
Telford, Thomas 40, 79, 185, 188, 192,
  204, 212
Thames & Severn Canal 198–9
Thames Barrier 128–9
Thames Tunnel 124–5
Thanet Canal 100
theatres and cinemas 17, 33, 83, 122, 125,
  148–9, 155
'Three Graces', Liverpool 90
Three Mills Island 130–1
Thrupp 145
Tilbury canal boat 118
Tixall Gatehouse 58–9
Tixall Wide 58–9
Tolkien, JRR 59
Toll Islands, Birmingham 60–1
Tontine Hotel, Stourport-on-Severn 55
Tooley's boatyard 146–7, 151
tow rope groves 112–13, 118, 119
towpath art 64–5, 131
Trans Pennine Trail 29
Trent & Mersey Canal 55, 68, 104, 105
Tuel Lane lock 10

UNESCO World Heritage Sites 33, 98, 126,
  188–9, 191, 195
Uttoxeter Canal 13

walking trails 29, 51, 55, 61, 69, 82, 83, 85,
  86, 99, 111, 133, 135, 154, 167, 185, 192,
  199, 203, 205, 212, 213, 215
Ward, Sister Mary 52–3
Wardle Lock & Canal 104–5
Warwick & Birmingham Canal 42–3
Wash, the 170–1
water birds/wild fowl see wildlife
water voles 172–3
Waterland (G. Swift) 167
Waterways Recovery Group 6, 9
Watt, James 212
Wedgewood, Josiah 50
Weedon Royal Ordnance Depot 48–9
West, Timothy 150–1
Wey & Arun Canal Trust 139
Wey Navigation 138–9
Whaley Bridge 33
Whitworth, Robert 76
Whixall Moss 202–3
Wicken Fen 166–7
Wigan and Wigan Pier 106–7
wild camping 167
wildlife 32, 69, 82–3, 107, 132, 136–7, 138,
  155, 159, 164, 166–7, 169, 171, 172–5,
  179, 184, 203, 204, 214, 215
Wisbech 171
Wisley Gardens, RHS 138, 139
Woodseaves cutting 204–5
World War II 5, 131
Wormleighton 47
Worsley Delph 108–9
Wrenbury 145
Wyre/Garstang Aqueduct 197

Index

Acknowledgements

Thanks to:

Bugsworth Basin Heritage Trust
Hugh Potter
Ian Edgar
Phil Brook-Little
Rosemary Chapman and Bob Wood
Nick Hayes
Brian Holt
David Jowett
Bob Williams
Canal & River Trust
Scottish Canals
Jennifer Barclay, our agent

Particular thanks to:

Andrew Denny
Miles Hedley
Kathryn Beer, our editor, who along with designers Phil Beresford and Austin Taylor, and cartographer John Plumer have worked so hard to make this book what it is.

All photography © **Steve Haywood** & **Moira Haynes** with the exception of the following:
Adobe Stock © 126, 161; **Alamy** © pp54, 55, 96, 114, 124, 150, 151, 171, 179; **Andrew Denny** © p45; **Getty** © pp12, 15, 17, 19, 30, 32, 33, 35, 36, 37, 39, 42, 43, 51, 53, 67, 68, 69, 71, 73, 79, 80, 82, 83, 85, 91, 93, 98, 99, 100, 106, 107, 109, 113, 117, 128, 129, 130, 131, 135, 136, 137, 147, 148, 153, 155, 159, 166, 167, 168, 169, 172, 173, 174, 177, 182, 183, 185, 186, 187, 189, 190, 191, 195, 200, 201, 203, 208, 211, 212, 213, 214, 215, 217, 219, 224; **Geograph** © pp31 Ian Rob; p44 Bill Boaden; p59 Jeff Buck; p205 Brian Deegan; **Supplied by National Waterways Archive, Canal and River Trust** pp56, 196; **John G Moore** © p220; **Michael Wooding** p115 (top); **Mikron Theatre Company** © p149; **Nick Hayes** © pp74, 110; **Peter Sandgrove** © p216; **RGM (royalgunpowdermills. com)** © p133; **Shutterstock** © pp16, 188; **Wikimedia Commons** © p13 (bottom right) Philip Halling; p40 Rodw; p41 Akke; p46 Minnie Bannister; pp57, 61 David Stowell; pp58, 105, 204 Roger Kidd; p60 Oosoom; p76 Dave Bevis; p101 Andrew Abbott; p103 54north; p104 Dr Neil Clifton; p111 Martin Lack; p118 David Smith; p119 Robin Webster; p120 Kallerna; p125 Secretlondon; p140 AstacopsisGouldi; p141 Des Blenkinsopp; p154 Akuppa John Wigham; p180 Tony Hisgett; p198 Mick Lobb; p209 Keith Lodge; p221 Son of Groucho; **Yorkshire Post and IWA** © p9

Maps by **JP Map Graphics Ltd** and map data © Crown Copyright, 2022